PORTRAIT OF A REBEL

BOOKS BY RICHARD ALDINGTON

BIOGRAPHY

Voltaire
Wellington
Four English Portraits
The Strange Life of Charles Waterton
Portrait of a Genius, But. . . (Life of D. H. Lawrence)
Pinorman
Lawrence of Arabia
Introduction to Mistral
Frauds

NOVELS

Death of a Hero
The Colonel's Daughter
All Men Are Enemies
Women Must Work
Very Heaven
Seven Against Reeves
Rejected Guest
The Romance of Casanova

SHORT STORIES

Roads to Glory
Soft Answers

POETRY

A Dream in the Luxembourg
Complete Poems

ESSAYS

French Studies and Reviews
Literary Studies and Reviews
D. H. Lawrence

ANTHOLOGIES

Poetry of the English-Speaking World
Fifty Romance Lyric Poems
The Religion of Beauty (The English Aesthetes)

TRANSLATIONS

Euripides: *Alcestis*
Medallions: Anyte, Meleager, Anacreontea, Renaissance Latin poets
Boccaccio: *Decameron*
The Fifteen Joys of Marriage (fifteenth century)
The Mysteries of the Nativity (from Liégeois of the fifteenth century)
Cyrano de Bergerac: *Voyages*
Voltaire: *Candide*
Choderlos de Laclos: *Dangerous Acquaintances*
Julien Benda: *The Great Betrayal*
Pierre Custot: *Sturly*

In Samoa with Chief Tui. The last portrait of Robert Louis Stevenson.

[*Frontispiece*

PORTRAIT OF A REBEL

The Life and Work of Robert Louis Stevenson

by

RICHARD ALDINGTON

LONDON

EVANS BROTHERS LIMITED

First published 1957

PRINTED IN GREAT BRITAIN BY J. W. ARROWSMITH LTD., BRISTOL

Z.5384

CONTENTS

ACKNOWLEDGEMENTS

For permission to reproduce the photographs in this book the publishers are indebted to: Exclusive News Agency; Clive Holland, Esq.; Picture Post Library; Robert Louis Stevenson Memorial House, Edinburgh.

They are also grateful to the Yale University Press, and the Oxford University Press for permission to quote from *R. L. Stevenson's Letters to Charles Baxter*, edited by De Lancey Ferguson and Marshall Waingrow.

ILLUSTRATIONS

I

'It mattered not what a man liked; the mere fact of his liking it made it sinful. Whatever was natural was wrong. The clergy deprived the people of their holidays, their amusements, their shows, their games, and their sports; they repressed every appearance of joy, they forbade all merriment, they stopped all festivities, they choked up every avenue by which pleasure could enter, and they spread over the country a universal gloom. . . . Men, in their daily actions and in their very looks, became troubled, melancholy, and ascetic. Their countenance soured and was downcast. Not only their opinions, but their gait, their demeanour, their voice, their general aspect, were influenced by that deadly blight which nipped all that was genial and warm.'

BUCKLE'S unqualified denunciation of Scottish life during the century from the Reformation to the end of the Solemn League and Covenant disturbances will not meet with everybody's agreement. Still, when trying to follow the fortunes of a man so essentially Scottish as Robert Lewis Stevenson, we do well to start off by noting the sombre religious history of Scottish society. Puritanism with them was more powerful and more prolonged than in England, more intellectual, or at any rate more argumentative, and more Calvinistic. Of course, by the time of Stevenson's youth (1850 to 1870) this tremendous discipline had weakened. Towards the end of the eighteenth century there was a marked softening of social manners, and it is hardly necessary to add that for several decades Edinburgh had some reason to consider itself a more intellectual capital than London. However much modified by time, the strict religious discipline was still there, especially for children; and mainly through his father, Thomas Stevenson, and his nurse, Alison Cunningham ('Cummy'), Robert Lewis Stevenson experienced it from the time he began to talk.

Inevitably with a person so complex as Stevenson such influences mainly provoked rebellion and even a downright disbelief, which involved him in endless and most painful clashes with his father. Such revolt is often an indication of the influences' power, and there was always an ineradicable Scotch Calvinist lurking under Stevenson's many *personae* or masks, ranging as they do from 'sprite' to amateur emigrant, from bohemian invalid to prayer-reading Samoan laird. Henley saw and resented it, not only in his jeer at the prayers written at Vailima but in the often-quoted line about Stevenson having in him 'something of the Shorter Catechist'. Other instances can easily be cited by anyone who has got beyond Stevenson as writer of boys' adventure tales and elegant essays. It is in that first boyish *The Pentland Rising*—tribute to the Covenanter heroes of his father and nurse—and in the similarly-named novel, long wrestled with, never completed to satisfaction, and destroyed. Grown-up, he went for choice wandering in the harsh Protestant Cevennes, admits ingenuously the pleasure he felt in meeting kindred spirits of that bleak religion, and, surrounded with Catholics, is at one with a French Plymouth Brother who 'knew the Lord'. You can see it even in such a trifle as that phrase from *Catriona*, 'the romance of destiny', with its graceful acknowledgement of predestination—not to be damned, but to dwell in the South Seas.

This contradictory reaction—repulsion and attraction—was inextricably tangled with Stevenson's attitude to his father with whom his relations were at once so close and so difficult, as we shall have to note more than once. Stevenson's interest in his family went beyond his own parents, and he would scarcely have been a Scot if he had lacked a pedigree. It may be studied, duly set forth in schematic form, showing the Stevensons' descent from a James Stevenson who in 1665 married a Jean Keir; and, more impressively, his mother's family of Balfour fetching their descent from an Alexander Balfour of Inchrye (born *circa* 1468) who married a Janet Wemyss. With his slightly spurious or adolescent love of 'romance' and 'adventure' Stevenson hoped he might be descended from Rob Roy MacGregor or at any rate from the clan. Obviously, he was never able to prove it, and the 'perfect evidence' he mentions in a letter written not long before his death amounts only to the fact—if it is a fact—that when the name of MacGregor was proscribed some of the clan called themselves 'Stevenson'. It may be so. Sir Walter Scott picturesquely says that they were 'Campbells by day and MacGregors by night'.

In default of a Scottish thief and outlaw as a progenitor Stevenson had to fall back on his father and grandfather, engineers and lighthouse-builders. He had enough sense to be proud of them, though the fact that he divided his filial allegiance between this squalid robber and men who, through sheer brains and character, achieved something worth doing in the world, is a measure of that devotion to factitious or even penny-dreadful 'romance' which contaminates some of his writing. The transition of the Stevensons from ordinary middle-class trading to the then pioneer profession of engineering and lighthouse-building is a curious little tale with a touch of tragical adventure and odd marrying to prefigure their literary descendant.

In the third quarter of the eighteenth century lived two Stevenson brothers, Hugh and Alan, the latter married very early in life to Jean Lillie by whom he had one son, Robert, born 1772. The two established a business in the West Indies, and both died in their early twenties pursuing a defaulting partner in an open boat. Jean and her baby were left penniless. How she provided for herself and her boy is not stated; but in 1787 she married again, an Edinburgh man, Thomas Smith, who specialized in Lamps and Oils. A year before this third marriage Thomas Smith was appointed engineer to the then new 'Board of Northern Lights' (i.e. lighthouses and beacons) and superseded the old coal flares with his oil lamps and reflectors.

Although only thirty-three when he married Jean Stevenson, Smith was twice a widower, with two daughters. This alliance of widower and daughters with widow and son might have been disastrous, but as in so many Puritan households the women occupied themselves with piety, domestic duties, and trying to boss the males, while the men were absorbed in money-making, their profession—and piety. Robert Stevenson (1772–1850) was not only his stepfather's pupil, he went far beyond him in the construction and improved lighting of lighthouses on the stormy and rocky Scottish coasts. And then a very curious thing happened. In 1799, when Robert was twenty-seven, he married Jean Smith, his stepfather's daughter! At first glance one would think this came within the prohibited degrees, but apparently not. Still, as Louis Stevenson reflects on his grandfather's unenterprising if unconventional union:

'The marriage of a man of twenty-seven and a girl of twenty who have lived for twelve years as brother and sister, is difficult to conceive.'

Obviously, it was the mother's doing. She had brought up the girl, and meant to make sure that her son did not lose his share of the Smith money and growing influence. Why Robert acquiesced in so unadventurous a union is impossible to say, but doubtless like other stern, determined, rugged fellows, in domestic affairs he did what he was told to do by the women.

However disappointing as a lover in a romance, Robert Stevenson was a man of high character and integrity, a person of great eminence in his profession. Apart from the lighthouses themselves, he left a written testimony of his work which his grandson edited and included in his *Records of a Family of Engineers*. Robert Stevenson's *Account* of the building of the Bell Rock Lighthouse in the years 1807–11 is certainly not the least interesting book included in his grandson's collected works. Indeed it stands well above the Osbourne and Louis pot-boilers and even some of the literary master's own less happy achievements. With the primitive equipment of that time it was almost an impossible feat to construct successfully and permanently 'a tower of masonry on a sunken reef far distant from land, covered at every tide to a depth of twelve feet or more'. Yet Robert Stevenson did it.

His character is unconsciously revealed by him in his account of how he dealt with a strike. The men, of course, worked in difficult conditions, involving irregular hours, exposure, hardship and danger. These they accepted like good Scots, but under the urging of the inevitable malcontent and his friend they quarrelled with their rations, which were per man: '1½ lb. beef; 1 lb. bread; 8 oz. oatmeal; 2 oz. barley; 2 oz. butter; 3 quarts beer; vegetables and salt' with extra beer and a glass of rum on occasions. They wanted more beer. Stevenson thought three quarts of beer enough, dismissed the two ringleaders, and gave the rest the alternative of dismissal or acceptance. They accepted. Of course, it was wartime, and they had the fear of the press-gang before them.

Three years after completion of the Bell Rock Lighthouse, the Commissioners of Northern Lights made a voyage of inspection in the lighthouse yacht, and had as guest Walter Scott, who has left a readable and entertaining journal of their travels. Scott speaks of 'the official chief of the expedition . . . Mr. Stevenson, the Surveyor-Viceroy over the commissioners—a most gentleman-like and modest man, and well known by his scientific skill'. Scott always mentions Stevenson with regard, and notes with interest that the islanders (wreckers to a man) complained that since the building of the lighthouses their income from wrecks had greatly decreased! Even more interesting from our point of view is the following paragraph:

'Having crept upon deck about four in the morning, I find we are beating to windward off the isle of Tyree, with the determination on the part of Mr. Stevenson, that his constituents should visit a reef of rocks called *Skerry Vhor*, where he thought it would be essential to have a lighthouse. Loud remonstrances on the part of the Commissioners, who one and all declare they will subscribe to his opinion, whatever it may be, rather than continue this infernal buffeting. Quiet perseverance on the part of Mr. S., and great kicking, bouncing and squabbling of the Yacht, who seems to like the idea of Skerry Vhor as little as the Commissioners. At length, by dint of exertion, come in sight of this long ridge of rocks (chiefly under water), on which the tide breaks in a most tremendous style. There appear a few low broad rocks at one end of the reef, which is about a mile in length. These are never entirely under water, though the surf dashes over them. To go through all the forms, Hamilton, Duff and I resolve to land upon these bare rocks in company with Mr. Stevenson. Pull through a very heavy swell with great difficulty, and approach a tremendous surf dashing over black pointed rocks. Our rowers, however, get the boat into a quiet creek between two rocks, where we contrive to land well wetted. . . . The rock was carefully measured by Mr. S. It will be a most desolate position for a lighthouse—the Bell Rock and Eddystone a joke to it, for the nearest land is the wild island of Tyree, at fourteen miles' distance. So much for the Skerry Vhor.'

Well, in the romance of his particular destiny, it turned out that Robert Stevenson was not predestined to achieve the adventure of the lighthouse of Skerryvore. That was reserved for his sons, Alan, and as a subordinate, Thomas, the father of Robert Louis, who considered it the greatest achievement of the firm. Perhaps this is the moment to note that both Robert and Thomas Stevenson, in addition to their professional duties, made a number of valuable inventions. Considering themselves servants of

Government they never took out patents or accepted any money for these discoveries, some of which were universally adopted. The result was that they received no credit for them, since other engineers and users did not know who were the inventors; and neither received any honours from the Crown. It is a kingly title.

When we turn from the Stevensons to the family of Robert Louis's mother, the Balfours, we do not find among the multitude of ascendants and collaterals anyone with the solid if 'unco' guid' merit of Robert Stevenson. Perhaps this is the place to note briefly that some of the genetical inferences made by his admirers and even by Robert Louis himself are a little far-fetched. Thus he is credited with 'foreign blood' which is supposed to have influenced both his character and his literary genius, because one of his maternal great-great-grandmothers was Margaret Lizars, herself (at least) the great-great-grand-daughter of a French immigrant of the sixteenth century named Lizars or Lisouris. Stevenson himself remarks exultantly that he had 'shaken a spear in the debatable land and shouted the slogans of the Elliots'. But his participation in Border warfare (a bloody, barbarous and discreditable form of robbery with violence) seems remote when we find it is based on the fact that his mother's great-grandmother, Cecilia Elphinstone had a mother who was an Elliot; and thus Stevenson's great-uncle John Balfour was a fifth cousin of Sir Walter Scott!

'When Adam delved and Eve span
Who was then the gentleman?'

It may well be that Professor James Balfour of Pilrig, who married Cecilia Elphinstone, found that he had acquired 'an exciting mother-in-law', but it is difficult to imagine how this fact (if it was a fact) can have influenced Robert Louis.

More to the purpose is that Stevenson used a 'David Balfour' as one of his heroes, and that there were Ministers among his Balfour ancestors including his grandfather, the Reverend Lewis Balfour of Colinton. In his early years, Robert Louis knew this Minister (then an old man) and has left in *Memories and Portraits* an admirably drawn sketch of his grandfather and the manse. He was 'a somewhat awful figure', inspiring the children 'with a kind of terror', yet capable of a warm tenderness which when suddenly revealed astonished his little grandson. He was evidently a man with a strong sense of justice even in trifles as well as a believer in discipline for children. In his old age, falling perhaps a little towards childishness, he sat eating barley-sugar after taking that most nauseous 'Gregory powder' with which many generations were unnecessarily tormented, but he would not allow the little boy to have a piece of barley-sugar—no Gregory, no sweet! Yet see what 'Romance' does! By virtue of that distant Lady Elliot (the 'exciting mother-in-law') Stevenson shook spears and shouted the slogan, yet try as he would he could not 'join myself on with the reverend doctor' though 'no doubt . . . he moves in my blood, and whispers words to me, and sits efficient in the very knot and centre of my being.' And Robert Louis goes on to speculate about the parts played in his make-up by various ancestors, more and more remote, including a fictitious 'French barber-surgeon' and an eventual though hypothetical 'Arboreal'.

What he refrains from noting is that at twenty this grandfather showed symptoms of 'a weak chest' which were happily removed by a winter in the Isle of Wight, from which he returned to beget thirteen children and to live to be well over eighty. But this 'weakness of chest' was even more marked and ominous in his youngest daughter, Margaret Isabella, who in 1848 at the age of nineteen married Thomas Stevenson, the seventh and youngest son of Robert Stevenson. And that weakness had a most obvious and even tragical influence on the life of her only son, Robert Lewis Balfour Stevenson (Robert Louis) who was born in Edinburgh on the 13th November, 1850.

Three persons profoundly influenced the early life of this child, his parents and his nurse, the more so since, in addition to the inevitable concentration of love on an only child, Robert Louis was sickly from the age of two. Between then and the age of eleven he not only endured the usual childish illnesses but suffered digestive upsets and feverish colds, as well as gastric fever, bronchitis and pneumonia. As everyone knows, he developed tuberculosis, and was never really well even in the South Seas, while he was constantly prostrated for weeks or even months by haemorrhages of the lung. It is misplaced, therefore, to deplore the possible or even probable harm done to his character by this devoted triple care, since without it he must have died, above all in a climate as harsh as Edinburgh's. There was not only the 'chest weakness' of his mother and her father, but a dubious medical history on the Stevenson side. The letters of Robert Stevenson show a harrowing series of children's deaths in the family, though, to be sure, the child mortality of a hundred and fifty years ago was appallingly high. If a large proportion of this influence was the nurse's in the early years it is due to the fact that Mrs. Stevenson was often ill herself during that time, and naturally the father had his profession.

There can be no slightest doubt of the devotion given so lavishly to this precariously held young life. Sir Graham Balfour has recorded the touching fact that Robert Louis's mother kept a diary from 1851—except for one year—until her death, and the books are so filled with Louis and his doings that she has recorded almost every month of his life. She kept every scrap of his manuscript she could get hold of, and she is said to have made a collection of all his press-cuttings, which in the case of so popular an author must have been very bulky. And whatever the later differences of opinion, so she remained until the end. As a widow of sixty she went with him on journeys to the United States and the Pacific which are more interesting to read in her gifted son's narratives and letters than they can have been for her to endure, since they were often tiring, sometimes dreary and even dangerous. After he died she returned to Scotland, and as she too lay on her death-bed her face suddenly brightened as she exclaimed 'Louis!' and then to those about her 'I must go', and died next day without recovering consciousness. It is not suggested that maternal love is uncommon, but even in a mother such selfless and lifelong devotion is worth recording.

We cannot expect such doting sympathy from the father, a man who relaxed from his professional duties with three favourite authors. The first was Lactantius, a third-century North African and fanatical convert to Christianity, who bequeathed us a genial work *On the Wrath of God* and another on the supposedly horrid deaths which overtook the persecutors of Christians. The second was a German Protestant theologian of the sixteenth century named Vossius. And the third was 'Cardinal Bona', whose works are not known to me, surprising reading for so uncompromising a Presbyterian. Readers will remember that when Robert Louis visited the monastery of Our Lady of the Snows in the Cevennes, two laymen tried to convert him, adding that he would doubtless make his parents Catholic too. On which Stevenson remarks: 'I think I see my father's face! I would rather tackle the Gaetulian lion in his den than embark on such an enterprise against the family theologian.' But the theologian also read *Guy Mannering* and *The Parent's Assistant*, and there can be no doubt whatever of his love for his little son, whatever their differences in later life. There are several anecdotes illustrating this. Perhaps the nicest is of the time when the little boy accidentally locked himself in a room, couldn't get out, and became hysterical. While someone went for a locksmith, Mr. Stevenson succeeded in calming the child by talking to him through the door.

On top of this parental devotion came that of the nurse, which Stevenson has celebrated in 'tributes' which some people have found a little ostentatious and theatrical. It may be so, but they are certainly not insincere. Alison Cunningham was even more recklessly theological than Thomas Stevenson, and entertained the child from his earliest years with tales of her Covenanting ancestors and the persecutions they endured from the ungodly sects who did not share their views. She said that when he was a little child she had read him the whole Bible three or four times over—appalling thought to dwell on—and she insisted on the Shorter Catechism, the curious doggerel Scots metrical version of the Psalms, and such works as Foxe's *Book of Martyrs* and *The Remains of Robert Murray McCheyne*, a godly young man who, alas, died early, but whose *Remains* are said to have comforted General Gordon himself in his last days at Khartoum.

There were, of course, some mitigations of these infant bean-feasts of theology. But in those earliest years the chief change of scene was to the manse of his grandfather, and the main relaxation from godly tales and reading lay in the direction of horrifying ghost stories, penny dreadfuls, and the crude but equally dreadful imaginings of his father. No wonder the child had nightmares. And no wonder that his earliest recorded doings and sayings were of the church, churchly. His mother's diaries note with deep satisfaction the frequency of the infant's church-going, his behaviour in church, and what he said about it afterwards. At the age of two years and eight months he started 'a favourite game' which was 'making a church'. He 'makes a pulpit with a chair and a stool; reads sitting, and then stands up and sings, by turns.' The godly infant made one blunder, however. He introduced the game to the house of his little friend Walter Blaikie, usually reserving the part of Minister for himself. On one occasion, striving for *vérisme*, he unwisely added white clerical bands to his nurse's black cloak which did duty as cassock. His friend's mother entered the nursery in the midst of this performance, and then was seen how much freer Scotland was than priest-ridden Ireland:

> 'She had not minded previous performances, but when she saw the clerical bands her anger was fierce. I remember it to this day,' writes Dr. Blaikie. 'To her the assumption was an act of utter sacrilege. She tore the bands from Louis's neck, and prohibited the church game for the future.'

A lad brought up in such surroundings had either to fall to the same level or rise in sarcastic rebellion, which the growing Stevenson most certainly did, to his credit. But what human being, subjected from his tenderest years, day in, day out, year in, year out, to this virulent and ruthless sectarian propaganda could escape some marks from it? The fact that Louis Stevenson did emancipate himself gives hope that the human race may yet survie the conditioning of Communist 'materialism'. Certainly it seems unfair in Henley (who had to endure no such infantile 'brain-washing') that he failed to give his friend credit for achieving sanity, and reproached him with the innocent sermons and prayer-meetings of Vailima and his leanings towards the Shorter Catechism. He might have done worse. He might, like the over-praised 'Cummy', have devoted himself to dropping sectarian Protestant tracts in Roman Catholic churches abroad or denouncing the repairs to Colinton Kirk as 'popish'.

There were of course alleviations and distractions in this grisly *régime* of propaganda, the most wholesome of which were the hours of play with his cousins and other children of his age. But how often in this child's life of sickness, with its sleepless nights of fever and coughing and its languid days in bed, such salutary escapes became impossible. The most sensible and salutary influence among the three adults, in whose company so great a portion of this childhood was passed, seems to have been the mother's. 'Cummy', when not urging him to her most undesirable heaven, terrified him with stories of ghosts and Covenanters and body-snatchers, and perverted his taste by allowing him to buy 'cut-outs' of sanguinary melodramas which the child coloured without cutting-out, and even so, over-excited his mind.

Mr. Thomas Stevenson, whose solid philistine worth was happily relieved by a vivid sense of humour in matters and persons not involving his own dignity, had also the strange habit—almost inexplicable in a disciple of Lactantius and Vossius—of lulling himself to sleep, not with pious thoughts, godly ejaculations, and imaginings of martyrs' ends, but with endless self-invented serial tales of pirates, highwaymen, Border raids, and all that post-Walter Scott and Ainsworth costume and old clothes romance which his son, grown adult, excellently tried to excuse in himself as 'tushery'. There is reason to believe that when Mr. Stevenson was not soothing his little boy's nerves with destiny and damnation, he was forming his literary taste by telling him the *romans-feuilletons* he invented between sleep and waking. When the sick child wakened from a 'feverish sleep' with 'little sallies of delirium' and 'such agony of terror as, thank God, I have never suffered since', his father gradually soothed him with feigned 'conversations with guards or coachmen or inn-keepers'.

His mother took him in the daytime to the zoo and, along with the Bible, read him books which he found later had begun to educate his taste, and cheered him with the cheerfulness of a temperament which, perhaps irreligiously, looked always on the bright side. No doubt all three nurses of the sick hysterical child always showed him a front of exaggerated cheerfulness, as every nurse must; but it was most genuine in the mother. The thought is perhaps a little far-fetched, but perhaps not, that the strain of factitious optimism in Stevenson's writings, for which he was censured (particularly by William Archer), may have been an unconscious hang-over from those days.

If we may believe the recollections of his nurse, Stevenson's career as a writer started not long after his premature plunge into theology and church-going had made him an amateur actor. According to her, he was only three when one day he dragged her into a room, locked the door, and in a stage whisper announced that he had made up a 'story' which she was to write down. It turned out to be only 'a child's havers', but she duly wrote them down and read them later to her mistress by the fireside. Mrs. Stevenson does not seem to have mentioned this event in her comprehensive diary, nor has the script been found. However, even if this precocious start may perhaps owe something to an old woman's fancy, there actually exists an essay *On Moses* in his mother's handwriting, dictated by Stevenson at the age of six. An uncle of his had offered a prize for an essay on this Scriptural subject, to be competed for by the numerous Balfour cousins and their friends. Opinion seems to be equally divided as to whether R.L.S. did or did not win the prize.

The reader may well feel that I am making too much of this infant and his trivial adventures, but they have a two-fold significance. Even in the nineteenth century heroes were mostly made by newspapers and periodicals, and Stevenson owed much of his fame to the friends who 'vetted' his literary career, and managed a good press for him, while in personal interviews his charm and wit and good temper won him plenty of publicity. The result of this is a hero-worship which has collected every possible personal reminiscence (some of them inconceivably trite and unimportant) and has recorded many traits and little episodes even of his most childish years. The mere fact that this was done on such a scale indicates the extent of the Stevenson cult. Far less has been recorded of more important personages; but the Scots are a clannish people.

These trivialities have another significance. It must be rare for some of the main influences or traits of a life and character to be revealed so very early. There is the dependence on devoted women, so that when at last Stevenson was earning a handsome income he surrounded himself in Samoa with his mother, his wife, and his stepdaughter, all eager to serve. Lloyd Osbourne, his stepson, took the place of the indispensable male playmate, Thomas Stevenson. The conflict, both inner and outer, with religion started in his infancy. All children are self-absorbed, and indeed all adults, but the infant Stevenson was remarkably so, while the lifelong play-acting had already begun when he wrapped himself in an old gown and preached his three-year-old sermons. The 'stagey' and factitious side of his not wholly sincere cult of Wardour Street adventure is prefigured in the tales of his father and the penny shockers in 'cut-outs' from the newsagent in Antigua Street. And above all there at the beginning is the start of that lifelong battle with ill health.

If revolt against too oppressive a Presbyterian respectability made Stevenson a lifelong bohemian of the upper crust, that gnawing demon at his lungs made him over-strung and restless and a world's wanderer. There is something arresting in the strange fact that, as this child of six was lying between waking and sleep, he was heard 'crooning', and what he 'crooned' was this:

'Had not an angel got the pride of man,
No evil thought, no hardened heart would have been seen,
No hell to go to, but a heaven so pure;
That angel was the Devil.
Had not that angel got the pride, there would have been no need,
For Jesus Christ to die upon the Cross.'

That a six-year-old should be harried by the problem of 'evil' and the theological sophistries invented 'to explain' it seems to indicate a certain ruthless imprudence in his guardians. No wonder the child suffered from 'little sallies of delirium'!

'I had an extreme terror of Hell,' says Stevenson in *Nuits Blanches*, 'implanted in me, I suppose, by my good nurse, which used to haunt me terribly on stormy nights. . . .'

It was the much-praised 'Cummy', then, who did that to him, and the fact leaves one musing over his words at the end of the essay on 'Nurses':

'I believe in a better state of things, that there will be no more nurses, and that every mother will nurse her own offspring. . . .'

2

THE schooling of such a boy must have presented his parents with a very difficult problem or set of problems. Even though he had the companionship of cousins and other playmates, an only child needed the stimulus and criticism of school and school-fellows. But there was the fact of his very delicate health, which boys could neither understand nor respect, and the extreme over-excitement of his mind due to 'Cummy's' injudicious curriculum of hell-fire, melodrama, martyrs and body-snatchers. One cannot avoid thinking that a salutary measure would have been the dismissal of 'Cummy' and the provision of a properly-trained nurse with some common sense in the treatment of children and the ability to give elementary teaching in the three R's.

A priori, one would think that Thomas Stevenson would have suggested just that solution, for, by one of those Shandeyan traits of whimsicality which later endeared him so much to his gifted son, Mr. Stevenson professed and doubtless felt the most complete indifference towards formal education. It is said that during the whole of Louis's school and university days his father never asked where he stood in class or troubled about progress or lack of progress! He himself had been an indifferent pupil, yet had succeeded in the science of engineering which in his day was hardly a subject of public instruction. What he knew he picked up from his father and elder brothers, and to the end his knowledge of mathematics was so imperfect that for his inventions and other calculations he always had to call in the aid of a mathematical friend. Why should not Louis do likewise? For Mr. Stevenson, at the time of Louis's boyhood and for years after, never had the faintest doubts that the 'romance of destiny' or the intention of Providence was that Louis should become a lighthouse engineer and thus carry on the honourable and successful tradition of the Stevensons.

Why, in 1857, the decision was made to send the child to an Edinburgh school is not related, but the choice shows the best intentions. He was sent to Canonmills School which had a good reputation 'for bringing on children' who were beginners. Fellow-pupils recollected that R.L.S. was in the lowest class, whose teacher was a woman, and that 'little Stevenson' was the 'butt of the school from the oddity of his appearance'. What was 'odd' in his appearance was not stated, but it is very probable that his being the 'butt of the school' was the reason why he was very soon taken away. If, as seems probable, he was there only a few weeks and went to and fro under the charge of his nurse, he cannot have profited much either by the school or its picturesque environs. In the same year, it seems, he was sent to another school (Henderson's School in India Street) and again for a few weeks only. It is not certain whether he was taken away because of a severe gastric fever or because of the ragging he received. A fellow-pupil remembered seeing him 'in a towering rage' with 'the rim of his straw hat torn down and hanging in rims round his face and shoulders'. There is, of course, nothing like school-life for showing a boy what 'the world really is' but he did not return to the school until October, 1859, some two years later. In any case, he must have had tutors (as was then the custom in Scotland) since, when he was eight years old, he discovered that he 'loved reading', while in 1861 he was sufficiently advanced to spend a year or two at the Edinburgh Academy.

Meanwhile, especially during the summer months the boy with his fine sensibility was gathering other and less trying impressions than those of the sick-room and his over-anxious guardians, of the streets of Edinburgh in weary little walks with his 'Covenanting' nurse, and of the hostility of schoolboys to someone a little different from themselves. Perhaps the most important of these impressions in Stevenson's life was that of his cousin R. A. M. Stevenson ('Bob'), his closest companion in boyish games, and later not only an ally but a leader in emancipation from the deadweight of 'respectability' which pressed on Stevenson's youth. Even more formative at the early stage before his grandfather died (Stevenson was then ten) was the summer life at Colinton Manse. Fortunately for us Stevenson's intense interest in himself led him to record his memories of that time not only in *The Manse of Memories and Portraits* but in the *Colinton Manse* quoted so fully by Sir Graham Balfour. The influence of the place on the sensitive, imaginative boy, of the games he played with his cousins or by himself, may easily be inferred from these pages. Even then at that early date his 'destiny' as a writer seemed obvious, for he writes:

> 'I would often get someone for amanuensis, and write pleasant narratives, which have fallen some degree into unjust oblivion. One, I remember, had for scene the Witches' Walk, and for heroine a kitten. It was intended to be something very thrilling and spectral....'

And there Stevenson leaves us with unsatisfied curiosity about this thrilling and spectral kitten, except to tell us that the kitten prosaically fed on 'pease-brose'. In another of the beautifully-written and readable essays which are among Stevenson's claims to permanent literary fame we find a very interesting passage on the 'Scottish child' which it is no straining of the text to see as the author's memory of influences in his own early years. Speaking of the influence of Scotland on her children he says:

> 'A Scottish child hears much of shipwreck, outlying iron skerries, pitiless breakers and great sea-lights; much of heathery mountains, wild clans, and hunted Covenanters. . . .'

One may perhaps be forgiven for saying in parenthesis that this particular set of traditional stories is much more characteristic of the Stevenson milieu than that of the 'Scottish child' in general. But here, as so often, Stevenson is wisely writing from his own experience. The generalizing is a mere device of style to excuse his self-absorption. He goes on, still giving his own memories as a child:

> 'Breaths come to him in song of the distant Cheviots, and the ring of foraying hoofs. He glories in his hard-fisted forefathers, of the iron girdle and the handful of oatmeal, who rode so swiftly and lived so sparely on their raids. Poverty, ill-luck, enterprise and constant resolution are the fibres of the legend of his country's history. The heroes and kings of Scotland have been tragically fated; the most marking incidents in Scottish history—Flodden, Darien, or the Forty-Five—were still either failures or defeats; and the fall of Wallace and the repeated reverses of the Bruce combine with the very smallness of the country to teach rather a moral than a material criterion for life.

Often, too often for one's will to admire, there is in Stevenson's writing a touch, and more than a touch, of artifice, of the factitious or faintly spurious, something of the *poseur* which unquestionably entered into the make-up of the living man. But here the feeling is genuine, although no generally approved sentiment is so often exaggerated or feigned as patriotism. Perhaps only Scots can feel how genuinely Stevenson was a Scot from identity of sentiment and response, but an Englishman in his own way feels it equally because he feels the difference.

A cynic might say that for somebody who loved Scotland so much, Stevenson spent an abnormally large part of his life out of it. But there is the perfect alibi of his health or lack of health. Stevenson has written well on many themes and countries, yet he seems at his best when writing of Scotland and Scottish characters, sometimes from places hundreds or even thousands of miles away. Even his love of France, one of the genuine traits in a make-up which includes much that might be considered pose, is Scottish rather than English. He loves the people and their literature, rather than the food and the comfort of France. It is perhaps a purely personal feeling, but Stevenson's verse in Scots, though not equal to his three or four finest poems in the *patois* of the Southron, is as a whole more interesting than the English. Again, while his letters, particularly the later ones, sometimes fall below his best and high standard and tend towards essays or sermons, they brisk up and re-kindle one's interest when he writes in Scots to his friend Baxter or to Bob Stevenson. Sometimes it suited his brilliant sense of humour better even than the English he handled with such skill.

Yet, as so often with Stevenson, the attitude is not wholly consistent, and in later years he certainly expressed a dislike for Edinburgh and Edinburgh people. What he loved was the romantic Scotland of landscape and legend. The realities of Edinburgh respectability and east winds were less fertilizing to a life which was lived so much in the imagination. In spite of which it seems obvious that his early excursions in Scotland impressed him more than the considerable amount of continental travel which were included in his 'destiny' during his teens.

Among the fancies of psychologists is a theory that a sense of insecurity is created in a child (and persists through life) if his home is changed too often and suddenly. Stevenson did have this feeling of insecurity, or at least he speaks of his 'fear of life'. This can hardly be attributed to insecurity of home life, which was always centred in Edinburgh, and from May of 1857 (Stevenson then being six and a half) was always at 17 Heriot

Row until his father's death in 1887. The earlier moves from 8 Howard Place and 1 Inverleith Terrace had been undertaken mainly because the houses were thought unsuitable to the delicate health of Robert Louis and his mother. As early as 1857 he had been taken on a tour round the English Lakes, but his first real travelling on any scale occurred in 1862–3.

It was Thomas Stevenson's ill health which in 1862 brought the family south to London and then to the Isle of Wight, which had been so serviceable to the weak chest of the Rev. Lewis Balfour. Robert Louis then saw Salisbury and Stonehenge. In the summer of that year they went overseas to Hamburg (still on account of Mr. Stevenson) where they stayed a month. Next year Mrs. Stevenson's health took all three of them and a girl cousin of Robert Louis's to Menton for two months, and from there they visited Genoa, Naples, Rome, Florence, Venice, Innsbruck and the Rhine. Perhaps he was a little too young, in spite of his supposed precocity, but these five months of travel in what were then some of the loveliest and comparatively intact towns of Europe seem to have influenced him very little. Unlike the aesthetes of his own and the preceding generation he seems to have been almost unmoved by what he saw, and a friend of Addington Symonds (Horatio Brown) in later years talked enthusiastically to him about Venice without so much as learning that Robert Louis had ever been in Italy. Menton and the lessons he had in French conversation there were what he chiefly remembered. Readers of Stevenson wonder how it happened that he came to know French so well in view of his broken schooling and his system of 'truantry' when he was at school. A clever lad conversing in a foreign language with a tutor who understands him will learn more in two months by that method than he would in twice that number of years of the mechanical plodding in class. Stevenson and his mother were again in Menton for the first five months of 1864, and presumably he again talked with the same or another tutor. True, he learned no grammar, but neither do French children until they have learned the language.

His early travels in Scotland were less extensive, mostly holidays in districts near Edinburgh, but they seem to have made a deeper impression on him, just as he remembered the scenery of the Rhône valley and forgot the towns of Italy. During a stay at Peebles he is said to have fought a duel with another boy—real pistols and powder but no bullets, a rather apt symbol of Stevenson's 'adventures'; and at North Berwick there was a boyish affair of the heart with a girl, though perhaps what he really loved were 'the long twilights on its sands, the glen and the burn running down it to the sea'.

Although Stevenson's health improved as he reached his teens, his formal education still remained desultory and ineffective. In the autumn of 1863 he was sent to an English boarding school, but a letter in would-be French to his mother ended up thus in English:

> 'My dear papa, you told me to tell you whenever I was miserable. I do not feel well and I wish to get home. Do take me with you.'

Many, perhaps most, parents, however much distressed by such an appeal, would have tried to resist it. Not so Mr. Thomas Stevenson. On his way to Menton he stopped at the school to pick up his son, who thus spent the first five months of 1864 in the South of France. He then rather significantly was sent to a school in Edinburgh 'for backward and delicate boys', where he nominally remained until he was seventeen and entered the University. Even when he attended school he paid little attention to subjects that did not interest him, though a fellow-pupil thought that Stevenson did work at French, Latin and geometry. Meanwhile, Mr. Thomas Stevenson continued his habit of stopping schoolboys in the street and, after looking at their school-books, would strongly advise them to pay no attention to such rubbish, but to play as much as they liked and to study only what happened to interest them.

Presumably he gave his son the same advice, and whether he did or did not, there can be no doubt that such was the course Robert Louis followed without any rebuke from his father. Clearly he was still so convinced that Providence intended his son to be an engineer that he was only anxious lest Robert Louis by attending too closely to regular studies might be tempted into the Church or the law or some other profession than building and fitting lighthouses. It never occurred to him that his son was preparing himself in his own way for what many besides Thomas Stevenson considered the precarious, semi-idle, self-indulgent life of a writer. Relying perhaps on his own experience as a boy and growing youth, Mr. Thomas Stevenson thought to correct any deficiencies in his son's education by giving the lad the run of his father's books.

There was shrewdness here in spite of the objections which would be made by the professional educator ('vous êtes orfèvre, monsieur Josse!') because a clever lad or even one not particularly gifted remembers better and is more influenced by what he finds out for himself than by what is imposed on him in the form of a curriculum he finds irksome and tedious. Thomas Stevenson's object, whether he admitted it or not, was for his son to grow as like himself intellectually and morally as possible. Naturally Mr. Stevenson's library was a replica of himself, and he could scarcely have imagined there was any danger in allowing his son to range freely over bookshelves which held mainly 'the proceedings of learned societies, some Latin divinity, cyclopaedias, physical science, and, above all, optics.'

What risk of the unconventional could be there, what 'horns of elf-land faintly blowing' to lure even the most guileless from the paths of Scottish Presbyterianism and engineering? None whatever if Robert Louis had been the same sort of person as his father and grandfather instead of a frail youth perilously freighted with a wayward temperament and literary genius. Even an Engineer to the Board of Northern Lights is not perfect, and there were a few books in that austere collection of what Charles Lamb would have called 'bilbia abiblia'. Stevenson has named some of them, and they included three of Scott's novels (including *Rob Roy*), the voyages of Captain Woodes Rogers, *The Female Bluebeard*, the *Mare au Diable* of Georges Sand, Harrison Ainsworth's *Tower of London* and four bound volumes of early *Punch* which happened to contain some of Thackeray's work. Obviously other books must have accompanied or preceded these. Thus, Stevenson mentions that he read *The Thousand and One Nights* in his grandfather's lifetime (i.e. before he was ten) and he was much impressed when his mother read *Macbeth* to him, though this may have been much later. It would be interesting to know when he discovered Montaigne, whose influence is so marked in the essays, but so mature a mind was hardly likely to please a youth who was in love with adventure stories. He seems to have read *Robinson Crusoe* when he was about twelve.

In 1887, more than twenty years after the period of his life we are now considering, Stevenson published in the *British Weekly* an article called *Books Which Have Influenced Me*. These are the books—or the characters from books—which remained with him, but in view of his early development it is likely that some at least of them began to influence him before he was twenty. He starts off, inevitably, with Shakespeare, with special emphasis on Hamlet, Rosalind and Kent; from which he passes to the d'Artagnan of *Le Vicomte de Bragelonne* and Bunyan's *Pilgrim's Progress*—a curious mixture. He says that Montaigne came to him 'early', but what does that mean? Did he read him with his tutor at Menton? Possibly, but as he says the influence 'was only sensible later on' I think it reasonable to infer that so mature an author must have come later in any effective way.

Rather startlingly, but keeping in 'order of time' Stevenson next mentions the Gospel according to St. Matthew. One can only say: 'Here was a youth with an open mind and a wide range of tastes', especially since the next work on his list is Walt Whitman's *Leaves of Grass*! Having said of St. Matthew that it contains those truths which 'we are all courteously supposed to know and all modestly refrain from applying', he then declares *Leaves of Grass* to be:

> '. . . a book of singular service, a book which tumbled the world upside down for me, blew into space a thousand cobwebs of genteel and ethical illusion, and, having thus shaken my tabernacle of lies, set me back again upon a strong foundation of all the original and manly virtues.'

When he proceeds to tell us that 'close upon' Whitman came Herbert Spencer, followed by Lewes's *Life of Goethe* (adding that 'I know no one whom I admire less than Goethe') we can well understand that in his university years he was in something of a turmoil intellectually. Nobody can say that it is impossible to assimilate and to control such diverse and even mutually destructive mental influences, for Stevenson obviously did so, but it is not wonderful that he puzzled others besides his father.

Stevenson's reading, however, is but a small part of his impulse to write and, above all, of the thorough training in style and expression which he gave himself, apparently from quite an early age; yet the authors named above had already in 1871–72 (when he was just of age) been increased by Horace, Pepys, Hazlitt, Burns, Sterne, Heine, Keats and Fielding, all of them marked 'most dear', and therefore presumably studied closely.

For the beginnings of his wish to write and deliberate study of writing we have to go back from his Edinburgh University years (1867–73) to an earlier period. We can dismiss as common to many children the little things he dictated to his nurse or mother before he had even learned to write (he never learned to spell with accuracy!) and the MS. magazines he started at school and at home. Still, it is interesting that in 1863 (when he was twelve) his contributions included such titles as *A Ghost Story*, *The Wreckers* (!) and equally prophetically *Creek Island, or Adventures in the South Seas*. Still more interesting, the testimonies of his school-friends Bellyse Baildon and John Ramsay Anderson indicate that as early as the Edinburgh School years Stevenson had started his self-imposed and self-taught task of 'learning to write'.

It is a truism that in the work of every creative literary artist there is 'inspiration' or the mysterious and spontaneous prompting of the subconscious mind, and there is 'execution' or the transference of these gifts by the conscious mind into words so appropriate that the reader will share what the author has felt. The common delusion is that nothing is easier than to say exactly what you mean and to convey that meaning uncontaminated to others; when, as a matter of fact, it is extremely difficult, as Stevenson himself has pointed out. Many writers, understandably, do not inform the world as to where they 'get their ideas', or the means by which they have learned to write as well or as badly as they do. In any case both author and reader might well feel that the revelation was a little egotistic, taking for granted the importance of the writer and his work, and even fringing the impertinent. Most fortunately for us Stevenson was much too interested in himself and everything which touched him to be subject to any such inhibition. The assumption that these entirely personal revelations were valuable enough to be recorded is no doubt characteristic of Stevenson, but it is also noteworthy that he and his friends had managed to create such a favourable prejudice in the Anglo-American reading public that they were eager to admire in him what they might have resented even in Meredith or Kipling. Somehow, with a little assistance from others, he had made himself a literary predecessor of later world's sweethearts and glamour-boys—the Rudolph Valentino of Parnassus. Which does not in the least detract from the exceptional interest of Stevenson's admirably presented descriptions of his mental processes and literary training.

In describing the process of his 'inspiration' Stevenson goes back to the early childhood period of sickness and 'Cummy' which has already been summarily sketched here. He was, he says, 'an ardent and uncomfortable dreamer', a condition, we may infer, due mainly to the feverish state of his health but also to the sensational theology which appalled his sensitive spirit. The two chief troubles of his life, 'hell and judgment' and 'school tasks' were, he says, often 'confounded together in one appalling nightmare'; and as he puts it with startling vigour 'the night-hag would have him by the throat, and pluck him, strangling and screaming, from his sleep'. It is an indication both of the child's sufferings and of his intense imagination that he felt it an alleviation when he suffered nothing worse than 'a flying heart, a freezing scalp, cold sweats, and the speechless midnight fear'!

Gradually from nightmares he progressed to more and more pleasureable dreams, of journeys and towns, and then of 'stories' in the eighteenth century, especially of Jacobites. Then in his dreams he read books, mostly of a 'tushery' kind apparently, but 'so incredibly more vivid and moving than any printed book, that he has ever since been malcontent with literature'—a statement to be taken a little cautiously, for throughout his life Stevenson's waking enjoyment of real books was intense and perfectly sincere. He is trying to make us see how vivid the dreams were, perhaps not altogether realizing that he was also telling us the power of creation of his subconscious mind.

A relapse to nightmare conditions followed, probably during the university period, but the physical basis of these images of horror is sufficiently revealed by the prosaic fact that while the dreams went on, the terror and horror were dissipated by 'a simple draught' prescribed by a doctor. It was after that, however, that he came to the beginning of a lifelong dream experience which, so far as I know, seems to be unique among writers—for de Quincey's and Coleridge's dreams were fantasies bred by opium. Like his father, Stevenson began to tell himself tales in the interval between waking and sleep, and then found that the tales went on in his sleeping dreams as if performed by 'little people' whose acting out of plots he remembered when he woke. They were less like 'drilled actors' than like children playing in 'man's internal theatre'. And from there he goes on to relate the extraordinary fact that his 'little people' gave him in his sleep the idea and even some of the scenes for *Jekyll and Hyde* and much of *Olalla*. He also gives the outline of a very striking story which he dreamed entire, but refrained from writing on commercial grounds—the public of that day would take any amount of blood and murder but would not endure sexual impropriety however dramatic, moving and tragical. That prejudice lost us a book which Stevenson, if he had possessed the moral courage as well as literary genius, might have made his finest achievement. 'We are such stuff as dreams are made on . . .' but has any other author thus fetched his plots and characters from the shadowy abysses of sleep?

Of course we must not take all this too literally and absolutely. Much of Stevenson's writing, and that for many readers his best and most enduring, had nothing to do with this dream-world of 'inspiration' but came wholly from the waking world and a conscious directing mind. There are no ghosts or 'little people' in the essays or so admirable a piece of realism and observation as *The Amateur Emigrant*. Which brings us back to the topic of Stevenson's long self-training and self-discipline as a conscious stylist. Baildon tells us that even at Mr. Thompson's School Stevenson had 'a fixed idea that literature was his calling, and a marvellously mature conception of the course of self-education' he had to follow. Anderson, less definitely, puts this as far back as the Academy period. At any rate he says that Stevenson 'used to appear in class in the morning with a scrap of paper' on which he had written verses, often making fun of his school-friends or the masters. There is some division of opinion as to whether Stevenson studied verse-writing as closely as prose-writing, but in any case little lampoons of this sort can hardly have been a serious part of the 'course of self-education' vouched for by Baildon.

Yet Stevenson's own words might be construed to mean that he started as early as the Academy days for he opens an account of his literary self-education by saying that it went on 'all through my boyhood and youth'. The only interest in the possibility of the earlier date is the fact that it would be truly remarkable if a boy of twelve or thirteen had actually and consciously begun a course of self-training as an author.

'I kept always two books in my pocket,' says Stevenson, 'one to read, one to write in.' On his walks, he explains, he tried to find the right words to describe what he saw; and whenever he sat down to rest he either read or noted the scene before him or wrote 'halting stanzas'. He 'lived with words', and did so 'consciously for practice'. And then he makes the curious statement: 'It was not so much that I wished to be an author (though I wished that too) as that I had vowed that I would learn to write.' But why do that unless one wishes to be an author? It is surely a barren accomplishment enough even if authorship is achieved, but really futile if it looks no further than an aimless virtuosity. The good Stevenson is unfair to himself, for, as we have seen, he was trying his hand at tales and verses all along, and he was not sixteen when he turned a pseudo-Scott novel on Covenanters into the brief historical sketch of *The Pentlands Rising*. Moreover, on his walks he tried to record conversations, and imagined dialogues in which he played a part.

His own criticism of this part of his self-training is that it taught him nothing more than 'the choice of the essential note and the right word'. It is all very well for a writer of Stevenson's achievement to treat these acquirements with a Holmes-like disdain as elementary and 'less intellectual', but there are only too many authors who never seek for them or, at least, never find them with any certainty of purpose. And not everyone will agree that a higher 'standard of achievement' was necessarily attained by his prolonged efforts at producing *pastiches* of famous authors he admired. There is the dread peril, which must have struck almost any youth less confident and self-assured, that the result might not be a passable emulation but an unintended parody. A generation later Marcel Proust in France produced a volume of brilliant *pastiches* of great writers which were intended as respectful parodies. In his Duc de Saint-Simon he catches the great master's almost inimitable manner with perfect felicity in the sentence—I quote from memory: 'C'était dans ces temps-ci qu'on voyait l'indécence de M. de Vendôme traité publiquement d'Altesse.' Stevenson is very disparaging of these exercises, describing them as 'monkey tricks', but who knows whether in some humorous mood he may not have forestalled Proust in the irony of literary compliment? But that does not answer the question whether writing *pastiches* of the great is a sound method of 'learning to write'. Perhaps it is, but perhaps it accounts for some of the mannerisms of style which annoy those readers who will not tolerate the presence of their author in his narrative and insist that he be as invisible in his prose as a manipulator of marionettes on his tiny stage.

Montaigne, Hazlitt, Lamb, Defoe and Sir Thomas Browne are some of the old favourites Stevenson numbers among his victims; and to them he adds Wordsworth, Hawthorne, Baudelaire, Obermann, and Ruskin. He wrote an epic about Cain in imitation of Browning's *Sordello*, and that doubtless read a little quaintly; made a verse story of Robin Hood in a Corinthian style fused from Chaucer, Keats and Morris, imitated Swinburne, and many lyric poets. His most remarkable and indeed baffling display of virtuosity was to write a tragedy in the style of Webster and then to treat the same subject in the manner of Congreve. Imagination is in travail to conceive how *The White Devil* could be transformed into an *Old Bachelor* even in the fancy of a conceited youth from a people whose worst enemies have never accused them of modesty. And finally, he asserts that a youthful tragedy about Semiramis in later years became *Prince Otto*, which is much less surprising than the former feat of literary alchemy.

'That, like it or not, is the way to learn to write'; says Stevenson dogmatically, adding the saving clause; 'whether I have profited or not, that is the way.' It may be so, though I should suspect it is more the 'way' of a French than of a British writer, and suspect also—though with no scrap of evidence—that the youthful Stevenson may have picked up the suggestion during one of those sojourns in Menton. Yet perhaps this is unfair, and he worked out the method for himself. If so, all the more honour to him for having from the beginning thought of writing as a craft or trade to be learned. Altogether admirable and indisputable is his reply to the inevitable objection that this is not the way to be original—'It is not; nor is there any way but to be born so'. And if only this truth were fully established along with the twin truth that no man by taking thought can make himself original but only temporarily conspicuous, how much false work in all the arts the world would be spared.

Stevenson, it will be noted, says nothing about translation as training for a writer. Translating gives practice in transferring the thought, descriptions, dialogue and style of another author into the translator's own tongue without the dangers of direct imitation. It is the difference between actually copying a picture and making an engraving of one. It is safer since a writer is less likely to remain unconsciously affected by the manner of a foreign author than by someone writing English. Of course, Stevenson may have done more early translating than is indicated by a friend's reference to rhymed versions of Ovid in the style of Scott. And of course every writer has his own methods, even in early days, which he is unlikely to change. Stevenson was less likely to change than others, once he had made up his mind. Mr. J. A. Steuart has recorded a significant remark made in conversation by an old friend:

> 'On the surface Louis Stevenson seemed all frivolity and flippancy; but beneath he was flint.'

That applies in matters more vital to his life and fortune than methods of literary training.

3

THE years 1867–1873 cover an interesting period of Stevenson's life—from a schoolboy to a man. In the first of those years he was entered as a student in Edinburgh University, and in the last he went off to Menton, alone, broken to some extent in both physical and mental health by the long intermittent struggle with his parents and his environment. In his parents he had to fight obstinate prepossessions as to the profession he was to follow, and an even more obstinate bigotry which took it for granted that their faith must be his; and the battle was made all the harder because this possessiveness was the expression of real love and devotion. They wanted him to adopt the family profession because, after all, it was the most natural and reasonable thing for him to do, ensuring an honourable and profitable career and keeping him near them; while adherence by him to their sect would ensure an eventual re-establishment of the family circle in heaven. Stevenson felt otherwise, as many sons of Victorian families did, but it is questionable if many had to fight quite so hard against such odds. The struggle with his environment—that is, mainly with Edinburgh people of his own class—is that which awaits every unusual person in a conventional and censorious community. Of course Stevenson had his friends and abettors, but they were few and his critics were many. Whatever the local adulation of him as a writer after he became a world success, the evidence seems to show that (with the exceptions mentioned) he was not then esteemed either as a person or a writer in Edinburgh, and never was in the country round Swanston.

In view of the testimonies, including that of Stevenson himself, to his inadequate schooling, the question naturally arises: how did he manage to get into a great university? In the first place we may reasonably suspect that the inadequacy of the education may have been exaggerated—it is a very common human trait to enjoy (and unconsciously to exaggerate) the tale of the brilliantly successful man who was a complete duffer at school. Even in school subjects a clever lad like Stevenson picks up casually what others less gifted must plod to acquire, and he makes a better use of whatever he has picked up. Many an Honours man might well envy Stevenson his knowledge of French and French literature, not to mention French life.

There are, however, excellent reasons why at that date his academical shortcomings, whatever they may have been, were no bar to his university career. At that time, there was no entrance examination to Edinburgh University. Anybody properly recommended and able to pay the fees could attend lectures, but no action was taken when students cut lectures, and there does not appear to have been a tutorial system which might have compelled some work. All has since been changed, but in those days of freedom and self-reliance the assumption was that the students were men not boys, and if they had come to work they would work; if not, that was their affair. If Stevenson absented himself from lectures, as he undoubtedly did, he could hardly put the blame on the quality of the lecturers. In Latin he had W. Y. Sellar, an excellent scholar; in 'Natural Philosophy' a collaborator of Lord Kelvin; and in Engineering, a man with the odd name of Fleeming (pronounced Fleming) Jenkin who, after an inauspicious start, became one of Stevenson's most valued friends, unflattering but affectionate.

Stories, which have the all too familiar ring of the apocryphal biographical anecdote, are told to illustrate wittily Stevenson's neglect of his work as an undergraduate; in spite of which there can be no doubt whatever that he did neglect it. He might easily have defended himself on the ground that a university education taken too seriously may make a professor, but will certainly mar a writer. When Jowett advised the highly erudite Swinburne to leave Oxford without taking a degree, it is a question whether the Master trembled for the poet's morals or his genius. That Stevenson did not profit academically by his university studies may be inferred from a rather severe comment made (in 1880 at Davos) by his friend J. A. Symonds, a Balliol man who took first-class honours, and was awarded a Magdalen fellowship:

> 'The more I see of him, the less I find of solid mental stuff. He wants years of study in tough subjects. After all a university education has some merits. One feels the want of it in men like him.'

Here the good Symonds was perhaps a trifle Oxonian. It may be doubted if he, with all his Balliol culture, could have written a paper *On the Thermal Influence of Forests* good enough to be read before the Royal Society of Edinburgh, or have won a silver medal for another paper (written at twenty) on *A New Form of Intermittent Light for Lighthouses*. Stevenson certainly did both, but the question is, how far was he helped by his engineer specialist father?

These two papers, which add nothing to Stevenson's renown as an author, are worth mentioning if only to show that he did make efforts to please his father by writing on scientific subjects. Yet it is doubtful whether such concessions, however well-meant, did not in the end complicate affairs. Stevenson must have known when he wrote them that he would not be engineer to the Board of Northern Lights, and therefore was in a sense misleading his father; but as he was still a minor he might well feel his duty was to obey. On the other hand it is obvious that Thomas Stevenson tolerated his son's idleness at the university mainly because he expected him to become an engineer once his salad days were over. One sees the difficulties and misunderstandings on both sides.

These scientific papers were not the only signs that Stevenson, during his university years, did make attempts to follow his father's wishes in choosing a profession. As early as 1863 he had gone with his father to visit lighthouses on the coast of Fife, though this was hardly a tour of instruction at that early age but rather a device of parental fondness to excuse the boy's going to school, over which he had 'shed tears of miserable sympathy' on a stray cat. A later excursion of inspection with his father took him over part of the voyage made half a century earlier by his grandfather with Sir Walter Scott. In the summer of 1868 he went to Anstruther on the coast of Fife 'to glean engineering experience from the building of the breakwater'. In letters home at the time Stevenson makes some effort at least to seem interested, reporting to his father that the masons have got 'ahead of the divers', promising to watch the masons at work and 'see how long they take to work that Fife-ness stone you ask about', and asking to be told what 'sort of things' he should look for. He mentions his work deciphering and copying-out a specification of some boat-builders who were 'the most illiterate writers with whom I have ever had any dealing'. But his real feelings are vividly expressed in a letter to his mother:

'I am utterly sick of this grey, grim, sea-beaten hole. I have a little cold in my head, which makes my eyes sore; and you can't tell how utterly sick I am, and anxious to get back among trees and flowers and something less meaningless than this bleak fertility*.'

And in the essay *Random Memories* devoted to this episode of his youth Stevenson says specifically that he had already made his 'own private determination to be an author', adding later that his 'only industry was in the hours when' he 'was not on duty'. If that was true of Anstruther, it must have been equally so when he moved on to the bleaker and windier and 'subarctic town of Wick' in Caithness, 'one of the meanest of man's towns, and situate certainly on the baldest of God's bays'. True, in his letters he keeps up what can only have been a pretence of interest in the work there and at Anstruther, offering to take the 'measurements and calculated weight of any stones that have been evidently moved by the sea'. But he surely gave away unwittingly the elementary state of his engineering knowledge when, in the same letter, he unguardedly asks his father the weight of a square foot of salt water and how many pounds there are in a ton! A future builder of lighthouses on dangerous half-submerged reefs and of harbour works on tempestuous seas ought surely to have got a little further than that! Yet he worked loyally enough, skinning and discolouring his hands by hauling at a wet hawser; and (perhaps more from curiosity than duty and certainly in spite of his father's fears) he went down with the divers working at the wall under-water. But surely the future writer and no engineer is revealed by this report of the destruction made by a storm. Note the picturesquely descriptive language.

'The end of the work displays gaps, cairns of ten-ton blocks, stones torn from their places and turned right round. . . . The roadway is torn away, cross-heads, broken planks tossed here and there, planks gnawn and mumbled as if a starved bear had been trying to eat them, planks with spales lifted from them as if they had been dressed with a rugged plane, one pile swaying to and fro clear of the bottom, the rails in one place sunk a foot at least. This was not a great storm, the waves were light and short. Yet when we were standing at the office, I felt the ground beneath me *quail* as a huge roller thundered on the work at the last year's cross wall.'

* Sterility?

To us who are wise after the event it may seem strange that Mr. Thomas Stevenson did not perceive and take warning from the fact that this and other passages in the youth's letters were the work of a born writer, not of a business man or a practical engineer. But men can be very blind when they have set their hearts on something, especially a Victorian father in a home where we are assured his 'slightest word or wish was sacred'. Apparently he went on believing that Robert Louis would become an engineer as planned until the very day (8th April, 1871) when he heard the shattering news from his son that he could not and would not make engineering his life's work. It was all the harder for the father to accept since this declaration (based on the 'flint' of Robert Louis's character) came close on top of the award of that medal.

There must have been pain on both sides, for even so complete an egoist as Louis Stevenson at the height of this contest of wills could not fail to acknowledge the limitless affection, consideration and care given him by his parents. That they made mistakes is obvious, but it would need a son far more obtuse and insensitive than Louis Stevenson to fail to see that he was the centre and motive of their lives. The wanton abandonment of a great tradition of scientific and public service—for so Robert Louis's declaration must have seemed to him—was made all the more intolerable since Thomas Stevenson had the greatest contempt for literature as a profession and a truly Scottish disbelief in the ability of his only son.

Two testimonies should suffice. Patrick Campbell, a Writer to the Signet, who had known Robert Louis from 1861, relates that at an Edinburgh dinner he introduced to Mr. and Mrs. Thomas Stevenson a young clerical friend, the Rev. Alexander Whyte:

> '. . . and I can never forget the astonishment of the father when he heard the unstinted praise of his son from the lips of a serious-minded young clergyman, and the look of incredulity with which he listened to it all.'

Unfortunately Campbell does not give us the date of this episode, though the later it occurred the more significant it is. As late as 1879 when the estrangement between Stevenson and his father was at its worst, the old man spoke of it freely to Sir James Dewar, speaking 'with anger and dismay of his son's journey' (to America to marry Mrs. Osbourne) 'and intentions, his desertion of the old firm, and taking to the devious and barren paths of literature'. Professor Dewar ventured to disagree, and, partly in joke, partly in earnest, offered to bet that in ten years' time Robert Louis's earnings would be larger than the Stevenson engineering firm had ever made.

> 'To his surprise, the father became furious, and repulsed all attempts at reconciliation.'

Six and a half years later the old man, near his end, insisted on being carried to apologize to his friend, for Sir James and not he was tending to be right. These two episodes, which seem as authentic as most biographical material, give us some idea of the appalling difficulties Louis Stevenson had to face in combatting the philistine prejudices and commercial outlook of his father. There is something very revealing in his anger at the suggestion that a mere 'writer' could possibly earn as much as the great engineer, and in a standard of values which made the earning of money the test of merit. It is not surprising that Robert Louis was only too glad to accept the compromise of reading for the Scottish Bar, though he must have known that with his temperament and his love of human truth he was even less fitted to be a barrister than an engineer.

Mr. Thomas Stevenson, however deeply devoted to his son, seems to have taken his duties as a parent with something of the grimness of his uncomfortable religion, and not always to have shown in their relations that sense of humour for which he is praised. Two instances of this may be cited among several, trifling indeed, but all the more annoying to a high-spirited lad because they were trifling. He imposed a fine of a penny for every time Robert Louis used a slang word in his father's hearing. In the first place this was a heavy tax on a pocket-money of half a crown a week in his student days, which was still only a pound a month when he was twenty-three. In the second case, a lad constantly hears slang, uses it, and drops the habit, while for a student of language and style so intelligent as Stevenson slang was part of his study—it is language in the raw, the crude state of what tomorrow may be colloquial and the day after that 'standard'. If we cut from the language everything that has at one time been considered slang since the time of Addison we should talk and write an oddly stilted and archaic speech. And the petty little oppression did not succeed anyway. Flora Masson (a daughter of the Edinburgh Professor of English) has left a note on a Stevenson dinner-party during Robert Louis's student days when she sat between father and son. Louis talked of Balzac, whom Miss Masson had never heard of, and Thomas Stevenson thought nothing of! Louis talked brilliantly, causing in his father, she thought, 'an indescribable mixture of vexation, fatherly pride, admiration and sheer vexation'. The talk turned on foreign words which Mr. Stevenson of course wanted to ostracize, and this

> '. . . made Louis Stevenson rattle off with extraordinary ingenuity whole sentences composed of words taken into our language from all parts of the world. . . . By a string of sentences he proved the absurdity of such a doctrine, and indeed its practical impossibility. The father was silenced; but for a moment he had been almost tearfully in earnest.'

The other occasion was when Mr. Stevenson discovered that his son belonged to a club of young students, the first rule of which was that members were to disregard everything they had learned from their parents. Instead of laughing at them and asking to be enrolled as a member, the model parent came down very heavily indeed and thereby turned a jest into something more nearly serious. In any event his handling of these and a hundred other symptoms of 'growing-up' developed rather than discouraged Robert Louis's inevitable revolt against the dour religion forced upon his frightened childhood and against the smug, purse-proud, conventional, repressive society that religion had created.

Trifles such as these have little importance in themselves, but they have a significance since they show how divided father and son were in their outlook, and how hard it was for Thomas Stevenson to conceive the possibility that he might be wrong and Louis right. During his son's student years in Edinburgh Mr. Stevenson had to endure other wounds to his pride through his son's defiance of his human environment and the dreary religion which was behind it all.

To begin with, a great many of Robert Louis's fellow-townsmen disliked his physical appearance, and the way he dressed or failed to dress. George Crabbie remembered him as 'a thin, lanky youth, with long hair, a sallow complexion', and the Rev. Archibald Bisset says he had 'a very noticeable stoop of the shoulders, and a poorly-developed chest'. An unnamed friend, quoted by J. A. Steuart, goes a good deal further:

> 'To begin with he was badly put together, a slithering loose flail of a fellow, all joints, elbows, and exposed spindle-shanks. . . . He was so like a scarecrow that one almost expected him to creak in the wind.'

It is true that another witness, but a woman this time (Margaret Moyes Black), says he was 'a very interesting personality', 'picturesque and distinguished', 'slim, and graceful'; yet Edmund Gosse, who was not of Edinburgh and saw Stevenson as early as 1870, thought him ugly. It is perhaps a bias, but my own impression from a study of the rather numerous photographs coincides rather with that of the lady than of these male friends. The photograph, of course, is dubious evidence—the camera usually lies—but the mature Stevenson has a singularly attractive look, with very intelligent eyes, and a smile which gives a hint of why so many people found him 'charming'. Strange to say, his appearance improved as he got older, partly because of the dentistry which changed the expression of his mouth very much for the better, and partly because he was no longer oppressed by Scotland, home and the Sabbath. If the early photographs are taken alone, it is impossible to deny that Stevenson then was rather 'homely', not because he looks 'emaciated' (as some testimonies assert) but mainly because of his really ugly mouth and a rather cowed expression. He does not look 'emaciated', at least in the early photographs.

There is an 'animus' in some of these recollections which do more than correct the usual treacly *de mortuis nil nisi bunkum* of the innumerable Stevenson sentimentalizers, who are as nippy in suggesting the false as they are unscrupulous in suppressing the truth. Other testimonies show that years after Stevenson's death and apotheosis as the literary hero of the British bourgeoisie, his youthful defiances still rankled. You would think a more or less humble undergraduate might be allowed a little laxity of dress without arousing so much almost vindictive annoyance, but then, if the British dearly love a Laird, they deeply loathe an

Artist. He looked 'like a quack or a gipsy', says one 'friend', who deplores a costume of 'duck trousers and a black shirt, with a loose collar and a tie that might be a strip torn from a castaway carpet'. It was noted that his black velvet jacket 'never seemed good or new', and this was charitably explained on the theory that 'there must be a family trunk full of old clothes that he was wearing out'. Margaret Black, even, regrets his 'weird attire'. The prejudice pursued him to London, where one afternoon Stevenson was walking in Bond Street dressed in a black shirt, red tie, black coat and velvet smoking-cap. Meeting him, the Oxonian snob though excellent writer, Andrew Lang, humorously implored Stevenson to go away and not compromise Mr. Lang's 'character'. This adoption of a free and easy costume must not be taken as a proof of personal modesty. Both Henley and Flora Masson have noted that Louis Stevenson never came upon a mirror without making use of it.

These are but symptoms of a deeper dislike. 'He was always posing', and 'his airs were more ridiculous than his clothes.' 'He had no friends'! At university lectures 'he was the worst behaved man' and paraded 'an offensive, provocative attitude of sneering'. This unnamed witness, who thought Stevenson had no friends, is contradicted by the Writer to the Signet, Patrick Campbell, who when asked why he had not been more often with Stevenson at the university, replied:

> '. . . I was not at all keen to see much of him, still less of the friends who surrounded him. We are, perhaps fortunately, not all cast in the same mould.'

The suggestion of this anonymous witness that Stevenson in his university days had 'no friends' at all is just not true. During that period he had made or was making such friends as his brilliant if somewhat erratic cousin 'Bob' Stevenson, his lifelong legal and literary adviser Charles Baxter, Sir Walter Simpson, the son of the discoverer of chloroform, and Professor Jenkin. These were in Edinburgh, while in 1873 in England he met Mrs. Sitwell and Sidney Colvin. True, Robert Louis and his cousin and Baxter invented some of those undergraduate jokes which seem much funnier at twenty than at forty. Bob Stevenson had been in France and was evidently a good deal more emancipated than Louis, to whom he apparently introduced the red sash then so commonly worn by the peasantry of the South. Bob was a resourceful young man. Arriving at the railway station one day he discovered he had come with insufficient money for his fare. So he went to the nearest pawn shop, raised the money on his dress trousers under the assumed name of 'Libbell', and caught his train. Robert Louis was much taken with the idea of 'Libbell' and the young men spent—fruitlessly—much energy and ingenuity in trying to delude their fellow-citizens into the belief that such a person existed. They also invented a couple of typical or eponymous Edinburgh characters called 'Thompson and Johnson', who occasionally turn up in the mature Stevenson's jesting letters in Scots. Unprosperous jests of this type are a common diversion or failing of undergraduates and other young men before the hands of time and commerce have quenched the spirit of youth; and do not seem to deserve very serious condemnation. Still, the echoes of such frivolous behaviour which reached Mr. and Mrs. Stevenson could not fail to displease respectable persons so anxious about their social status. In Samoa, more than twenty years later, Stevenson's mother was particularly anxious that Louis should do nothing in the 'war' of head-hunters and Consuls which might lower the social prestige of the Stevensons! Around 1870 they can hardly have approved of ribaldry about 'Thompson and Johnson' and 'Libbell'. Indeed, as Robert Louis's religious doubts developed concurrently with his university idling and these abortive hoaxes, Mr. Thomas Stevenson angrily accused Bob of destroying Robert Louis's faith in the religion of his father—a charge which he honestly withdrew when cool reflection showed its injustice, for a spirit like that of R.L.S. needed no encouragement in order to rebel.

Mr. Campbell, the lawyer who congratulated himself on not being 'made in the same mould' as Stevenson, was far nearer the truth than the anonymous witness. If his parents had been asked at the time they would almost certainly have agreed with Mr. Campbell in thinking that far from having 'no friends', their son had too many of the wrong sort. Whether his religious doubts and self-questioning led to a temporary revulsion against the self-righteous persons of his own class, or whether he was merely extending his training as an author by 'studying low life', Stevenson himself has told us how he spent his time in the disreputable haunts of disreputable people. The company included thieves and street women, and frequenting these places 'disconsidered a young man for good with the more serious classes, but gave him a standing with the riotous'. Stevenson was known to the other frequenters of his favourite 'howff' as 'Velvet Jacket', and records with pride that the women were gentle with him and that at any time he could have entrusted them with his money without the slightest danger of loss. In a letter written much later in his life he mentions casually that he seemed to have an attraction for 'harridans'. And not only harridans. On his excursion to Earraid in 1870 Stevenson, not yet twenty, remarked that he loved to travel alone because of the people he met and 'grew friendly with'. 'Ah,' said the man to whom he was speaking, 'but you've such a pleasant manner, you know—quite captivated my old woman, you did—she couldn't talk of anything else.' It was Stevenson's skill in putting that 'pleasant manner' into his writings which accounts in part for his popularity.

What did Stevenson do in this 'howff'? Well, he says that he took his notebook and worked at writing lyrics, and we may perhaps infer something of the mood of revolt which took him there from these lines:

> 'O fine, religious, decent folk
> In virtues flaunting gold and scarlet,
> I sneer between two puffs of smoke,
> Give me the publican and harlot.'

If this seems a strange end-product of the study of Montaigne and St. Matthew we must remember the writer's cult of a 'romance' which was not altogether free from the spurious, and his lifelong pleasure in watching himself play a part for which he dressed appropriately—in his Edinburgh student days he was the shabby, bohemian artist who likened himself to the dissipated Robert Fergusson, just as at the end of his life he played and dressed for the part of the wealthy gentleman planter. It is perhaps not unfair to point out that those who most severely censured Stevenson for these harmless little vanities were usually persons too unimaginative to be anything but social stereotypes.

This playing at wickedness in 'haunts of vice' was of course part of the 'idleness' for which Stevenson was blamed during his student years, though one would think that complete rest would be the proper treatment for a young man threatened with tuberculosis. More recently, on the evidence of poems such as that just quoted and of passages from letters to Mrs. Sitwell—both of which were long suppressed in the interests of Stevenson royalties—he has been accused of wishing to ally himself in marriage with a youthful harlot referred to as 'Claire'. The Edinburgh gossip so freely tapped by Mr. Steuart has elaborated the theme. When young Robert Louis could no logner endure the condemnation of Edinburgh society, when his religious troubles caused his father to scowl and his mother to weep, the young man fled to his 'howff' and the 'unblushing daughters of Venus', some of whom did him 'a lasting injury'. What 'injury' is not stated, so the reader's imagination may roam freely over any possibility he likes. Claire's real name was Kate Drummond, a Highland lassie who 'possibly' told him 'Highland stories, with the qauint, rich turns of phrase and the soft musical cadence which are the heritage of the Gael'—though how anyone could know or even reasonably infer this forty or fifty years later is not explained Anyway, Stevenson is said to have wanted to marry Kate, but could not do so, since he had no money and his father (not unreasonably) refused to finance such an unworldly proceeding.

Of course, there may be something in the story. In his violent reaction against Edinburgh Phariseeism, the young man may really have had some such project. Or, more likely, it was another of the hoaxes on the lines of 'Libbell' and 'Thompson and Johnson' which was taken a good deal more seriously than its author intended. What is certain is that even after he was of age Robert Louis was allowed only a pound a month pocket-money. Anything he needed was paid for, but ready cash he was not allowed. The question is: did Stevenson seek out this 'low company' because he had so little money, or was he deprivedn of money because his father knew what company the young man was keeping? Stevenson implies the former, but it seems just as likely that the latter is the real explanation. Possibly the Kate Drummond story is nothing but malicious gossip, in spite of the seeming confirmation of the unpublished poems and letters, but if there had been any truth in the story the least a father could do was to make sure his son hadn't the price of a licence and a wedding-ring, though to be sure these might have been borrowed. The moral of all this is clear: the habit, by no means confined to the 'Victorians', of family insistence on suppressing any biographical evidence which they disapprove, in the long run defeats itself and leads to suspicion that 'the worst' remains untold. In spite of historians and the newspapers, the truth eventually becomes known. Stevenson's public reputation was 'doctored' from the beginning for sales reasons—by his father, by Colvin, by Balfour and most of them. Fanny Stevenson was too good a business woman and too much interested in the Stevenson royalties not to realize that the gullible public who made a saint ('as happy as kings') of Stevenson must be kept gulled. From the fuss made about this alleged episode one would think the lad had been accused of embezzling four hundred pounds (as told so amusingly by R.L.S. in *John Nicolson*) instead of romantically wanting to marry a harlot, which, if true, was creditable to his heart though perhaps not to his common sense.

4

THIS situation of war or at any rate antagonism between Stevenson on the one side and his parents plus Edinburgh respectability on the other, oppressed him during those university years—and indeed for some time after, until he won a kind of independence through marriage. No doubt the young man was often 'tiresome' in many ways, deliberately flaunting his bohemian views and determination not to conform, getting into scrapes, pestering his mother for money, and in many ways consciously or unconsciously creating an animosity against himself which survived his success, his death and the popularity created by the hagiographers. Add to this his religious doubts and the refusal to be an engineer, and we can see how he irritated his father's arbitrary and domineering temperament and outraged his mother's domestic subservience. Yet, after all, it was only reasonable that a young man should refuse a profession which did not interest him. His father, who was heart and soul in the work, had made a failure of the harbour works at Wick. How probable that Robert Louis, lacking his father's guidance in the future and without real enthusiasm, would achieve worse disasters! He had been 'reasonable' in yielding to his father's wish that he should read for the Scottish Bar, and did eventually succeed—heaven knows how—in being called. And even here we may not unfairly ask if Mr. Thomas Stevenson was not mainly sacrificing to 'respectability' and 'what will people say?', for the position of a briefless barrister is worse than that of a not very saleable author. It was ignorant philistinism in Thomas Stevenson—common enough in his time and since—which made him refuse to see authorship as a profession, as indeed anything but the 'idling' which Robert Louis tried to defend in one of his essays. And surely it was only an elementary human liberty for the young man to work out his own religion. In that respect his crime or blunder, as we shall see, was that he was honest enough to let himself be found out.

Still, uncomfortable as the situation was, we must not allow it to appear more gloomy than it really was. One of Stevenson's greatest difficulties was that he could not walk out of his father's house and make himself independent by work. Without having any tremendous 'message' to deliver, Stevenson's vocation for letters was too strong for him to concentrate on other work, and he was too frail physically for the rough-and-tumble either of Fleet Street or commercial life. Stevenson himself rather optimistically wondered later if he might not have succeeded at the Bar? But then, as he cheerfully adds, he by then would have been dead. The physically weak, only son of well-to-do parents might not unreasonably expect them to provide for him; and so they did, but too suspiciously and penuriously. Indeed, Mr. Stevenson later informed his son that an infidel could not expect to inherit Christian money!

So there was nothing for Robert Louis to do but to put up with the situation as best he could. And there were alleviations and indeed privileges in his student life. There was Swanston, there were vacation travels, there was the 'Spec', there were amateur theatricals with the Jenkin family, there was the fun of the inevitable undergraduates' magazine and of course the disappointment of its no less inevitable failure. And towards the very end of this epoch came new friends, new openings out, a little surcease from parental over-watching.

Swanston Cottage has perhaps been over-romanticized, as so much in Stevenson's life. It was only a few miles from the centre of Edinburgh, though far less suburban in situation than it is now. Mr. Thomas Stevenson took the lease in May 1867, and kept the place as a summer residence for fourteen years. Robert Louis spent a good deal of time there, with his parents, or alone, or with a friend; and the place and its memories make an important showing in that literature of personal experience and recollection which is among the more permanently interesting part of Stevenson's work. There he found his old Scots gardener as well as the shepherd who began by shouting angrily at him as an intruder among the nervous sheep, and ended up as a friend. There too he found scenery which he remembered long afterwards when he came to write *St. Ives*. It is not possible to resist quoting at least a scrap or two of Stevenson at his most attractive best where sharp observation and subdued laughter are not too much impeded by a style which so often a little tended to mannerism. The gardener, Robert Young, is sometimes thought to owe something to Scott's Andrew Fairservice, but it is really no more than a common place of nativity. Who can fail to enjoy Stevenson's enjoyment of his countryman?

> 'He shrank the very place he cultivated. The dignity and reduced gentility of his appearance made the small garden cut a sorry figure. He was full of tales of greater situations in his younger days. He spoke of castle and parks with a humbling familiarity. He told of places where under-gardeners had trembled at his looks, where there were meres and swanneries, labyrinths of walk and wilderness of sad shrubbery in his control, till you could not help feeling that it was condescension on his part to dress your humbler garden plots. You were thrown at once into an invidious position. You felt that you were profiting by the needs of dignity, and that his poverty and not his will consented to your vulgar rule.'

The whole portrait is worth close reading, for seldom has a writer portrayed at once so kindly yet so ruthlessly the—possibly unconscious—compensation of the menial for his lot by such efforts at humiliating with his own past (and imaginary) grandeurs the only too solid superiority of his present paymaster. The now almost extinct English butler was fairly handy at this stately pantomime, but it was particularly the appanage of the 'sturdy Scot' which perhaps is one reason why so few sturdy Scots find domestic employment abroad. Contrast this portrait of the proud menial with the unconscious dignity of the lone shepherd, John Todd, who 'remembered the droving days' and had even known prison for the violences which must occur between rivals shepherding anxiously their flocks along tracks where there was ever dispute about pasture and resting places.

> 'His face was permanently set and coloured; ruddy and stiff with weathering; more like a picture than a face; yet with a certain strain, and a threat of latent anger in the expression, like that of a man trained too fine and harassed with perpetual vigilance. He spoke in the richest dialect of Scots I ever heard; the words in themselves were a pleasure and often a surprise to me, so that I often came back from our patrols with new acquisitions. . . . He touched on nothing at least but he adorned it; when he narrated, the scene was before you; when he spoke (as he did mostly) of his own antique business, the thing took on a colour of romance and curiosity that was surprising. The clans of sheep with their particular territories

on the hill, and how, in the yearly killings and purchases, each must proportionately be thinned and strengthened; the midnight busyness of animals, the signs of the weather, the cares of the snowy season, the exquisite stupidity of sheep, the exquisite cunning of dogs; all these he could present so humanly, and with so much old experience and living gusto, that weariness was excluded.'

Although the experiences in the portraits of the old gardener and shepherd date from Stevenson's student days, the expression and very likely most of the reflections came at a period of greater maturity. It is a truism that Stevenson's work is often autobiographical or at least contains fragments of autobiography, but we may doubt whether this is really such a defect as the pedantically 'objective' critics imply. But, granting the obvious self-absorption and even vanity involved, we can see therein the artistic merit of keeping his writing within his experience. Even such flights of fancy as *Treasure Island* and *Dr. Jekyll* contain more personal reminiscences than might be supposed. In any case, these friendships with Robert Young and John Todd are specific examples of a trait in Stevenson important to his work as well as to his personal life; namely, his ability to please people of very different kinds and to get on good terms with them. The tendency of artists and writers is naturally to make friends with those of their own kind; and they are quite right, for here the understanding and consequently the friendship are deepest. The advantage, especially for a writer, of friendly relations with other types of human life is too obvious to need stressing, yet the lack of it is one of the most fatal errors of 'highbrowism'. Stevenson had not the politician's ubiquity of relations with everybody who may be useful. Indeed, he seems to have made little enough impression on the other inhabitants of Swanston and that little was not good. They considered him 'daft', and explained his fame in later days as the result of what he had picked up in his talks with John Todd!

We may supplement these glimpses of Swanston days with a purely personal and literary recollection:

'My next reading was in winter-time, when I lived alone upon the Pentlands. I would return in the early night from one of my patrols with the shepherd; a friendly face would meet me in the door, a friendly retriever scurry upstairs to fetch my slippers; and I would sit down with the "*Vicomte*" for a long, silent, solitary lamp-lit evening by the fire. . . . I carried the thread of that epic into my slumbers . . . no part of the world has ever seemed to me so charming as these pages, and not even my friends are quite so real, perhaps quite so dear, as d'Artagnan.'

To most people this praise of Dumas and the *Vicomte de Bragelonne* will seem exaggerated, the more so since everyone now knows that Dumas was rather a syndicate than an individual. Why attach so much importance to that author and that book? The problem is worth a moment's thought. Both as a person and as an author Stevenson had a complex character, including a very observant realist, something of a *poseur* or self-conscious stylist both in art and life, a slightly factitious romanticist, a facile but genuine poet, and a hard worker with an eye to success, and yet the true artist's sickening mistrust of success. Might it not be said that one of Stevenson's main ambitions as a novelist was to put style on Scott and Dumas? They have what the stylists so often lack—narrative skill, continual movement, action—and what is a novel but character in action? Stevenson thought Scott and Dumas had 'life', and so in a way they have, but not 'life' as it comes to us from *L'Education Sentimentale* and *Moby Dick* and the colossal Russian steam-roller *War and Peace*. In Scott and Dumas the 'life' is too often factitious, the characters conventional, the action generally violence and motiveless agitation, the emotions as unsubtle as an advertising poster. The death of Milady in the *Musketeers*, of Mordaunt in *Vingt Ans Après* and the kidnapping of Monk in the *Vicomte* are but samples of an all-pervading melodrama. And the padding of these franc-a-line serials!

No formula-answer or 'critical definition', however oracular, will do very much here; but I should like to call the reader's attention to the following passage in a letter from R.L.S. to his mother, written when he was not yet twenty-two:

> 'An opera is far more *real* than real life to me. It seems as if stage illusion and particularly this hardest to swallow and most conventional illusion of them all—an opera, would never stale upon me. I wish that life was an opera. I should like to live in one. . . .'

I find that both 'illuminating' and 'suggestive', but beg the reader to draw his own deductions.

Swanston and the life there are held to have influenced strongly both Stevenson's life and work, so much so that one of the collected editions of his writings was named 'The Swanston'. However true this may be, the Swanston life must not be allowed to obliterate all notice of certain Edinburgh activities during these student years, if only because they are at any rate a partial answer to the gossip about his being so unpopular and disreputable.

In 1869 Stevenson was elected a member of the 'Speculative Society' which dated from the eighteenth century, and had included among its members Walter Scott, Benjamin Constant and Jeffrey. As the membership was limited to thirty and the objects of the Society were purely intellectual, the election may be held to show some esteem for the young man on the part of his contemporaries, especially when you think that he had the higher honour of joining the University Conservative Club. True, Stevenson seems to have used the Society's rooms partly if not largely as an aid to his sagacious truantry from formal university work. By an unexplained anomaly these rooms were not under the jurisdiction of the Senate though they were in the university buildings, so the Speculative Society formed a refuge for undergraduates who wished to defy the regulations against smoking. Stevenson certainly did that, but he did also attend the meetings which included the reading of an essay and a debate. It has often been pointed out that in *Weir of Hermiston* the son of the hanging judge proposes a motion that the penalty of capital punishment should be abolished, and that this was a reminiscence of Stevenson's own youth, since he himself brought forward exactly that motion at a 'Spec' meeting but found no seconder. So scandalous was this proposal in the last century that not only was Stevenson its sole defender in the 'Spec' but his biographers felt they must apologize for him and hasten to add that in later life Stevenson gave no support to a proposition which has lately been tentatively accepted by the first of Parliaments.

We learn from Stevenson himself that the 'Spec' rooms were the scene where he and friends planned a new college magazine to be written and published by themselves. The new magazine to make them if not rich at least famous is the perennial *ignus fatuus* of passing generations of undergraduates, and this one soon passed into oblivion like nearly all of them. Robert Louis has reprinted one of his contributions, and it is no other than the excellent character sketch of the 'old Scots gardener', Robert

Young, we found at Swanston. Obviously he must have re-written this early effort before he gave it to the great public which then read all he published so eagerly, but however poorly the original may have been written it must have been far above the usual undergraduate trash. It may seem surprising that apparently nobody at the time noticed the essay while Robert Louis expressly says that the lady of his heart at that time received it in silence. But then Dr. Johnson has remarked how surprising it is that 'there is so little literature' in the world, meaning of course knowledge and appreciation of literature.

Certainly it was not to his literary talents as displayed thus prematurely that Stevenson owed his introduction to and subsequent intimacy with Professor Jenkin and his family. Indeed he won their friendship before he ever joined the 'Spec' and he owed it not to his writing but to his own 'very agreeable manners' which he complained jokingly had never been 'a source of livelihood' to him. I am not so sure. Those 'very agreeable manners' which enabled him to charm casual acquaintances also brought him lifelong friends, and those friends were always eager to defend him publicly, while by re-casting him in the mould of their own wishful thinking they created the kind of Stevenson the public wanted, the falsely glamorous Stevenson against which Henley protested. And that helped sales enormously. I think Stevenson had some inkling of this even before his popularity began, because J. A. Symonds recording a conversation with R.L.S. says that he (Symonds) believes a writer stands or falls entirely by his own efforts, which Stevenson denied. The careers of the two men show how right Stevenson was. An influential *claque* is almost essential to the successful literary performer unless he happens to be born with the natural popularity of a Dickens or an Edgar Wallace or a Kipling. Any Clausewitz of literary strategy will confirm this.

The conquest of the Jenkin family began—one might almost say 'of course'—with Mrs. Jenkin, who gave Balfour a most interesting account of her first meeting with R.L.S., and it is worth stressing because it shows how Stevenson attracted instantly other intellectual men and women. Mrs. Jenkin called on Stevenson's mother, and found her sitting apparently alone in a room lighted only by the fire—how that touch brings back the pre-electricity days of a century ago! 'Suddenly from out of a dark corner beyond the fireplace, came a voice, peculiar, vibrating; a boy's voice, I thought at first.' Mrs. Stevenson introduced her son, and the visitor asked herself who was this 'young Heine with a Scottish accent', who talked as Charles Lamb wrote? He escorted her to the door when she left, and she found when they came into the light 'a slender, brown, long-haired lad, with great dark eyes, a brilliant smile, and a gentle deprecating bend of the head'. She invited him to pay a visit, and told her family at dinner that she had discovered a poet.

Like so many reminiscences of friends lately dead, this one is prettified and sentimentalized, but there is no reason to doubt that something of the kind introduced Louis Stevenson to Professor Jenkin as a friend rather than as a truant pupil who cut lectures and then impudently asked for a certificate of attendance. Jenkin made so great an impression on the young man that Robert Louis eventually wrote his life, which must have meant the expenditure of much time and energy on a book which could hardly interest anyone outside a small circle of friends. One of them went so far as to state his opinion that it was the best thing Stevenson ever wrote.

For a considerable period Stevenson seems to have been a constant visitor to this home, where he found a more cheerful atmosphere than in Heriot Row, with the company of young people of his own age and the amusement of amateur theatricals. On the more serious side Jenkin did the young man a real service by allowing him to express freely his religious doubts and perplexities without exploding into ferocious and gloomy diatribes of theological disapproval, as Thomas Stevenson did. Jenkin was far more tactful and effective, skilfully counter-attacking Stevenson's extreme anti-orthodox views. However, Jenkin's influence was insufficient to keep Stevenson's away from his 'howff' and thieves' kitchen and whatever intrigues with young women may have occurred.

From all this one gets the impression that those student years 1868–73 may have been idle, in the sense that they were not devoted to the usual studies which are supposed to lead to financial and social success, but were far from being inactive. In any case Stevenson must have done some work as a law-student, or he would not have been called to the Bar. In addition he had his unremitting labours in the study of literature and preparation as a writer, his friends of various types, the 'Spec' and so forth. Yet if not actively unhappy he was restless. However much he may in later years have idealized his 'auld Reekie' there can be little doubt that at this time he longed to get away from it. He would go to the main railway station and wistfully watch the expresses starting south, and at night the distant train whistles in the silence seemed 'horns of elfland faintly blowing'. The explanation is obvious enough, yet one hardly sees what could have been done, unless his parents had been quite different people. They kept him too much on a string, and treated an exceptionally intelligent and gifted young man as if he were a bad, untrustworthy and yet dearly loved schoolboy, pestering him to study for a profession he didn't like, to profess bigoted religious views he had abandoned, and to acquiesce in a solemn philistinism against which all the best in him revolted.

The situation was difficult and at times painful to both sides yet commonplace even to banality since it merely reproduced the ever-recurring conflict of youth and age, the child full-grown rebelling against an over-prolonged parental care and wish to guide which have become irksome and frustrating. Small wonder that with all his gift of sympathy and imagination, which enabled him to understand even then his parents at least partially, his constant preoccupation was to find some seemingly valid excuse to get away from them for more than a week or two.

In the summer of 1872 he thought he had found the ideal pretext. His friend Sir Walter Simpson, also a law student, proposed to spend the summer session at a German university. Robert Louis caught eagerly at the idea, which seemed to have everything in its favour. One can imagine him pleading for it eagerly, perhaps too eagerly—he would learn German, he would work at law, he would meet young men of another civilization and yet have the companionship of the baronet—one almost thinks 'chaperonage'—and of course his behaviour would be exemplary and he would write home constantly to report. . . . Remember, he was of age, and surely entitled to think that he could take care of himself for a few weeks in the purlieus of a foreign university. Not at all. His mother discovered so much anxiety at the thought of even this modest emancipation that he had to try to be content with two or three weeks alone with Simpson at Frankfurt, and then had to join his parents at Baden-

Baden. Evidently, so long as his parents paid for him he was to run loose on a very short tether. That he might have 'got into mischief' of one kind or another is possible and even probable, but as he himself remarked in his whimsical way, it is better for a boy to break his neck than his spirit.

This unsuccessful attempt to obtain a little longer spell of freedom would not call for more than this bare mention but for a passage in one of Robert Louis's letters from Germany. The published letters written home, mostly to his mother, are full of gaiety and good spirits. In one of them he describes going to a *Wirthschaft* outside the town, and how to his great surprise he was asked if he were not a Scot? On his admitting the charge, he was stunned by voluble praises of a Scots *Doktor* 'a professor—a poet—who wrote books—*gross wie das*—' a remarkable person, seemingly, named Scobie (Stevenson had never heard of him) who was 'in some undecipherable manner connected with the Queen of England and one of the Princesses'. And, Stevenson proceeds:

> 'He had been in Turkey, and had there married a wife of immense wealth. They could find apparently no measure adequate to express the size of his books. In one way or another, he has amassed a princely fortune, and had apparently only one sorrow, his daughter, to wit, who had absconded into a *Kloster*, with a considerable slice of the mother's *Geld*. . . . Although the first torrent was exhausted, yet the Doctor came up again in all sorts of ways, and with or without occasion, throughout the whole interview; as, for example, when one man, taking his pipe out of his mouth and shaking his head, remarked apropos of nothing and with almost defiant conviction, "*Er war ein feiner Mann, der Herr Doktor*", and was answered by another with, "*Yaw, yaw, und trank immer rothen We'n*".'

This seems almost too good to be true, except that only a great man could have invented such a scrap of dialogue. Whether we pay Stevenson the compliment of thinking that he made it up, or content ourselves with allotting him the slighter praise of Boswellizing admirably his German peasants, there can be no doubt that the episode is admirably observed and rendered. It has already the mature Stevenson skill in handling words as well as his gift of friendly laughter with a zest of malice and infinite enjoyment of these unintentional comics. Certainly Stevenson's self-training in writing had been far indeed from idleness since it enabled him to sketch the little scene so ably before he was twenty-two. One is divided between surprise that so young a man should write so well, and surprise that his parents seemingly saw nothing remarkable in the writing. The letter was just sentimentally 'treasured' along with the little boy's scribbles and the youth's first crude efforts at composition and the rest of his letters. If the parents had seen the remarkable literary promise in that letter (page 44 of the Tusitala edition) there would not have been such an episode as that (already related) where Thomas Stevenson felt and showed complete incredulity when his son's literary ability was praised by a young clergyman.

As many writers on Stevenson have recognized, the year 1873 was a crucial one for him both as a person and as a writer. In that year the religious differences between Robert Louis and his parents (particularly his father) reached their crisis of unpleasantness. But the 'romance of destiny' which struck him this most disagreeable blow, which affected the health of all three and his most of all, like the fabled lance of Achilles which both wounded and cured, brought him new but lifelong friends through whom his first real emancipation was attained and through whose influence he made a real start as a published author.

Bob and Louis Stevenson and three or four other students had started a private 'club', mysteriously called the L.J.R., which held meetings (only a few) in a pub supposed to have been frequented by Burns. The stated objective of the L.J.R. was the ostensibly blameless if rather difficult establishment of 'Liberty, Justice and Reverence', from which of course the mysterious initials were derived; and this laudable utopia was to be attained through 'socialism' and 'atheism', and (*inter alia*) the abolition of the House of Lords. This programme of what is now practically orthodox *politique de gauche* happened to fall into Thomas Stevenson's hands and froze his blood with horror, particularly as it contained the already noted phrase about 'disregarding everything our parents have taught us'. As I have pointed out, the sensible thing for Mr. Stevenson to do would have been to laugh and ask to join the 'club', but he chose instead to take this (crude and infantile) document very seriously. The age of the Barretts of Wimpole Street is not yet ended in backward sections of the community, and it was still in its heyday at that time. The father tackled his son, whose slightly hysterical account of the interview is to be found in a letter to Charles Baxter written on the 2nd February, 1873:

> 'The thunderbolt has fallen with a vengeance now . . On Friday night after leaving you, in the course of conversation, my father put me one or two questions as to beliefs, which I candidly answered. I really hate all lying so much now—a new-found honesty which has somehow come out of my late illness— that I could not so much as hesitate at that time; but if I had foreseen the real Hell of everything since, I think I should have lied, as I have done so often before. I so far thought of my father, but I have forgotten my mother. And now! they are both ill, both silent, both as down in the mouth as if—I can find no simile. You may fancy how happy it is for me. If it were not too late, I think I could almost find it in my heart to retract, but it is too late; and again, am I to live my whole life as one falsehood? Of course, it is rougher than Hell upon my father, but can I help it? They don't see either that my game is not the light-hearted scoffer; that I am not (as they call me) a careless infidel. I believe as much as they do, only generally in the inverse ratio; I am, I think, as honest as they can be in what I hold. I have not come hastily to my views. I reserve (as I told them) many points until I acquire fuller information, and do not think I am thus justly to be called "horrible atheist"; and I confess I cannot exactly swallow my father's purpose of praying down continuous afflictions on my head.'

An ethical debate might be held to discuss whether Robert Louis was right or wrong in answering his father's questions with an intransigent declaration of 'infidelity'. During the famous Tichborne trial which occurred in that decade Chief Justice Cockburn asserted on the Bench that there are exceptional circumstances which justify a man in telling an untruth, a proposition from which counsel for the defence vehemently dissented. Was this Stevenson imbroglio one in which the son would have been right to dissemble? Obviously the thought came to Robert Louis since he puts it down in this unhappy letter. Yet if he had lied, he would surely have involved himself in an almost intolerable and (certainly to so honest a man) repugnant series of further dissimulations, hypocrisies and distasteful religious practices. One feels he had to tell the truth, but at what a price of contention and misery!

How formidable and destructive was the sectarian wrath of this Cameronian parent may be judged from another remarkable letter from Robert Louis written seven months after the other, in

September 1873. It is necessary to explain that a young relative of the Stevenson family was seriously ill, and that from what proved to be his death-bed he had sent for Thomas Stevenson and had (erroneously, it seems) warned him that his nephew Bob was actively engaged in destroying the religious faith of his beloved son. Perhaps it would be more accurate to say 'was confirming him in his infidelity' since Robert Louis had already admitted to his father that his faith was gone. Here is this new scene of pious bullying as vividly recorded by Louis:

> 'I was sitting up here working away at John Knox, when the door opened and Bob came in with his hands over his face and sank down on a chair and began to sob. He was scarcely able to speak at first, but he found voice at last, and I then found that he had come to see me, had met my father on the way and had just brought to an end an interview with him. There is now, at least, one person in the world who knows what I have had to face, and what a tempest of emotions my father can raise when he is really excited. I am so tired at heart and tired in body that I cannot tell you the result tonight. They shook hands; my father said that he wished him all happiness, but prayed him, as the one favour that could be done him, that he should never see him between the eye again.'

Tantaene animis caelestibus irae? Why, indeed, should so much anger be the main result of so much piety? And what was the object of this dreadful scene which must have been extremely painful to both sides, but particularly to the unsuspecting and light-hearted Bob? According to Robert Louis, continuing his letter next day, there was none:

> '. . . it had no practical issue except the ludicrous one that Bob promised never to talk Religion to me any more. It was awfully rough on him, you know; he had no idea that there was that sort of thing in the world, although I had told him often enough—my father on his knees and that kind of thing.'

Making all allowances for the intensity of Thomas Stevenson's religious convictions and the purity of his motives, one cannot help suspecting that such scenes—for Robert Louis's words imply that he had often suffered them—were also embittered, perhaps unconsciously, by the Victorian father's helpless rage at finding that the offspring was grown up and bent on a way of life of his own. Mr. Thomas Stevenson must have had some inkling that he exaggerated since he wrote next day 'apologizing for anything he may have said' but—how characteristic this is of such persons!—'adhering to the substance of the interview'. And he must have made life very unpleasant for his family, for Robert Louis goes on:

> 'If I had not a very light heart and a great faculty of interest in what is under hand, I really think I should go mad under this wretched state of matters. Even the calm of our daily life is all glossing, there is a sort of tremor through it all and a whole world of repressed bitterness. I do not think of it, because it is one of those inevitable fates that no thinking can mend. . . . Now, don't get bothered about this. It has been as bad before any time this last year, and then I had no one to talk my bitterness to.'

Passing lightly over the merely literary interest of the fact that in these earlier and much livelier letters the inveterate stylist cared nothing about minor inelegancies, we have to look for a moment at the correspondent to whom this last letter was written since she is important at this stage of our story. Was Robert Louis in love with Fanny Sitwell? Of course he was. The fact is undeniable since the passages cut from his letters to her by Colvin have been made available. The further fact that she insisted on Robert Louis's destroying her letters to him might be held to imply some reciprocity, though there is every reason to believe that it was one of those 'innocent' affairs which do sometimes happen, for her real interest was in Sidney Colvin. It was through Mrs. Sitwell that Stevenson met Colvin, and through Colvin and his influence that the young man got his first real emancipation from the loving tyranny of home and his start as a published writer.

In July of 1873 Robert Louis was allowed to make a visit to his cousin (née Maud Balfour) in Sussex, where her husband, the Rev. Churchill Babington was Rector of Cuckfield. It was there he first met Fanny Sitwell, who saw his rare qualities as quickly as Mrs. Jenkin had seen them a few years before. She wrote to Colvin to tell him of 'the fine young spirit' she had discovered, and Colvin hastened his visit in order to meet him. Perhaps it is only fair to give Mrs. Sitwell's (Lady Colvin's) own account of a relationship which, at any rate on the female side, was probably more important to Stevenson than any except his mother and his wife. After saying that Mrs. Babington had mentioned that she expected her young Scottish cousin, Mrs. Sitwell says:

> 'That afternoon I was lying on a sofa near an open window when I saw a slim youth in a black velvet jacket and straw hat, with a knapsack on his back, walking up the avenue.'

This of course was Stevenson, who was rather shy, until Mrs. Sitwell's boy took him to see the moat in which they could fish:

> '. . . they came back in a little while evidently fast friends. From that moment Louis was at his ease, and before twenty-four hours were over the little boy's mother was a fast friend too of R.L.S and remained so to the end of his life.'

She goes on to praise Stevenson's talk as 'like nothing I had ever heard before', confirms that she wrote Colvin to come as soon as possible to meet 'a brilliant and . . . unmistakeable young genius'. After describing how this visit made the Stevenson-Colvin friendship, she ends up:

> 'For nearly three years after this Louis wrote me long letters almost daily, pouring out in them all the many difficulties and troubles of that time of his life. A number of these letters have been published, or part-published, in the volume of letters edited by Sir Sidney Colvin, and a great many more, too sacred and intimate to print, are still in my possession.'

The month of respite from theological cares and urgings to work for a profession he had no intention of following seems to have been most beneficial. There is no need to suppose that Colvin and Mrs. Sitwell were necessarily superior in mind to the people Stevenson knew in Edinburgh, but they had a more liberal outlook. Above all they liked him and sympathized with his ambitions. In Mrs. Sitwell Stevenson found a well-bred woman of culture willing to help with sympathy in his personal troubles (even if they included Kate Drummond, as some believed) and in Colvin the almost indispensable literary sponsor. In spite of the foreignness of Sussex to him—'the hopeless gulf there is between England and Scotland'—he wrote his mother, perhaps injudiciously that he was 'too happy' to write letters, though he tried to persuade himself and her that he was reading 'a little law' and 'some German'.

After such a glimpse of happiness in congenial society he suffered all the more from such scenes as that between his father and Bob Stevenson. Lucky indeed for Stevenson was it that he had that strong inner core of determination, for in spite of a happy day with his mother (including a restaurant luncheon) when his father had to be away, the scenes recurred. He mentions 'another disagreeable' only three weeks after his return. He speaks of his ill health but, hopefully, is working at writing essays, and records the important news that the Lord Advocate had suggested, in Thomas Stevenson's hearing, that Robert Louis should go to the English Bar. At this date it is impossible to say whether the all-important legal peer gave this advice because he thought young Stevenson would be no particular acquisition to Scottish law practice, or whether he knew something of the situation and suggested this as an escape. At any rate Robert Louis jumped at the idea, and prepared to move to London in mid-October when he suddenly was afflicted 'with a bad sore throat, fever, rheumatism and a threatening of pleurisy'.

In spite of what he says to the contrary, Louis must still have been ill when he managed to get away to London, for his weight was down to eight stone six pounds. At any rate, when he arrived in London, Colvin and Mrs. Sitwell insisted on his consulting the then eminent physician Sir Andrew Clark, who for reasons unexplained was as highly thought of by Robert Louis's parents as the Lord Advocate. It seems probable that Sir Andrew was tipped off as to the state of family affairs aggravating this illness, diagnosed nervous exhaustion and a threat of tuberculosis (only too accurately) and insisted that the patient must be well fed, must go abroad, alone, and suggested the French Riviera. When Mrs. Stevenson tried to insist on going with her son, Sir Andrew insisted against. 'Clark is a trump', Robert Louis reported happily as he prepared to leave for Menton. The parents, he added, meant to give him six weeks at the outside, but, he adds, 'methinks I shall manage to disappoint them'. And lest too much weight may be given to the carefully created legend of the utterly devoted mother we may note this scrap:

> 'I have had a slight spar with my mother this afternoon about my movements tomorrow. She said, "You shall not have everything your own way, I can tell you." I said, "I don't expect it, but surely I may please myself as to where I am to sleep." She caved in incontinently and asked it as a favour, whereupon I facilely gave way and promised.'

He could afford to be magnanimous, for with the aid of Mrs.

Robert Louis Stevenson, aged 4—after a chalk drawing.

[*To face p. 64*

Thomas Stevenson, who planned that R.L.S. would become an engineer.

Margaret Isabella Stevenson profoundly influenced the life of her son.

To face p. 65]

Sitwell, Colvin and the specialist, Robert Louis had won a freedom which should have been granted him long before. Even at this stage, but for Sir Andrew's peremptory veto, they had planned to send him, like a little boy, to Torquay with his mother! True, there were plenty of efforts to haul him back into servitude, but he was never again really without hope both for his life and his art. An addition to the letter just quoted runs:

> 'I go tomorrow to Dover. Thursday night I shall be in Paris; Friday, Sens; Saturday, Mâcon; Sunday, Avignon. . . . I do look forward to the sun and I go with a great store of contentment—bah! what a mean word—of living happiness that I can scarce keep bottled down, in my weatherbeaten body.'

Ordered south! For how many unhappy persons in that consumptive epoch that was no more than a deferred sentence of death. The menace was there in Stevenson's case, but there can be little doubt that for him the dreaded sentence was an order of release, at any rate of respite. There were still difficult Edinburgh years ahead, but there were to be more and more escapes until the final one. The tiny world which still has some respect for literature owes a debt of gratitude to Sir Andrew Clark.

5

LOUIS STEVENSON was a good traveller; it is part of the charm of his writing which still attracts more readers than the highbrows think. He was very seldom in a hurry, he prepared himself beforehand by learning something of the language and history of the country visited, he had an eye for the unexpected and the knack of getting into touch with persons he met. It is not unfair to add that he does not seem to have known or cared very much about architecture and the fine arts, so that in spite of his 'style' and some affectations of dress and manner he ranks rather as a bohemian than an aesthete. We must remember that he was nearly always ailing and often really ill, and that, short of real manual labour, few occupations are so physically tiring as sightseeing. He could at times bear the fatigues of a walking-tour, but lacked either strength or urge to spend much energy in museums and galleries.

These remarks may seem contradicted by the essay *On Roads*, Stevenson's real début as a writer, which through Colvin's influence appeared in the November *Portfolio*. The article as re-published seems over-written, with little of Stevenson's characteristic gifts. It is sententious without being pithy, and is perhaps too generalized—we want to follow Stevenson along *a* road and not to hear his sage reflections on *the* road, a more or less Whitmanesque abstraction. But it was young work, and the writer himself laments having to revise it in such sickness that he felt as if he were standing on his head! The paper is noteworthy by its place chronologically at the head of his genuine publications; after November 1873 not a year from then until his death passed without his work appearing in magazines or in book form. He was fortunate in having kindly and intelligent friends to help in launching him, for among the infelicities of a writer's life may be reckoned both a false start and the necessity to continue after he has ceased to please. Stevenson was spared both these misfortunes.

In one of the letters recording his leisurely journey from Dover to Menton Stevenson laments their absence of 'style'.

This is a matter of taste on which there can never be complete agreement, but if by 'style' Stevenson meant the manner—if not mannerism—of his *Roads* then readers not enslaved by literary theories may rejoice in the freshness and spontaneity of letters happily uncontaminated by 'style'.

Stevenson's second published essay *Ordered South* (*Macmillans*, May 1874) came out of his own winter experiences as an invalid at Menton, and it is a great advance on *Roads*. It has passages of real observation and eloquence, and thoughts worth the pains of finding 'the right word'. But for contact with the living reality we must go to the letters. He crossed from Dover on the 6th November (1873) and it was lucky for him he was a good sailor, for the sea was very rough and most of the passengers suffered the miseries of *mal de mer*. In Paris he was cold and perhaps a little lonely. At Sens he noted—not the cathedral and its famous treasury or the museum but—a blind poet selling his own books in the streets. At Avignon—*mistral* of course. Yet he was able to sit and enjoy the view from the Rocher des Doms, and found the sun 'beat down furiously' in Villeneuve across the Rhône; but he confessed to feeling restless and that he was 'easily upset'. We can guess the state of 'nerves' to which he had been driven by family theological quarrels and loving guidance from a little episode which happened soon after he reached Menton. He had to run over to Nice to consult an English specialist, but although the doctor confirmed Sir Andrew Clark in thinking there was no active tubercular condition, the ordeal seems to have upset Stevenson completely:

> 'I could not remember French, or at least I was afraid to go into any place lest I should not be able to remember it, and so could not tell when the train went. At last I crawled up to the station and sat down on the steps, and just steeped myself in the sunshine until the evening began to fall and the air to grow chilly. This long rest put me all right; and I came home here triumphantly and ate dinner well.'

He must have been near to a nervous breakdown, and later he laments in a letter to Mrs. Sitwell that he cannot respond to the beauty about him, that his soul is blind, that as an intellectual being he has not 'begun to re-exist', and then:

> 'If you knew how old I felt! I am sure this is what age brings

with it—this carelessness, this disenchantment, this continual bodily weariness. I am a man of seventy: O Medea, kill me, or make me young again!'

Certainly his nerves were in a bad state, for a week later he ruefully recalls an upsetting disagreement with a clergyman whom in fact he rather liked, and then in his discouragement goes on to say that if Colvin does not think 'I shall be able to support myself soon by literature, I shall give it up and go (horrible as the thought is to me) into an office of some sort'. There must have been something very wrong with a young man, so clearly 'destined by romance' to be a writer, for him to fall into such gloomy self-mistrust. These feelings may be set down as part of a fit of 'the miserables'—due to ill health and solitude—which vanished when Colvin arrived, but he also contrived to torment himself with scruples which evidently were more permanent since he speaks of them in the excellent but unfortunately incomplete *Lay Morals*. In an epoch when so many persons are indignantly certain that the world owes them a living, these scruples may seem far-fetched, though from the standpoint of an old-fashioned sense of responsibility they were highly honourable to the young man. He felt that through his father the world had made him large advances of money and that if he died young, as he then believed he must, there was no way he could make repayment. Therefore, he decided that he must live as cheaply as possible, even grudging himself necessities, until he either died or the certain hope of recovery brought the further hope that he might earn and repay. In the letter he winds up:

'If I didn't hope to get well and do good work yet and more than repay my debts to the world, I should consider it right to invest an extra franc or two in laudanum. But I *will* repay it.'

This is the kind of morbid excess of conscientiousness which Henley, if he had ever heard of it, would have explosively denounced as one of the deplorable results of taking the Shorter Catechism too seriously or at any rate the eighth commandment. But there was in Stevenson something which made him akin to that sympathetic Mr. Edwards who lamented that though he tried to be a philosopher 'cheerfulness was always breaking in'. In less than two weeks after this sinister threat about a shillingsworth of laudanum, cheerfulness broke in—or out—in this most delightful and characteristic piece of Stevensonian fun:

'I live in the same hotel with Lord Salisbury. Ahem. He has black whiskers and looks not unlike Crum Brown, only rather more of Crum B. than there is in the Edinburgh edition. He has been successful (or rather his wife has) in making some kids; rather a melancholy success; they are weedy looking kids in highland clo'. They have a tutor with them who respires Piety and that kind of humble your-lordship's-most-obedient sort of gentlemanliness that noblemen's tutors have generally. They all get livings, these men, and silvery hair and a gold watch from their attached pupil; and they sit in the porch and make the watch repeat for their little grandchildren, and tell them long stories, beginning, "When I was private tutor in the family of", &c., and the grandchildren cock snooks at them behind their backs and go away whenever they can get the groom to teach them bad words.'

The threatened fatal dose of laudanum dwindled to a mild experiment with opium, and pretty soon Colvin turned up, and the pair went off to practise misanthropy at Monte Carlo by dining with Sir Charles Dilke, attending a Christmas tree function, and lounging the hours away in a boat or in the public gardens. And so effectively was dread of breaking the eighth commandment banished that on returning to Menton in January Stevenson gaily informs his mother that he has gone to a better hotel where he is paying thirteen francs a day—at least twice as much as he needed to pay if he meant to practise that rigid economy to himself for fear of cheating society. Then Colvin had to go to Paris on business, and Stevenson, far from relapsing into gloom, enjoyed himself thoroughly in the society of two Russian ladies and their children and a graceful little American girl, all pleasantly recorded in letters home. Two months in the Midi, with no theological rows and—we may guess—mighty little burning of midnight oil over Scots or English law, had made a marvellous change. His troubles seem to have been an occasional nightmare and an uncertainty as to whether one of the Russian ladies was flirting with him seriously or trying to make him look silly. By the end of January 1874 we come on this fragment of pessimism:

'I think you will find everything very jolly here, I am very jolly myself. I worked six hours today. I am occupied in transcribing *The Bottle* which is pleasant work to me. . . .'

In spite of the circumambient jollity this *Bottle—The Curate of Anstruther's Bottle*—was never completed, like many others of his early attempts at fiction. And he was able to joke by letter with his father—of whom in spite of everything Robert Louis remained very fond—about a cloak Colvin had brought him from Paris:

> 'My cloak is the most admirable of all garments. For warmth, unequalled; for a sort of pensive, Roman stateliness, sometimes warming into Romantic guitarism, it is simply without concurrent; it starts alone. If you could see me in my cloak, it would impress you. I am hugely better, I think: I stood the cold these last few days without trouble, instead of taking to bed, as I did at Monte Carlo. . . .'

Evidently Sir Andrew Clark had diagnosed correctly and prescribed cleverly, for the letters grow more and more cheery, and he managed so well that his string of six weeks was somehow lengthened to twenty before he left Menton for Paris. During that time he had plenty of opportunity to become friendly with the two Russians and their children—particularly the 'little button', Nelitchka—who figure in the Menton letters. From passages suppressed in the early Colvin-edited 'Letters' but now available it appears that the relations with Mme Garschine were not quite so platonic as Colvin's editing makes out, and that the 'little button' was at times a little nuisance, though in the Colvin letters and in the essay on the movements of young children Nelitchka is always perfect.

Stevenson admits that he did not understand the attitude to him of these Russian women, and after all who does understand Russians? From some of the episodes he relates we might infer that they looked on him at first as a 'queer Dick', and that they wavered between making a butt of him and a genuine liking and even some respect for his gifts—and then every now and then they could not help laughing at him. We must remember that at twenty-three he had still not developed into the rather handsome distinguished man with whose later photographs we are all familiar. His mouthful of misplaced teeth, his smooth oval face, long hair and large eyes gave him an effeminate look which later disappeared. The little Nelitchka, on first seeing him, thought he was a girl, and Andrew Lang—afterwards a fairly close if not uncritical friend—meeting him for the first time at

Menton thought him 'more like a lass than a lad' and even put him down as 'one of your aesthetic young men'.

An example of how the Russian women laughed at him is told by himself against himself with great good humour but not perhaps complete realization of the contempt involved. Mme Zassetsky went with Stevenson to the photographer, arranged Louis in a pose to suit herself and said to the photographer, in French of course: 'This is my son, who is just nineteen. He is very proud of his moustache, so do try to make it show.' Most young men of twenty-three would feel there was more malice than fun in such a joke. After they separated he never saw them again, and before long they ceased to write. In a more sentimental age the whole curious relationship would doubtless have been described as one of those 'ships that pass in the night and speak each other in passing' episodes.

Was Stevenson wholly wise to leave the comparative warmth and shelter of Menton for Paris early in damp and draughty April? His mother didn't think so, and even sent him a telegram expressing disapproval, to which he replied not quite truthfully that he 'only did it to be the sooner able to come home'. The fact is that the supposedly atheistical Bob was in Paris, as the Stevenson parents well knew, and that was the main reason why Robert Louis went there. The friendship between the cousins was deep and sincere, and they evidently stimulated each other mentally. It may have been due to a temporary emotional state arising from the religious rows, Louis's illness and flight south, but in November 1873 Bob had thus expressed himself about his cousin:

> 'He cannot get on at all without me, he writes; he finds that I have been the whole world for him; that he only talked to other people in order that he might tell me afterwards about the conversation.'

And Stevenson goes on to tell his correspondent (Mrs. Sitwell) how astonished he was to hear this, and that he was left with 'a strange sense of weight and responsibility'. Perhaps it was partly that sense of responsibility which took Stevenson to Paris, but alas for good intentions! He went down with 'a very violent cold' and far from his being able to help Bob, Bob had to help him. It is characteristic of Stevenson's heroic devotion to his art that in the midst of this illness he did not give up his work but dictated for Bob to take down several pages of a draft essay on Victor Hugo. Unluckily, here as in other aspects of the man, his admirers whooped it up into something splendidly unique as if no other consumptive man or woman had worked, thereby provoking persons so different as Henley and George Moore into pointing out how poor girls with consumption had to work for a pittance until they collapsed into paupers' graves. Stevenson was never called on for that height of heroic suffering even in some bad days we shall have to pass with him, but a lesser man would have given up and thrown himself on the responsibility of his parents.

In spite of what Stevenson had written his mother about being on his way home, his real hope was to go direct from Paris to Göttingen to meet Prince Galitzin (a relative of the Russian ladies) and study under a famous German professor of Roman law. What the real attraction was he doesn't say, probably nothing more than a further respite from theology and Edinburgh. With the unconscious cynicism of the penniless dependant he wrote that he meant to leave Paris for Germany 'without delay' if he would get permission: 'by permission, I mean money'. Alas, he had to admit that he was so ill there was nothing for it but 'to crawl cautiously home', in perplexity at receiving 'quite a nice note' from his father. If the real reason of his trip to Paris was his wish to be with Bob, then it was an unfortunate impulse, for that sudden and frustrating illness was a warning of the struggle with sickness which made up much of Stevenson's years to come. The comparative good health of the next few years was often threatened, especially in winter, in Scotland, helped by his excursions south in summer, until the grand breakdown of 1879.

The omens of return were not altogether adverse. Robert Louis found his father more gentle and tolerant, at least for a time. And in May, the month of his return, *Ordered South* appeared in *Macmillan's Magazine*. His parents read it, thought it 'heathen', but let it pass. The judgment is a little startling, and unlikely to occur to most readers of Stevenson, unless indeed heavily afflicted by Scottish theology. I have just re-read the article with that criticism in mind, and see no basis for it unless perhaps in his reference to Hazlitt's rich man who had laboured all his life and bought a collection of pictures and the poor man who had learned to understand and to enjoy them—'the one man has made for himself a fortune, and the other has made for himself a living spirit'. Equally astonishing is it that they were seemingly quite unimpressed that a young man of only twenty-three should appear in *Macmillan's Magazine*. In those days it had a high standard, and even Walter Pater did not get accepted there until he was thirty-seven. Of course, in Stevenson's case it was Colvin's doing. Through the same zealous friendship he was allowed to review Lord Lytton's *Fables* for *The Fortnighty Review*, and his rather ineffective study of Victor Hugo appeared in *The Cornhill* for August. And on his return his father had agreed to make him an allowance of seven pounds a month. In the modern world of depreciated currencies and inflated prices this will seem ludicrously insufficient. Stevenson, who was no canny Scot over bawbees but a spendthrift, certainly found it so; but even after the Boer war and before the catastrophe of 1914, thirty-five shillings a week was enough for a young man willing to live a spartan life for the sake of an art, especially if he earned a little extra as Stevenson did. If he often bewails his poverty in his letters, the fault was mainly his extravagance. When he was making almost the income of a Cabinet Minister he squandered it—fortunately for them, real artists nearly always do.

How much the medical verdict of Sir Andrew Clark and the escape to Menton had been a step in Stevenson's 'emancipation' is demonstrated not only by the allowance but by the fact that only a month after returning he was off to England, staying with Colvin at Hampstead. Colvin had him elected to the Savile Club where he met the editor of *The Academy*, to which he later contributed, and of *The Saturday Review* from which at least favourable puffing might be hoped. With this early experience we can understand Stevenson's amazement at J. A. Symonds's naïf faith that literary success may be obtained by merit alone. Luckily for him Stevenson knew better.

This escape was for only a week or two, though it was followed by many others. Back at Swanston he is to be found writing sentimental nonsense to Mrs. Sitwell:

> 'I am so tired; but I am very hopeful. All will be well some time, if it be only when we are dead. One thing I see so clearly. Death is the end neither of joy nor sorrow. Let us pass into the clouds and come up again as grass and flowers; we shall still be this wonderful, shrinking, sentient matter. . . . Consciousness and ganglia and such-like are after all but theories.'

How often one feels that R.L.S. in so many ways was but a preliminary sketch of D. H. Lawrence! That particular statement was wrung from Stevenson by anxiety over his cousin Bob, who was thought to be dying of diphtheria. Bob fortunately recovered, and almost immediately it was Robert Louis who was 'seedy, very seedy', 'quite unfit for work'. But note his resilience. He was very soon able to go off on one of his annual trips on the lighthouse yacht, and even was able to boast: 'I work like a common sailor when it is needful, in rain and wind, without hurt, and my heart is quite stout now.' So the days and weeks moved past with ups and downs, work on his *John Knox* and *Walt Whitman*, projects of other work never fully or even partly carried out, a trip to Wales with his parents, and so back to Edinburgh and Swanston in the autumn. He was also that year in Buckinghamshire, at Cambridge and Oxford; another escape, one surmises from theology, for after all the effort at good will and reconciliation comes this sad little note:

> 'I have discovered why I get on always so ill, am always so nasty, so much worse than myself, with my parents; it is because they always take me at my worst, seek out my faults, and never give me any credit.'

In a later letter he gives us an interesting glimpse of his daily life during November 1874:

> 'Breakfast 8.30; during breakfast and my smoke afterwards till ten, when I begin to work, I read Reformation; from ten, I work until about a quarter to one; from one until two, I lunch and read a book on Schopenhauer or one on Positivism; two to three work, three to six any thing; if I am in before six I read about Japan: six, dinner and a pipe with my father and coffee until 7.30; 7.30 to 9.30 work; after that either supper and a pipe at home, or out to Simpson's or Baxter's: bed between eleven and twelve.'

It will be noted that the strained relations between father and son did not prevent them from smoking a friendly pipe together, while in a letter written from the country Stevenson reports that his father is 'such fun here', 'always skipping about'. And the austerity of his work programme must have been sometimes relaxed by diversions or the accidents of life. Thus we hear of a symphony concert, where Mozart made him think of the 'colour and scent of rose-leaves' and Cherubini of 'green bronze'.

From other sources we know that he enjoyed taking part in the amateur theatricals of the Jenkins and their friends, and that when a hard frost came he went skating every day. One night he found a little boy lost, and in his warm-hearted way spent hours trying to find the child's home. And though before the end of the year he had to confess another miserable scene with his father, who was in bad health and then revealed that he would not leave his son money unless he was a Christian, the pattern of Louis Stevenson's days hardly justifies his neurasthenic outburst: 'O, I do hate this damned life that I lead. Work—work—work—that's all right, it's amusing; but I want women about me and pleasure.'

The next two years of Stevenson's life—1875–76—held some interesting events for him. Probably the least important in a positive sense was that in July 1875, he passed his final law examination and was called to the Scottish Bar. Although he celebrated the event by shouting the news from an open carriage to everyone he passed and by having his photograph taken in wig and gown, the real excitement was the sensation of relief that he had satisfied the bourgeois ambition and prejudices of his parents, and at last, at twenty-four, was free from the obligation to work as a student on things which did not interest him. True, he did put up a brass plate at Heriot Row, walked like other barristers in the great hall, and even received one or two complimentary briefs. But, on the whole, from his point of view it was 'good riddance to bad rubbish' as children say, and before long he gave up even the pretence of legal practice. The truth is that Stevenson was as glad it was all over as a galley-slave when they cut the chains from him. There was another cause for rejoicing. Rather inconsistently Mr. Stevenson allowed his wife to give Louis a thousand pounds from her jointure. If they could not bequeath money to an infidel, why give it to him in his lifetime? Fortunately a mother's heart is generally superior to logic and consistency, though it may be doubted if the gift of so comparatively large a sum to a feckless loon (in money matters) like Louis was altogether wise. Certainly, it gave him some freedom and leisure, but much of the money soon went as 'loans' to friends whose necessities to borrow were far stronger than their scruples about repayment. It is one of the many good points in Stevenson's character that, though he often groused about lack of money and worked hard—too hard—to earn it, he never 'husbanded the golden grain' but 'threw it to the winds like rain' and while he had money never hesitated to share it with others.

Far more important to his real life—the life of the mind and the affections, not of money and social-political obligations—was the meeting with W. E. Henley. There is not much of the 'romance of destiny' about the long business of his training for the Bar except that we might say Stevenson was 'predestined' both by Fate and his own temperament and determination, *not* to be a practising advocate; but there was something romantic in the odd chance of his meeting with Henley. In a novel such a chain of coincidences would be censured as improbable. Henley was really poor, not a player at poverty like Louis Stevenson who if the worst came to the worst could always return as the penitent prodigal and be fed. Henley's poor bookseller father was dead, and his poorer mother struggled to feed younger children. At sixteen a foot was amputated because of a tubercular infection of the bone. He was a cripple, living precariously as a free-lance writer, though a far finer poet than Stevenson as it turned out, and by no means negligible as a prose writer. Then the other foot became infected, and the surgeons he consulted in England looked at him compassionately and said 'amputate'.

Henley rebelled. With both feet gone what would he be but a pauper in a wheel-chair? Lister's fame had reached him, and he made his way to Edinburgh by the cheapest method of transport—by ship—and presented himself to the great surgeon, with exactly tenpence ha'penny in his pocket. Lister agreed to take him into Edinburgh hospital, operated, but did not amputate. This was in August 1873, and in January 1875 Henley was still in his hospital bed, knowing nothing of Louis Stevenson, nor Stevenson of him. But a Henley poem had been accepted by *The Cornhill*, whose editor, Leslie Stephen, was already in touch with Stevenson. In February Leslie Stephen came to give a lecture in Edinburgh, and, conscientious man that he was, called on his contributor in hospital, and then went again, this time taking Stevenson whose description of the meeting has been so often quoted.

With his warm sympathies and bohemian faith that 'artists in distress' should help one another, Stevenson easily responded to the 'poor fellow, a sort of poet who writes for him, and who has been eighteen months in our infirmary' and made up his mind to 'try to be of use to him'. This he undoubtedly did, but neither could possibly have guessed that this fortuitous meeting in a public hospital ward was the start of the warmest and closest literary friendship of Stevenson's life. No doubt Bob Stevenson and Charles Baxter, friends from boyhood days, were closer to him, but none of his literary faction, not even Colvin, meant as much to him as Henley, who with Bob and Baxter was taken into an imaginary 'Three Musketeers' relationship.

Henley was still in his early convalescence when in spring Stevenson 'ran over to Paris' and was shepherded by the more knowing Bob among the bohemian characters of the Latin quarter and then to the 'artists' colony' of Barbizon and the forest of Fontainebleau, an area which was to produce another momentous coincidence in Stevenson's life. Either just before or just after this Paris trip, Henley had recovered sufficiently to go out of doors for the first time in nearly two years. Stevenson carried him down the stairs and back again, a 'business' as he says, for a man so delicate, but Henley's rapture as they drove in a carriage 'was as wine' to Stevenson, who inferred from his questions that Henley 'plainly has been little in the country before'. The 'artifex' Stevenson so essentially was—artist and actor—must have enjoyed these two afternoons with the penniless cripple by contrast with his evenings. The Jenkin amateur theatricals had culminated just at that time for Stevenson in his playing in full costume the part of Orsino in *Twelfth Night*, 'in all the pomp of Solomon, splendid Francis the First clothes, heavy with gold and stage jewellery' while he lived 'upon principally champagne and lobster salad, with a company of people nearly all of whom were exceptionally good talkers'. We should perhaps moralize on this at least to the extent of noting the harsh difference between the real poverty of Henley's bohemia and the 'champagne bohemia' of Louis Stevenson.

The value of Stevenson to Henley, especially at that time of loneliness and near destitution, is easy to see. Stevenson brought him books and hope, introduced him to Bob and Baxter and Walter Ferrier, was in a sense his Maecenas, for it was through the Edinburgh connexion that Henley achieved the editorship of the *London* and, much later, the *Scots Observer*. But why was Henley so much to Stevenson that even the famous 'quarrel' could not kill his affection? Very likely because Henley was the only genuine poet Stevenson had then met—the Savile Club men being merely men of letters. And then Henley was not 'respectable'. He had a touch of the bohemian outlaw whose full-blown character in Villon so much attracted the romantic pseudo-rebel in Stevenson. Henley was the antidote to what was so ladylike in Stevenson's parentally regimented life, and also, let us hope, to the 'harridans' and 'howffs' to which he fled in over-reaction.

Again, the lure of bohemia called Stevenson back to the Fontainebleau 'colony' revealed in the spring by Bob, when at last in July the long trial of dilettante studentship was ended by the rationally so improbable happy ending of a call to the Bar. He was chaperoned by his friend, Sir Walter Simpson, for if 17 Heriot Row still scowled on Colvins, Sitwells, Leslie Stephens and above all Henleys, an Edinburgh baronet could do little wrong. 'My son is abroad with Sir Walter Simpson' was indisputably a better excuse for failure in respectability than a confession that he was drinking in taverns with a crippled English pauper, an atheist cousin, a very young Writer to the Signet and such riff-raff.

France, especially bohemian France, occupied a portion of Stevenson's time for several years, and his experiences there may be traced in his work: those of Paris in the opening chapters of *The Wrecker* and in the *Story of a Lie*, those of the Fontainebleau area in the disconnected but readable *Forest Notes*. The longer excursions, one by canoe, the other with a donkey, recorded in his two early travel books were more consciously undertaken and exploited for literary purposes. At all events, his summer weeks in France in 1875 were mainly a relaxation from Edinburgh, partly in the company of French artists at Barbizon, partly on walks with his friend Simpson, and partly in extending his knowledge of French literature. A good deal less of all this is recorded in the extant letters than one would expect and wish, but no doubt he was often too much occupied or too tired or too happy to write letters.

There is a description in the later essay *Fontainebleau* of Stevenson's headquarters in the forest, Siron's inn at Barbizon, but that in *Forest Notes* is more detailed and written when his impressions were fresh:

> 'The doves coo and flutter from the dovecot; Hortense is drawing water from the well; and as all the rooms open into the court, you

can see the white-capped cook over the furnace in the kitchen, and some idle painter, who has stored his canvases and washed his brushes, jangling a waltz on the crazy, tongue-tied piano in the *salle à manger*. . . .'

A 'man in velveteen' calls for a vermouth and makes it a double; another man 'in pure white linen from top to toe' talks of his day's painting with one 'in corduroy'. There is 'an outbreak of jubilation' as some artist friend walks unexpectedly in. It is a pleasant picture (perhaps not wholly innocent of Murger's influence) of the picturesque setting, good fellowship and careless living which ought to mark every 'artists' colony', and very seldom do. Perhaps the twentieth-century artist is more nervous, more persecuted by 'progress' and bureaucratic tyrannies than his nineteenth-century predecessor, but it is rare indeed to find much if any of the geniality and carefree existence Stevenson attributes to Siron's. Bills were never presented until asked for, and then you paid five francs a day, but . . . . Monsieur Siron added under the rather appalling vocable *estrats* the amount he considered you ought to pay of the collective expenditure above the basic rate. There was a sort of hotel in Jermyn Street which ran on rather similar lines, but it wouldn't work now. And it didn't always work in Stevenson's days though he claims, no doubt with reason, that the bilkers were always English or American. Showing, however, no blind partiality for his French friends, he goes on:

> 'At the same time, the great influx of Anglo-Saxons had begun to affect the life of the studious. There had been disputes; and, in one instance at least, the English and the Americans had made common cause to prevent a cruel pleasantry. It would be well if nations and races could communicate their qualities; but in practice when they look upon each other, they have an eye to nothing but defects. The Anglo-Saxon is essentially dishonest; the French is devoid by nature of the principle that we call "Fair Play". The Frenchman marvelled at the scruples of his guest, and, when that defender of innocence retired overseas and left his bills unpaid, he marvelled once again; the good and evil were, in his eyes, part and parcel of the same eccentricity; a shrug expressed his judgment upon both.'

This must refer to a period rather later than 1875, but the observation is unluckily only too exact.

It was at this inn and on his walks alone in the forest or to greater distances with Simpson that Stevenson did the reading for his essays on Villon and Charles d'Orléans. At the same time, like others of his generation in England, he had been smitten with admiration for Théodore de Banville's brilliant modernizations of the medieval verse forms—ballade, rondeau, rondel, triolet, villanelle, chant royal. They are very difficult to write successfully even in modern French, and in English they tend to a feebleness of rhythm and thought which shows the poet more concerned with his rhymes and refrains than with the ideas and feeling he is supposed to be expressing. Henley, strange to say, was the most successful among the English poets though Dowson later handled the villanelle with superb skill. Stevenson destroyed his own efforts in this formal verse where virtuosity is an essential, and perhaps with reason, if they were no better than the rondeaux accidentally preserved in one of his letters to Mrs. Sitwell. One can't say they are bad, but they are far below Henley's standard, and beside Banville's don't exist. Banville was a poet to delight Stevenson, somewhere between Musset, Heine and his own pupil Verlaine, romantic, touching, sentimental, but a wit and a sharp one, with laughter both genial and derisive, and a fellow-feeling for those lovers of beauty, rhythm and justice who 'wherever they may be are never in their own land, worshippers of fallen Gods, champions of lost causes, seekers after a paradise that has gone'. And Stevenson was not altogether unworthy of his master.

It was during this summer of 1875 that Stevenson experienced a slight and brief taste of what life must have been for his hero, François Villon, with his genuine reasons for avoiding the police. The little story is amusingly told in the *Epilogue* to *An Inland Voyage*, and many readers naturally suppose that the episode happened after the canoe trip, but in fact the walk in the valley of the Loing and its abrupt ending at Châtillon-sur-Loing was earlier. Stevenson was arrested by the police and incarcerated as a vagabond, and might have enjoyed some days or even weeks of preventive arrest—French justice is seldom in a hurry—before the British consular service got him freed, but for the fact that Sir Walter Simpson was making the same journey.

The profession of *clochard* in France seems to an outside view to present advantages in an over-taxed, over-regimented, over-

'Cummy' (Alison Cunningham), Robert Louis's nurse, to whom he dedicated *The Child's Garden of Verses.*

[*To face p.* 80

Robert Louis Stevenson, the briefless barrister.

To face p. 81]

crowded epoch, especially in the summer months. Even during the incredible conditions of liberty and prosperity which Stevenson's generation enjoyed in many parts of Europe, there were compensations. But Stevenson was evidently unaware that a tramping beggar, especially a foreigner, must have his *papiers* to show, and he realized too late that the war of 1870–71 still left disagreeable memories and fanciful rumours of espionage. He also admits he was ill-inspired to wander the roads in a costume at once so threadbare and eccentric, especially since (as he proudly boasts) his very face aroused suspicion in all save the Edinburgh and London police. It is less remarkable than he thinks that he was refused entry to the Monte Carlo casino—the door-keepers have their standards of respectability, and foreigners are often refused when they present themselves in what they think appropriate holiday attire for a poor Latin country. Twice that day Stevenson had been mistaken for a genuine tramp, by a rural postman who was much hurt that the tramp would not display the indecent postcards the postman was certain he had for sale, and once by a poor woman keeping a café. His knapsack was ill-garnished, and its most valuable exhibit was a two-volume edition of the poems of Charles d'Orléans which Stevenson was translating into a notebook.

He has related all this and his dialogue with the police Commissaire with much gusto and Boswellian accuracy, the upshot of which was that he was accused of being a German who had come to sing Charles d'Orléans at the local fair—a deduction which does little honour to the Commissaire's capacity as a sleuth. Stevenson protested, even offering to sing as an alibi, but went unheard and unbelieved, and soon found himself conducted under escort to a dismally chill and damp cellar. And there he might have stayed until he died of pneumonia but for the arrival of his friend, who to the stricken amazement of the Commissaire was not only 'respectable' but 'elegant', with plenty of money and a passport! Even here this highly-trained functionary contrived to make deductions which to an English mind seem little short of ridiculous, if not subversive. Observing that Sir Walter's passport described him as 'Baronet', the policeman said: 'Then your father is a Baron?' On the victim's denial, the Commissaire said triumphantly: 'Then the passport cannot be yours'. *Q.E.D.* It ended up by Stevenson's release from his dungeon, but the pair were forced to take the evening train to Paris to avoid further trouble.

Bohemian life in France early in the Third Republic offered attractions and freedoms we can scarcely conceive, especially for someone who had behind him a fond if bigoted father with a good middle-class income, but evidently there were limits in the matter of dress and lack of identity papers. For half an hour Stevenson, shivering on the dirty bed in his chilly dungeon, was free to imagine he was sharing the feelings and experiences of Villon. It was a distinction to have been at least once in prison.

6

In the years immediately following his call to the Bar Stevenson's life seemed and to a considerable extent was similar to that of many other young men of the period who had modest incomes or allowances, artistic tastes and literary ambitions. They hung about London clubs, as Stevenson did at the Savile, and spent a good deal of time abroad, as he did. The more intelligent and industrious wrote articles about their studies and travels and musings, as Stevenson did, and like him even aspired to 'travel books' and remunerative fiction. Where hundreds failed he succeeded, and it is no detraction from his merit to say that he owed much of that first success, small as it was, to the influence of such friends as Colvin, Stephen, Gosse and even Henley.

A short study of Graham Balfour's useful chronological list of Stevenson's publications for the years 1875–78 inclusive will show the justice of these remarks. Apart from a short pamphlet rather astonishingly named *An Appeal to the Clergy of the Church of Scotland* and one or two poems, his publications fall into one or other of the categories named. It is a little difficult to see what right 'an infidel' had to offer his unasked advice to the Scottish clergy, but the pamphlet was doubtless written to please his father and perhaps to show that R.L.S. was not such an atheist as he was painted. The other publications include literary studies of Poe, Charles d'Orléans, Villon and Whitman; then come most of the Essays which eventually appeared in *Virginibus Puerisque*. His first published story, *A Lodging for the Night*, did not appear until October 1877, and only in 1878, a successful year, did he triumph with two short stories and a serial of *The New Arabian Nights*—but that was published in the *London* by Henley and could not have paid him much. Finally we have the travel essays and books, the latter including *Walking Tours*, the notes on Carrick and Galloway, the *Forest Notes*, *An Inland Voyage* and *Picturesque Notes on Edinburgh*.

This is perhaps not a crowded schedule for a period of four

years, but it is most certainly not the record of an idler. Considering the care with which Stevenson wrote and re-wrote, those articles and books must represent a great many hours of hard work. It is not the fashion now to praise men for working hard, the ideal being to work ever less and less for more and more, and long ago Anatole France cynically but truly remarked that in art real industry does not consist in working hard but in working well. It is true—a magical lyric scrawled by an absinthe-soaked Paul Verlaine on a café table is worth twenty laborious novels of social realism. But let us give Stevenson his due. If he lived on his father's bounty at an age when most young men of his class were providing for themselves, he did not waste the infinitely valuable leisure granted him. If Mr. Thomas Stevenson was not pleased with his son's record in 1878, he ought to have been. Stevenson had two magazine publications in January of that year, one in March, two in April, two and a book in May, a serial from June to October in *London*, and another from June to December in *Portfolio*, magazine articles again in July, September and October and November, and a serial in *London* in November! The mystery is that with all that success Stevenson had so little money—he must have been heinously underpaid. Yet in spite of this tangible evidence of work and success, Stevenson's father remained unconvinced, and it was not until 1883 that he added a codicil to his will which restored Robert Louis to a share of his patrimony.

In spite of this honourable production Stevenson nevertheless gives the impression that he had nothing extremely urgent or important to say. In spite of his ill health, he is an amused and interested spectator of life and the world of men and places as he happened to touch them, of books and their authors, and comments on them with a certain mannered cheerfulness. The newspaper events of his own time scarcely intrude at all into his books or even into his letters, yet this 1874–78 era covers Disraeli's last administration with its acquisition of Cyprus and the Suez Canal shares, its bluff of war with Russia (for which it was totally unprepared) and its 'Peace with Honour' which prepared the war of 1914. Doubtless Robert Louis registered and brooded over these startling events like other people, but he held the view that yesterday's headlines are not the material for this or the next century's literature. The experiences of the individual alone matter to that, and at the outside public events are but a background; except in the South Seas.

Some time elapsed before the 'romance of destiny' jerked Stevenson out of this rather enviable life. Meanwhile, he sought for themes in books and in travels, much as his artist friends at Barbizon sought for 'motives'. Perhaps it was the search for a 'travel motive' a little different from the many, which suggested to Stevenson the uncomfortable January walk through snow and fog in Scotland. The ensuing essay is daintily put together, as so much of Stevenson's work is, but the originality of a winter walking-tour hardly compensates for the barrenness of the experience. The thinly snowed landscape comes to us rather as bleak than majestic, and too many of the human contacts were with 'poor bodies' or mere drunks. Perhaps the most noteworthy little fact is that on this journey Stevenson stopped at Ballantrae.

With one or two exceptions Stevenson spent the first eight months of 1876 in Scotland, chiefly in Edinburgh. Although of course the town remained his headquarters for some time he tended to pass more of each year away from it for various reasons, among them his state of health, his longing for a more varied life, and a new interest of a female kind which the romance of destiny provided for him in the autumn. Although it is the second of his published travel books and did not appear until 1878, the *Edinburgh Picturesque Notes* may be glanced at during an epoch rather barren of letters. Can a man be said to write a travel book about his native city even when it is a capital? Strictly speaking it is perhaps inaccurate, but when you consider how many people spend their lives in a town almost unconscious of it except as a static environment too familiar for curiosity, and then how much time Stevenson expended in purposeful exploration, going out of his way to verify some scene of history or perhaps merely to see certain aspects and less familiar regions of his town, the book may legitimately rank as 'travel'. Although *Edinburgh* is one of the books comparatively neglected by Stevensonians it has a good travel book's value for the few who do look into it—that of arousing their interest in a town they have never seen.

The book is happily free from that distressing 'I'm sure we should all be as happy as kings' sentimentality which made Stevenson's literary fortune with Thackeray's 'great stupid public', and yet avoids the trap of jesting invective which might easily have caught so witty and malcontent a citizen. The frank but not unjustified depreciation Scottish parents visit on their children Stevenson turns against his mother city. 'Edinburgh pays cruelly for her high seat in one of the vilest climates under heaven', and as his paragraph marches on with the winds and rain and 'cold sea fogs out of the east', the 'raw and boisterous winter', 'shifty and ungenial' summer, 'downright meteorological purgatory' of spring, 'dark weather and perpetual tilting against squalls', we are not surprised to find it end with a vignette of the inhabitants leaning over a railway bridge and envying those in the trains running South! Only insensitive people are insensitive to good and bad climate, and a spirit so receptive of impressions in a physical envelope so frail must indeed have suffered. A climate so gloomy was matched with a gloomier religion, from both of which Stevenson fled, and yet was attracted by use and wont, and the fascination of oppression.

He is not so outspoken about his fellow-townsmen, yet the passage where he speaks of them 'thronging by, in their neat clothes and conscious moral rectitude' seems to have given more offence than his more severe confession, 'we are wonderful patient haters for conscience' sake up here in the north' and his rejection of Edinburgh's sabbath bells as 'a harsh ecclesiastical tocsin, the outcry of incongruous orthodoxies', with more to the same or worse effect, showing, as his writings so often do, the energy of his revolt against an uncharitable and tormenting religion over-zealously censorious of trifles. 'Shakespeare wrote a comedy of "Much Ado About Nothing". The Scottish nation made a fantastic tragedy on the same subject.'

These, it may be said, are hardly 'picturesque notes', but from a biographical point of view such self-revelations are more immediately useful than eloquent descriptions of the Old and New Towns, though we must note his evocation of Deacon Brodie, godly citizen by day and masked burglar by night, whose figure haunted Stevenson until it was 'laid' not by the unsuccessful play he wrote with Henley, but by the inspired allegory of Jekyll and Hyde. The chapter on the grisly old cemetery and its macabre tombstones recalls 'Cummy's' sensational morbidity, especially in the long quotation about the digging up of the heads of the executed Covenanters after forty-five years! More acceptable is the evocation of the Edinburgh Law Courts where 'by a ferocious custom' the barristers, mostly briefless, must 'parade in wig and gown from ten till two' . . . 'intelligent men have been walking here daily for ten or twenty years without a rag of business or a shilling of reward'. We may guess that passage was written for his parents to read and note that at least one of these legal peripatetics thought it 'the most arduous form of idleness', leaving them to form the obvious conclusion. Indeed Stevenson's practice at the Bar was not lucrative. In later days his mother let slip that they had agreed he was to give her the shilling and keep the sovereign of every guinea he earned; and under this pact she netted four shillings. It was hardly worth the toil and time and the two thousand pounds which went to secure that barren title of 'Advocate at the Scottish Bar', only to have the fact disbelieved by an ignorant French policeman.

On the 30th of July, 1876 Stevenson was still in Scotland, and if not actually in Edinburgh close by at Swanston. The belief that he planned his canoe trip with Simpson along the canals and rivers of Belgium and France to recover from one of his periodic illnesses seems in this case unfounded, although it is quite true that he thought moderate outdoor exercise, such as a walking tour, the best treatment and that Henley speaks of having 'nursed' him about this time. At any rate, a letter written at least a month before the 'inland voyage' started gives no indication of ill health, but does show the trip planned from Antwerp to Grez for that year, with a continuation 'next spring' from Grez to the Mediterranean. The letter also shows that he hoped to use the experiences for 'a jolly book of gossip'.

The second half of the 'voyage' was never undertaken, perhaps fortunately since Stevenson nearly drowned himself in the Oise when it was somewhat in flood—what might have happened to our canoeists on the swift and dangerous Rhône when the snows were melting? Sir Walter had taken Stevenson yachting and had taught him canoeing in a two-seater on the Clyde, but it seems doubtful if Stevenson was really qualified to pilot so frail a craft over troubled waters. The idea of an 'inland voyage' was good enough as a title, though at least three previous books are mentioned relating similar 'voyages' and a reference by Stevenson himself seems to imply a fourth. Stevenson's book was not published until May 1878, and the discriminating publisher who picked it out was Kegan, Paul and Co. The publication was not a success, and the book only gradually acquired readers through the growth of the Stevenson cult.

An Inland Voyage is well worth a little attention, not only because of its interest as the first 'real' book of a young man who became a highly successful professional writer. Anyone who doubts either Stevenson's literary skill or the success with which he 'puts over' the peculiar charm of his literary personality, should be convinced by this first book alone. The discrepancy between the triviality—one might almost say insipidity—of the experiences related and the charm of the narrative as writing is quite startling. Only a hardened prejudice or desperate lack of appreciation in a reader could protect him from ending the book without a real liking for the author. The reader is interested by Stevenson, not by the canoeists' 'voyage'. What in fact did they do? They went by dull canals and flooded rivers much of the time in rainy weather, seeing little but the towing paths or the banks; they made a long 'portage' by train from Brussels to Maubeuge; until they reached Noyon and Compiègne they hardly saw a place worth recording; in their rain-soaked clothes carrying rubber knapsacks they were mistaken for peddlers and once rudely refused by a small-hotel keeper; and Stevenson nearly drowned himself. He makes the most of the little daily incidents and the chance acquaintances in rough lodgings, as well as of the cathedral of Noyon and the Compiègne Town Hall with the three mechanical figures striking the hours, but they are nothing but excuses—what we are really invited to admire is Stevenson.

Already he had the art of putting himself on good terms with his reader by a little judicious flattery of our species which the said reader naturally takes to himself with a nod of acquiescence and condescending approval for so shrewd an observer. '. . . We usually find ourselves a great deal braver and better than we thought' says the author on his second page. Do we? Again . . . 'the good in a man's spirit will not suffer itself to be overlaid, and rarely or never deserts him in the hour of need.' It may be so, but such a sentiment looked less questionable in the comfortable shelter of the 1870's than in the middle of the twentieth century. He finds lessons of consolation and good in everything. '. . . To see the barges waiting their turn at a lock affords a fine lesson of how easily the world may be taken.' The life of a bargee, has so many attractions 'it is not easy to see why' he 'should ever die'.

And then, 'discomfort, when it is honestly uncomfortable and makes no nauseous pretensions to the contrary, is a vastly humourous business. . . .' Again 'there is an upright stock in a man's own heart, that is trustier than any syllogism'; and 'the true materialism is to be ashamed of what we are'; and 'if we were charged so much a head for sunsets, or if God sent round the drum before the hawthorns came in flower, what a work should we not make about their beauty!' All comfortable doctrine, and the more so since placed in opposition to criticisms of society, mercantilism, work in offices, jacks-in-office, the decline of English manufacturing skill and probity, respectability and so forth, all done with a geniality which would provoke approval from a respectable nonconformist Mayor who had spent his life in an office directing the factory-production of ever more shoddy articles. I do not find it surprising that this book was a great favourite with Mr. Thomas Stevenson, who whole-heartedly vetoed publication of the astringent, reality-facing *Amateur Emigrant* a few years later.

We have now to note a still more interesting aspect of this first Stevenson book which is probably little known to all under the age of eighty. In its point of view of life, its 'philosophy'—if one may use so pretentious a word of so unassuming a line of thought—Stevenson set down or possibly invented the main lines of a character and way of life which endured up to the disasters of 1940. *An Inland Voyage* sketched the outline of the true uncommercial traveller (which Dickens certainly was not, though he coined the phrase), the writer or painter or 'artist' who shrugged off the advantages and rewards as well as the responsibilities and duties of money-making man in exchange for freedom and art. 'The moon and sixpence,' as Somerset Maugham put it so admirably. What was the ideal? To cut free from squalid money-making and office-servitude, to flee one's own country for the freedom of anonymity, to live in poverty for art's sake, to work hard under pretence of idling, to share one's last sovereign with a friend, and—hopefully—at last to justify rebellion by success. Until 1940 and socialism put an end to it, how many British artists of all sorts tried to follow his precepts, perhaps without having read them? In this and others of his writings Stevenson made articulate the vague but persistent feeling of revolt against a system and a set of values whose main end-product was ennui.

Hence his sympathy for those persons he thinks have kept intact 'those clean perceptions of what is nice and nasty, what is interesting and what is dull, which envious old gentlemen refer to as illusions'. He delighted in the poor strolling players who keep their hearts up in poverty and discomfort with the thought that after all they were 'artists'—Dickens loved the type too—and in all persons who seemed to be living life for its own sake, down to those mysterious French contemplatives who spend their lives dabbling a rod and line in seemingly fishless waters. He had hit on the great truth that people who have to be passively amused and cannot amuse themselves are defective. Canoeing in the rain along a continual prospect of barges and canal banks was far better than social climbing at Edinburgh dinners in a stiff shirt, and at the worst made a frame for 'philosophizing'.

According to Graham Balfour and Rosalind Masson the first meeting between Stevenson and his future wife, Fanny Osbourne, occurred at the moment when the 'inland voyage' ended at Grez. Others added a pretty story that Louis arriving at Chevillon's inn at night with a companion saw Mrs. Osbourne for the first time through the window and instantly remarked: "That's the woman I'm going to marry' or some such words. 'Whoever loved that loved not at first sight?' but so important a decision in the first second would seem 'so sudden' even for a romantic. Yet he confirmed something of the kind later. Even the account of the first meeting given by Lloyd Osbourne, Stevenson's stepson, who was present though only a schoolboy, seems to support the end of the inland voyage story until you come to the sentence where he speaks of Robert Louis's 'dusty knapsack'. Now if he had just come off a long canoe trip the knapsack would hardly have been 'dusty'. Yet, another eye-witness and member of the Grez 'colony', Birge Harrison, supports the Graham and Masson story. Other evidence shows that Stevenson and Fanny had met earlier in the year at Grez, so that the September 1876 meeting was not a surprise but a reunion. The actual date is of small importance, but the conflict of evidence about a matter of fact on which pretty stories were built, shows the difficulties of biography. I may add that the position of Colvin's note in his edition of the 'Letters' seems to support the September meeting, and that the scholarly Andrew Lang says the pair first met 'at Fontainebleau'!

When there is so much difference of opinion about the mere event of their meeting, the reader will not be surprised to learn that there is great disagreement about Fanny Osbourne, her part in Stevenson's life, and the effect of her influence. Without making a catalogue of testimonies and opinions, one may put it that estimates vary from making her indispensable to him, his 'Sine Qua Non' (to quote the title of one book on her), down to insinuations that she ruthlessly bossed him, caused quarrels with his friends and relatives, interfered with his writing unintelligently, and worked him to death.

Fanny Osbourne (née van de Grift) was an American, born in 1840, and the mother of three children, separated from her husband. When Stevenson met her the youngest of the three children had recently died in Paris in painful circumstances of sickness and poverty, and Mrs. Osbourne had with her at Grez a daughter Isobel (Belle) aged about seventeen, and her schoolboy son, the 'Lloyd Osbourne' of the Stevenson saga. In 1876 she was 36 and Stevenson 26. It is a curious fact that three of the women with whom the young Stevenson fell more or less in love, Mme Garschine, Mrs. Sitwell and Mrs. Osbourne, were all older than he, and all grass widows with a child or children through whom Stevenson made his first appeal to the mothers' hearts. There is no reason to suppose that this approach by way of the child formed part of any strategy of seduction. Among the many attractive features of Stevenson is a genuine liking for children and a remarkable ability to get quickly on good terms with them. It seems all the more unfortunate that he never had a child of his own. In his *Child's Garden of Verses* Stevenson has re-lived scenes and emotions and dreams of his own childhood with a vividness which still keeps them alive. For some reason a certain school of 'modern criticism' thinks that writers who enjoy the evocation of childhood are unintelligent, though why it should be intelligent to forget the most impressionable and imaginative part of life is not explained. At any rate Stevenson had this gift of sympathy with child life which served him well both as a person and in his work.

There seems little doubt that even if Stevenson had not made love to Fanny Osbourne during his first stay with her at Grez he must have done so during the autumn, and probably they came to some sort of understanding, though there is some evidence that at first she was more attracted by Robert Louis's cousin, Bob Stevenson. In any case their situation was difficult. At that time Fanny had been married for nearly nineteen years—her wedding with Sam Osbourne occurred before the American Civil War, when Louis was seven! She had more than once left her husband because of his alleged infidelities, and at one time he had been so long away that she had thought him dead. But he had always turned up again and she had always re-accepted him. Apparently she and her children were dependent on what he could allow them, which explains the desperate poverty in Paris which Lloyd remembered as a time when he was always hungry. The studies of mother and daughter at Julien's were evidently little more than the usual excuse for females alone in Paris, while Fanny's efforts as a writer during that period brought her one magazine publication, and that only because her work 'went with' the drawings of an artist friend. Between her precarious little income and her responsibilities she must have lived in perpetual anxiety, and she was not 'much of a catch', in the vulgar phrase, for a young man of family trying to be a writer.

All the more honour to him, then, that he followed his heart, and did not allow himself to be discouraged. If, at this early stage, Robert Louis really proposed that she should seek a divorce and then marry him, she might well be excused if she looked on this as the sort of wild talk young men do put out when they are or think they are in love. There is some evidence that Grez bohemians had spread exaggerated stories of the wealth to which Robert Louis was heir, but we may be confident that so honourable a man would have told her what the real position was. Perhaps it is true that some of that mysterious thousand pounds (whether maternal or paternal in origin) which rewarded his call to the Bar went to Fanny, as some undoubtedly went to Henley and other friends. Stevenson's open-handed generosity with money was only equalled by the delicacy with which he gave or 'lent' it. We need not doubt that he would do all he could to come to the aid of Fanny and her children, so long as the remnant of the rapidly dwindling thousand remained. At the same time both he and Fanny would have had to admit that, however great his talent and his potential earning power as a writer, he could not possibly support a wife and one or two stepchildren. The gilded chariot of Love's young dream seemed to have driven straight into a squalid impasse. But Stevenson evidently did not allow such trifles to cool his assiduities; and when the party returned to Paris in the autumn Stevenson's men friends could only regret that he was at least half lost to them, since he spent all the time possible with the Osbournes.

Stevenson's published letters do not give us much help over the year 1877, which he spent between England, Scotland and France; yet we must note the fact that a letter to his mother, dated January, gives the address '5 Rue Douay' which happens to be Fanny's address at the time. He gets no nearer to 'confessing' Fanny than the general statement that he dines every day at a *crémerie* 'with a party of Americans, one Irishman, and sometimes an English lady: elderly, very prim. . . .' Probably Mrs. Stevenson by this time knew her boy well enough not to be taken in by that 'elderly, very prim' false scent.

In any case, this particular phase of his 'romance of destiny' did not evolve either so swiftly or so smoothly as might appear, while the propounders of the 'Stevenson as Galahad' myth evidently did not know that Sam Osbourne came over to Paris when his child died and was with his wife at Grez in 1876 when she met Louis. A few weeks later Osbourne returned to America. In any event and whatever the exact chronology of their falling in love, there can be no doubt that this unresolved situation with its seemingly insoluble difficulties must have been a major preoccupation with both of them, particularly with Louis, during the two or three years between their meeting and their marriage. It was fortunate for them both that Fanny was as shrewd and what is called 'practical' as well as strong-willed, for at that date any 'romantic' running away together would have completely wrecked Louis's literary career and doubtless would have received from his father both commination and an abrupt slamming of the family door in his face—for Louis had already been turned out of his home at least once.

The problem, then, was: how could they be united respectably thus retaining the family allowance, public esteem, and the support of literary London? In bohemian Paris there was no particular objection to a married woman with children eloping with a young man ten years her junior, but it would not have been kindly judged in Victorian England, let alone Scotland. But for the fact that Fanny was an American, and that the laws of California enabled her to divorce without much difficulty, expense or scandal, their situation would have been as hopeless as that of poor Mrs. Sitwell and Colvin, who had to wait until they were in their romantic sixties to be united. What would Louis and Fanny have done if she had been a British subject? They would either have sighed in vain or starved in fact.

With this constant preoccupation on his mind, Stevenson's movements become less important in detail, particularly since he had now emancipated himself from perpetual family servitude. He travelled between Scotland, London and Paris, as many writers of his day did, spending as much time with Fanny as he possibly could, either in Paris or at Grez. Whether they were imprudent enough to live together seems undecided, but just as they had the same Paris address in January 1877 so in September they both had 5 Rue Ravignan as address. There she nursed him when he seemed likely to be going blind, and from there she took him to London where she began to meet his friends—Henley and Stephen as well as Mrs. Sitwell. A letter from Stevenson to Henley written from Edinburgh early in 1878 leaves no possible doubt as to the full intimacy of the two lovers by that time, and apparently they made no particular secret of it to his friends. That the news went no further is a tribute to the friends' discretion and to fear of Mrs. Grundy. With Sam Osbourne far off in America there was no need for a hasty and dramatic elopement.

This halfway situation was well enough for a time, at any rate as long as the thousand pounds lasted. But even that sum—several times as valuable then as it would be now—plus his allowance plus his earnings, could not be expected to last long with a man so careless and generous as Stevenson, particularly since he and Simpson lost money by buying and fitting up a barge which had to be sold at a loss. These perennial money crises in Stevenson's life—he was from time to time worried about money until the day he died—were due even in early days as much to his extravagance as to real penury, and at this time the crisis was complicated by the knot of problems involved with Fanny. There seems no means of knowing when she made up her mind she would transfer herself permanently from the faithless if fascinating Sam to the faithful Louis. Perhaps it was due to her shrewd advice that Louis, instead of confronting his father with the fatal ultimatum of an elopement, sent for him to come to Paris, and perhaps to some extent revealed the truth.

How far Robert Louis in fact confided in his father cannot be determined, and the phrase from which the confidence is inferred (apart from Colvin's testimony) is simply a reference to the 'Scotch Presbyterian who has been to Paris under such strange circumstances'. Why in Paris? Was it merely to bring Thomas Stevenson away from Edinburgh and into a less censorious ambiance, or was it to let him meet Fanny? There does not seem to be any evidence that he ever saw Fanny until August 1879. In any case, if Stevenson had told his father the whole truth, the brutal facts stripped of 'romance' and periphrases would have run thus: 'I am in love with Fanny Osbourne, a married woman ten years older than myself, with two children, and we have lived together. All the same, we hope her husband will allow her to divorce him, and then I can marry Fanny which of course means that I must support her and her family.' This took for granted a certain magnanimity in the absent Sam, while Thomas Stevenson must have realized that most of the 'supporting' would fall to him. With his social and religious prejudices (although he approved of divorce for women only), he might tend to see the situation in rather harsh terms—either Louis was 'breaking up a home life of twenty years' or Fanny was an adventuress anxious to get rid of an unsuccessful husband and to achieve the security of the Stevenson family money. In either case he would have been unjust, and Robert Louis's eloquence would have been called in to show that here were two people caught up in an emotional situation beyond their control which must somehow be made to fit in with the arbitrary arrangements imposed by society. As an American Fanny at first would have difficulty in realizing the disproportionate horror and censure evoked by 'divorce' in the British Isles of those days, but she evidently learned. In her certificate of marriage to Louis she described herself as 'widow', not as 'divorced'.

In any case the genuine affection existing between father and son underneath all the quarrels and differences brought them closer together, though it seems improbable that Thomas Stevenson's conscience would have allowed him to sanction such a scheme beforehand, whatever he might do when confronted with the *fait accompli*. Their talks must have turned on religion, which is confirmed by a letter written by Louis early in 1878 and dated from a café in the Boulevard St. Michael, of all places! He propounds a theory of Christianity and asceticism, but inevitably diverges to Stevenson himself:

> 'I feel every day as if religion had a greater interest for me . . . I cannot transfer my interests, not even my religious interests, to any different sphere. . . .'

He speaks of his 'very acute sufferings', feels he is growing 'an old man', a 'little sharp, I fear, and a little close and unfriendly'. A friend of his is dying, he has had to write painful letters—'I am lonely and sick and out of heart'. And so forth, ending with a postscript of appeal to his father '. . . don't expect too much of me. Try to take me as I am.' The tone is wholly at variance with the philosophy of 'we should all be as happy as kings' but the letter was evidently written, as he says, on a day of sickness and discouragement. It is worth study and meditation for those who care to look it up if only because Stevenson at twenty-seven is shown still trying to clarify his religious feelings, and genuinely. I do not think there is any reason to believe he brought up the subject merely to gratify his father, who in any case would have been satisfied with nothing less than complete acquiescence in orthodoxy, *his* orthodoxy.

The financial responsibilities which would obviously result from marriage with Fanny must have weighed on Stevenson particularly as the last of the thousand pounds disappeared. The year 1878 was almost a record in his life for the number of serial publications, and it is natural to suppose that this was due to his eagerness to achieve professional success for Fanny's sake. Probably that motive did exist, but we must remember that Stevenson was now reaping the literary rewards of several years of intense work. He had to offer the essays which now make up *Virginibus Puerisque* as well as the earliest of his fiction he preserved, including *The New Arabian Nights* which we know was partly Bob's idea, and eagerly discussed by Louis, Bob and Fanny as it was being written.

The natural inference is that Fanny's influence was already at work on Robert Louis as a writer, diverting him from essays to fiction. This can be only partly true. Setting aside those mysterious and rather disquieting 'little people' who acted stories in Stevenson's dream life for him to write when awake, we know that he had always been trying to write fiction—as early as sixteen he had attempted a Scott novel. There still exists from early days a schedule of stories he intended to write, most of which he probably never did write, but the intention was there. *A Lodging for the Night* and *The Sire de Malétroit's Door* are still 'literary' inasmuch as they derive from his study of French medieval literature. *Will o' the Mill* is rather a parable-sermon than a real story, on the theme of the man who from a timid yet mellow selfishness refuses himself to life, and vegetates and dies alone. This may have been a passing mood in Stevenson, but it certainly was not typical of him. And it can hardly be said that *Will o' the Mill* is staged on the contemporary scene. With *New Arabian Nights*, fantastic and in a sense unreal as the stories are, there is a big step towards modernity; and as Fanny later wrote an introduction to a reprint of the book, discussing its genesis, we may reasonably infer both her encouragement and direction. She was evidently willing to take on the Puritan wife's burden of acting as her husband's conscience, which in this case included his literary conscience.

How far Fanny was qualified to bring out the very best of Stevenson's literary gifts is a question. We can only say that he did submit all his work to her and accepted her judgment, while Mr. Thomas Stevenson thought so highly of her that before he died he made Louis promise never to publish anything without her approval. But it seems highly likely that father and Fanny had much the same conception of literary merit, i.e. what would be an immediate success with the public. Fanny could see that essays and literary studies and charming travel books would never provide the money which would be needed if they were to marry, especially if Mr. Thomas Stevenson withdrew the regular allowance. The people who enjoyed that sort of thing were too few, and the way to the great public was the way of fiction. Tastes have changed, for whereas in those days people liked to read what they thought was fact presented as fiction, they now like to read wishful-thinking fiction presented as fact. But in those days the great market was for avowed fiction, so that for all practical purposes Fanny was quite right to encourage Louis to make a lively story out of Bob's fanciful notion of a Suicide Club, and to follow it with others in the same vein. The title is a bid for popularity as much as the character of Prince Florizel which hardly needed Fanny's later revelation for readers to perceive was respectful flattery of the Prince of Wales. Fanny cannot be reproached for failing to see that Conan Doyle would have treated the tales more successfully, since this happened years before Doyle began to write, so that here again we may be allowed to give Stevenson credit as a predecessor. Unluckily, as we have seen, *The New Arabian Nights* appeared first in Henley's *London*, which had little or no money for contributors; and then remained unpublished because Mr. Kegan Paul thought them 'too fantastic, and likely to injure the reputation of their author'—a literary opinion more fantastic than the tales themselves. The book was issued in August 1882 by Chatto and Windus, and was immediately successful, since it was reprinted in November. As Fanny Stevenson sarcastically winds up her introduction:

> 'There was not a single story, poem, article, or novel written by my husband that was not similarly condemned by some one of his friends and literary advisers.'

Today's great thought for literary critics!

The planning, if not the actual writing of the *New Arabian Nights*, was followed by an improbable event. R.L.S. became temporarily a secretary, and startled his friends by appearing in a new, clean suit of clothes. True, the secretary's employer was only his old friend Professor Jenkin, who had been appointed a member of the jury at the Paris Exposition of 1878. The only indication I find as to the manner in which Stevenson discharged these unaccustomed duties is contained in the remark of an Edinburgh notable who states, a little sardonically perhaps, that during *l'Exposition* he received a number of letters from the professor, but not one was in the handwriting of the secretary.

Early in the month of August 1878 Fanny brought her children to London, and then left for the United States. What understanding she and Louis came to before she left is not specifically stated, but presumably the general plan was for her to seek a divorce and then, when she was legally free, to marry Louis. If we try to see the situation from Fanny's point of view we can see that the final decision rested with her and was not easy to make. She had two children dependent on her, and at that time neither Sam nor Louis was a particularly good provider, but she had a legal claim on Sam and none on Louis. No doubt he made every kind of solemn promise, but 'men were deceivers ever'—how was she to know that he might not grow cool with absence, meet some other charmer (there had been plenty in his life) and leave her stranded? It is fairly clear that Belle and the young Irishman O'Meara were in love, but in some way and for some reason he failed to come to the point. Why should Louis be more scrupulous? After all she did not know him then as she learned to know him later or even as we now know him. She knew he was subject to moods, to fits of hysterical emotion and reaction, and did not in all probability realize the 'core of flint' that was in him. The next year must have been one of perplexity for her, and natural hesitation may account for the long delay in the divorce.

What is certain is that the parting was a bitter one for Louis Stevenson, and Lloyd Osbourne has given us a glimpse of his future stepfather turning from the train at the London terminus and walking swiftly away, tall and thin and resolute, without one backward glance. By the beginning of September he was in the little French town of Monastier, working hard to finish his *Edinburgh Notes* and *New Arabian Nights*. Le Monastier (which does not rate a notice in the *Guide Michelin*) is about fifteen miles south of Le Puy, and it was from there that Stevenson started on his not very extensive travels with Modestine, the donkey. The title, *Travels with a Donkey*, was not altogether happy for either by accident or design someone reviewed it as travels *of* a donkey, and in my youth in London it was often called *Travels with Sidney Colvin*.

While he tarried in this village we get one or two glimpses in his letters of the charming Louis Stevenson who so easily made friends, especially in friendly and 'democratic' France, and could still enjoy life though his heart was journeying with Fanny to California. He was taken into the company of the local bureaucrats, whom he amusingly translates as 'the Conductor of Roads and Bridges, the Receiver of Registrations, the First Clerk of Excise, and the Perceiver of the Impost'. So little does administrative France change under the changes of revolutions that it is a hundred to one that exactly similar and equally amiable officials are still in that village, probably eating lunch and dinner, and welcoming any likely stranger at the same table in the same restaurant, but not, unluckily, with the same menus. In the days before the adjective 'Gargantuan' had become impossible Stevenson applied it rightly to a lunch at Le Puy, consisting of a large slice of melon, ham and jelly, a plateful of gudgeon, eight small crayfish (he means *écrivisses*) a fillet steak, the breast and leg of a partridge with green peas, cheese of Mont d'Or, a peach, and 'a handful of biscuits, macaroons, and things'. For this '*repas plantureux*' he paid three francs or about sixty cents! And the politicians, bureaucrats and journalists tell us how much better off we are under their rule than our downtrodden ignorant predecessors of eighty years ago! And remember that was only a few years after the disastrous Franco-Prussian war and only fifteen years after the American Civil War had rocked the foundations of the world.

The ostensible object of these travels was to explore the country of the Cevennes, the home and guerrilla battlefields of those stout-hearted French Protestants who defied the persecutions of Louis XIV (breaking his kingly grandfather's word by revoking the Edict of Nantes) and gave plenty of trouble to a Marshal of France and an army of French regulars. Their kinship with the Scottish Covenanters is obvious, but there were differences. True, both Scots and Camisards 'had a remarkable confidence in God', but 'in Scotland they had all gloomy and bedevilled thoughts', whereas the Protestants of the Cevennes 'had only bright and supporting visions'. They fought hard and slew their enemies, but 'with a light conscience' and when they heard the singing of psalms they felt 'an animating ardour, a transporting desire'. How are we to account for this difference, which naturally interested Stevenson still quivering from the horrors of 'Cummy's' tales of the Covenanters? A different climate and landscape, he thinks, but perhaps a different race and a different culture—from some of those peaks you can see the Mediterranean over which Odysseus sailed.

The travels certainly had an interested motive. 'Another book ought to come of it,' he wrote his mother. But apart from reviving memories of the Camisards and, by way of contrast, visiting a Trappist monastery, the trip seems ill-planned. He left it until too late in the year, much of his route was through dull country and by semi-barbarous hamlets. He did not know how to drive his donkey or how to adjust her burden without galling the poor beast until peasants took pity on his ignorance, and he spent '80 francs and two glasses of beer' on a sleeping bag which he used only a few times. It is the same story of the skilful essayist and stylist making a charming book out of trifling encounters and not very interesting experiences. The pleasure of the book is in the details, as in the matter of *le père Adam* who sold the donkey and claimed that he had cherished her to the extent of giving her white bread while he fed on coarse 'black' bread. 'But,' adds Stevenson:

> 'He had a name in the village for brutally misusing the ass; yet it is certain that he shed a tear, and the tear made a clean mark down one cheek.'

Travels with a Donkey is said by Stevenson himself to be filled with love messages to the absent Fanny. No doubt I am obtuse, but I don't find many. Apropos of beating the donkey he remarks:

> 'I am worthy of the name of an Englishman, and it goes against my conscience to lay my hand rudely on a female.'

But was it really necessary to reassure Fanny on that point? Was it news to her that he felt abashed at having to share a bedroom in a very rustic inn with a cooper and his wife? After a rainy walk his thoughts at eventide 'began to turn upon dinner and a fireside', and in the monastery he reflects that 'the arts and sciences, and professional male jollity' are 'deserted at once for two sweet eyes and a caressing accent'. This last remark is to the purpose, but we are already halfway through the book, and for a long time we look in vain for a 'message' even so vague as the assertion of man's felicity if he finds 'but one' to whom he can speak out his heart freely. And that is all, until near the end of the book he hears a woman singing and wishes he could have answered her:

> 'What could I have told her? Little enough; and yet all the heart requires. How the world gives and takes away, and brings sweethearts near only to separate them again into distant and strange lands; but to love is the great amulet which makes the world a garden; and "hope, which comes to all", outwears the accidents of life, and reaches with tremulous hands beyond the grave and death.'

A lovely compliment to any woman, and when Fanny read it she was doubtless not displeased. Only, the author must have reached her about as soon as the book.

7

THE months which followed Fanny's departure were a time of increasing restlessness and discontent for Stevenson. The Cevennes trip of course had as its main object the production of another travel book but there was also the motive of finding a means of killing time; and after his return from France he constantly shifted from London to Scotland and back. Certainly he worked, but some of it was almost sheer waste—collaborating with Henley on a play about Deacon Brodie. These plays with Henley were a financial will o' the wisp for Stevenson, and it is unfortunate that he spent much time on them which could have been better used. Unquestionably, plays are and were then the most paying form of literary work, *if* you have the gift of writing successful ones; and neither of them had. Henley is not solely to be blamed—in later years Fanny was urgent in pushing Louis to write plays, which perhaps goes to show that her supposedly unerring gift for criticizing his work was not so unerring, and that her standards were rather a matter of possible profit than of fame.

If *Deacon Brodie* the play was a failure both as art and pot-boiler—and indeed today it is almost unreadable—Deacon Brodie the historical character fascinated Stevenson from his childhood, an Edinburgh cabinet-maker of ostentatious respectability who was secretly a burglar. The tale appealed to the romantic Stevenson who liked to think he might be descended from Rob Roy MacGregor, and whose greatest popular success was the vivid allegory and sermon of Jekyll and Hyde. Perhaps there was in Stevenson himself something of a double personality, which would explain his lifelong interest in the theme; but it is easy to carry this too far. There was doubtless more play-acting than reality in Stevenson's double life, such as it was, which at this very period (1879) included such contrasts as meeting George Meredith at Box Hill and wandering the streets of London in disreputable clothes in the hope of being arrested as a vagabond. Why he wanted that when he so much disliked being actually arrested as a vagabond in France remains unexplained. Whatever

Stevenson's sexual relations with other women before he fell in love with Fanny—and at least three seem definitely established—it is hard to believe the story that at this very time he was 'carrying on' with two other women (one called Margaret Stevenson) who met and came to blows at Swanston! Stevenson's behaviour at this time is more consistent with a state of anxiety about Fanny than with an amateurish Don Juanism. It is perhaps unfair but one can't help feeling that much of Louis Stevenson's supposed erotic activities in this respect were less in the manner of Count Almaviva than of Monsieur Léon Berthelini, the hero of *Providence and the Guitar*.

Still, J. A. Steuart implies that he had this Margaret Stevenson story from Charles Baxter and Henley, who must have known this side of Stevenson's bohemian life better than anyone. In which case we have the not unprecedented situation of a man genuinely in love with one woman who makes love to others in her absence; and after all he was separated from Fanny for a year. If the scene of violence between the women did take place that would explain why Stevenson went to live with Henley after being turned out of his home by his father, as well as Henley's later indignation at the plaster saint R.L.S. manufactured by Balfour and the crew of boosters. In this connexion we should perhaps note that the essay on Burns (whose publication caused so much rage and resentment among the Scottish admirers of the plaster saint Burns of national hero tradition) was composed during the summer of 1879. In that essay Stevenson tried to face the facts recorded of Burns and his numerous love affairs, and in his letter to Gosse remarks that there was in Burns 'something of the vulgar, bagmanlike, professional seducer'. His essay, on the other hand, opens with these interesting remarks:

> 'To write with authority about another man, we must have fellow feeling and some common ground of experience with our subject. We may praise or blame according as we find him related to us by the best or worst in ourselves; but it is only in virtue of some relationship that we can be his judges, even to condemn.'

What then was Stevenson's 'relationship' to Burns? True, they were both Scots; and both were poets, but rather as Macedon is related to Monmouth by Fluellen. They come together again with Stevenson's reflection that:

> 'Schools and colleges, for one great man whom they complete, perhaps unmake a dozen; the strong spirit can do well upon more scanty fare.'

In speaking of the love affairs he is not so downright in the essay as in the Gosse letter. 'A man brings to love a deal of ready-made sentiment,' he says; and again Burns 'stands unsurpassed in his power of self-deception' (about falling in love) and hits out hard in this sentence:

> 'With a leer of what the French call fatuity, he bids the belles of Mauchline beware of his seductions; and the same cheap self-satisfaction finds a yet uglier vent when he plumes himself on the scandal at the birth of his first bastard.'

It seems improbable that, in spite of his opening remarks, Stevenson was either confessing or attacking himself. If he was in any sense identifying himself with Burns in these respects he had changed from the man who in 1876 wrote the charming little essay *On Falling in Love*, which he defines as 'the one illogical adventure, the one thing of which we are tempted to think as supernatural'. The remarks on marriage in the preceding section of *Virginibus Puerisque* are more sententious and would-be wise. 'To marry,' he says in an over-quoted epigram, 'is to domesticate the Recording Angel,' but he does not say whether the Recording Angel is male or female, though of course we must infer the latter. Surely he was thinking of himself when he wrote this:

> 'Times are changed with him who marries; there are no more by-path meadows, where you may innocently linger, but the road lies long and straight and dusty to the grave. Idleness which is often becoming and even wise in the bachelor, begins to wear a different aspect when you have a wife to support. Suppose, after you are married, one of those little slips were to befall you. . . .'

Well, might we not 'suppose' that one or even two of 'those little slips' might occur while he was hoping to get married? We lose ourselves in conjectures, and so, unfortunately, we do when we try to interpret the imperfectly known facts of the next and most dramatic move in Stevenson's romance of destiny. What we know can be put in a sentence: at the beginning of August 1879 Louis received a cable from Fanny and decided at once to go to California. If we knew what the cable said. . . . But we don't, so that no certainty is possible.

There is one curious little fact about this separation worth recording, and it is this—Louis tells a friend that he is not writing to Fanny because she knows how he feels and there is nothing more to be said. This sounds more like a lame excuse than an explanation. Absent lovers may be perfectly aware of each other's feelings but wish to be reassured, and frequently. It seems incredible that Louis—so skilled a writer, moreover!—should not want to give her news of his life and to hear of hers. The phrase must refer only to some temporary condition, for if they were not writing how could he learn of the vicissitudes of feeling through Fanny which is supposed to have passed? Perhaps he did not wish to give Sam Osbourne written evidence which might be used against him in a divorce.

At all events, there was the cable and there was the decision. Did Louis confide in his father? Perhaps, from which we may infer that in spite of that patriarch's eccentric belief that no man should be divorced but any woman might on mere application, he did not approve at that time of marriage with Fanny Osbourne. Edmund Gosse, who was with Stevenson during much of his last day in London before he sailed says that Louis's 'family and the inner circle of his friends were equally certain that it was neither needful nor expedient that he should make this journey'. Gosse further says 'it was hoped the withdrawal of supplies would make the voyage impossible' and adds later that 'we' (i.e. himself and his wife) 'to the last were trying to dissuade him from what seemed to us the maddest of enterprises.' Gosse notes that towards the end of the evening both he and Stevenson were 'in a pretty hysterical state'. This 'hysterical' condition remained a menace to Stevenson and was probably far more a consequence of the wrong treatment he received in childhood than of his ill health or unstable temperament. Fanny had already had a disagreeable experience of it during a cab drive.

The 'cutting off of supplies' explains why Stevenson made an otherwise almost motiveless journey to London, seeing that he was in Edinburgh on the 29th July, 1879, and sailed from Greenock to New York on the 7th August. Obviously he went to London not merely to say good-bye to the Gosses and other friends, but to raise funds for his desperate journey. In spite of his realization that he ought to save money if he hoped to marry Stevenson had continued to live in his usual careless, extravagant fashion. From

Monastier he wrote his mother asking for fifty pounds (his allowance had been raised to one hundred pounds a year, but had not been paid for six months, on account of one of the endless differences with his father) and then had spent too much on his donkey and sleeping bag and so forth. Among other needless waste, due to lack of forethought, he threw away a cold leg of mutton, a loaf of white bread, a milk bottle and an egg-whisk! In the 'spring' of 1879 he wrote Gosse that he was 'shorn and bleating: a poor, lone, penniless man of letters'; yet in May (?) or perhaps June he spent no less than twenty pounds on copies of his *Donkey* to give away—a fantastic sacrifice to literary strategy. From France a little later he thanks his father for money, and yet in July arrives in London with only four shillings, and carelessly begs from his mother—'unless some money is sent I shall probably have died of hunger in the meanwhile'. So that he could scarcely have saved much in a year when Fanny's cable arrived, and the emergency so long foreseen and so ill provided for was upon him. It seems almost a miracle he got away at all, but all through the difficult months ahead (much of the experience very unromantic 'destiny') we must remember that 'core of flint' in his character. And, though Henley would have protested, I cannot but think that Stevenson was also supported by the essential religious if unorthodox views expressed in *Lay Morals*, which were in fact written in March of this year 1879. There we may find the explanation of the irregular love affairs which so much scandalized contemporary fellow-townsmen and later critics of the Stevenson plaster saint myth, and an indication of the mood in which he started to join Fanny:

> 'Thus, man is tormented by a very imperious physical desire; it spoils his rest, it is not to be denied; the doctors will tell you, not I, how it is a physical need like the want of food or slumber. In the satisfaction of this desire, as it first appears, the soul sparingly takes part; nay, it oft unsparingly regrets and disapproves the satisfaction. But let the man learn to love a woman as far as he is capable of love; and for this random affection of the body there is substituted a steady determination, a consent of all his powers and faculties, which supersedes, adopts, and commands all the others. The desire survives, strengthened perhaps, but taught obedience and changed in scope and character. Life is no longer a tale of betrayals and regrets; for the man now lives as a whole; his consciousness now

moves on uninterrupted like a river; through all the extremes and ups and downs of passion, he remains approvingly conscious of himself.'

We can see why the little Sanhedrin which determined what Stevenson should and should not publish definitely put off publication of that book until two years after Stevenson's death, when it was included in *Juvenilia*, though in fact he was twenty-eight when he wrote it. And the final words about remaining approvingly conscious of himself may perhaps be thought to justify the judgment on Stevenson, for writing which Henley was so much abused by those who did not want the truth and were congenitally incapable of seeing it.

> 'Withal, if he wanted a thing,' says Henley, 'he went after it with an entire contempt for consequences. For these, indeed, the Shorter Catechist was ever prepared to answer; so that, whether he did well or ill, he was safe to come out unabashed and cheerful. He detested Mr. Gladstone, I am pleased to say; but his gift of self-persuasion was scarce second to that statesman's own.'

Though born in England, Mr. Gladstone also was of Scottish descent.

The expedition to join Fanny in California, to which all this was preliminary, marks a great change in Stevenson's life. He was perfectly well aware of it, as of everything which concerned him and his destiny, and has recorded all but the more intimate phases of his life with especial interest and detail during the period of exactly one year which elapsed between his sailing from Greenock alone and returning from New York with Fanny and Lloyd on the 7th August, 1880. It was a very severe test of his character and integrity, from which on the whole he came out excellently, though he must fairly soon have failed but for financial help from home. As he said of himself cheerfully but perhaps a little cynically, he always fell on his feet but then the legs were always his father's. His failure would not have been due to any lack of courage and hard work, but simply to the fact that his health gave way under the combined strains of physical fatigue, mental over-work, anxieties and hardships. Indeed, it seems obvious that active tuberculosis with lung haemorrhages were a result of the extremities to which he was reduced—which in turn evokes the question of what his parents and friends were thinking of to allow so frail though stout-hearted a man to go without money help for about nine months? Of course, none of them wanted him to marry Fanny; but if they thought cutting off supplies would stop the marriage they mistook both the sincerity of Louis's love and the strength of his character.

Louis Stevenson, as 'amateur emigrant', did not in fact cross the Atlantic in the steerage. By paying two guineas extra above the steerage passage money of six guineas he was able to travel in the 'second cabin', separated from steerage by only a thin partition, but with a table to work at, a slightly better diet, and exemption from the emigrant 'processing' in New York. Nobody can say that he did not work hard in difficult conditions. During the voyage he worked to complete *The Story of a Lie* and must have made many notes for *The Amateur Emigrant*, while during the interminable and exhausting train journey of nearly two weeks he must again have made notes. I am a strong man and Stevenson was a weakling, and I have found that three days and three nights in an American train without a sleeper are quite enough. He endured four times that, and took it on top of the discomforts and disagreeables of his second-cabin crossing.

The Amateur Emigrant, we learn from Graham Balfour, was 'the work which Stevenson's friends criticized most severely', was bought back from the publisher by Louis's father and suppressed until after the author's death. Why? Well, Charles Baxter as a lawyer might well have criticized it, since the steamship company, several members of the crew and more of the steerage passengers might even at that time have brought actions for libel. But the real reason was that the author frankly revealed himself as forced to travel in circumstances of actual poverty, associating with poor and almost destitute persons, and occasionally producing reflections too true to be palatable to the buying public. In the interests of the 'romantic' Stevenson the suppression was no doubt justified, but if his 'friends' criticized his book on the ground that it was a failure from a literary point of view they were even more mistaken than Fanny's sarcastic remark about their judgment indicates.

Whatever its faults, and what book—especially a good book—is without them? *The Amateur Emigrant* was the most mature piece of work Stevenson had yet produced. To call it *reportage* is to miss its significance, for it goes much deeper than that.

The presentation is so vivid that as we read we share and re-live Stevenson's experiences and feelings until they become our own. Here, as in other respects, Stevenson is the predecessor or 'herald' of D. H. Lawrence, though Lawrence never seemingly encountered experiences and people so disillusioning, not to say squalid. *The Amateur Emigrant* goes far deeper into social inequalities and class brutalities than reminiscences of playing 'Velvet Jacket' in a 'howff' or of half an hour in a French prison could possibly have justified. The callous brutality of the crew to steerage passengers, the food thrown at them (of which the best was the leavings of the first-class passengers), the conviction of the emigrants that nothing in the world matters but money and that they could only get it by a social revolution, the removal of all glamour from emigration—these and a score of other observations honestly set down 'would never do' for the prosperous of that age, but are most interesting to read now. The book is an authentic fragment of that 'history of the English people' which the English historians have never written and probably never will.

The Amateur Emigrant is far from being 'social realism', for the author has no particular political axe to grind though, as a Tory, he likes people and is suspicious of humanity. The characters individually are not all ugly, and Stevenson would not be Stevenson if he had not discovered almost at once a likeable child, 'an ugly, merry, unbreeched child of three, his lint-white hair in a tangle, his face smeared with suet and treacle' but moving with 'such grace and good-humour' that 'he might fairly be called beautiful'. We may set that against his amazement at the daintiness of these artisans who rejected as not 'fit for pigs' the porridge, soup and bread Stevenson found 'if not luxurious, at least sufficient'. They were too self-conscious to dance and were bitterly opposed to war, attributing 'their own misfortunes and frequently their own taste for whisky to the campaigns in Zululand and Afghanistan'. Stevenson's critics would have been momentarily cheered by his reflection that 'there is nothing more becoming than a genuine admiration; and it shares this with love, that it does not become contemptible although misplaced'. (This is more benevolent than true.) But they would not like the merciless thumb-nail sketch of the man who never said anything that was 'true, kind or interesting' though they might have accepted the Russian whose song was 'as deep as a cow's bellow and wild like the White Sea'. But then comes this cool appreciation:

> 'As far as I saw, drink, idleness and incompetency were the three great causes of emigration . . .'

which destroys the myth of the 'new countries' that in Europe the weak and vicious stayed at home and the strong and virtuous emigrated and begat descendants, to praise their own non-existent heroics and virtues out of nationalist vanity! On top of that we have the portrait of Mackay, then down and out, now a type which is ruling much of the world to ruin:

> 'His eyes were sealed by a cheap, school-book materialism. He could see nothing in the world but money and steam-engines. He did not know what you meant by the word happiness. He had forgotten the simple emotions of childhood, and perhaps never encountered the delights of youth. He believed in production, that useful figment of economy, as if it had been real like laughter; and production, without prejudice to liquor, was his god and guide. . . . Anything, whatever it was, that seemed to him likely to discourage the continued passionate production of corn and steam-engines he resented like a conspiracy against the people. . . . One thing indeed is not to be learned in Scotland, and that is, the way to be happy. Yet that is the whole of culture, and perhaps two-thirds of morality. Can it be that the Puritan school, by divorcing a man from nature, by thinning out his instincts, and setting a stamp of its disapproval on whole fields of human activity and interest, leads at last directly to material greed?'

Turning from Mackay in particular to his fellow-passengers in general Stevenson could praise the best of them as 'not rough, nor hasty, nor disputatious', but 'helpful, gentle, patient and placid', and he even thought their gentleness 'lay more nearly at the spring of behaviour than in many more ornate and delicate societies'. And yet he has to confess:

> 'One and all were too much interested in disconnected facts, and loved information for its own sake with too rash a devotion; but people in all classes display the same appetite as they gorge themselves daily with the miscellaneous gossip of the newspaper. . . . They did not perceive relations, but leaped to a so-called cause, and thought the problem settled. Thus the cause of everything in England was the form of government, and the cure for all evils was, by consequence, a revolution. . . . They would not hear of improvement on

their part, but wished the world made over again in a crack, so that they might remain improvident and idle and debauched, and yet enjoy the comfort and respect that should accompany the opposite virtues. . . .'

These are but specimens of the observations set down in this book, some of them no doubt less striking now than when Stevenson made them, others as melancholy to read as must have been Cassandra's unheeded prophecies when time had fulfilled them. But the whole book is well worth study for anyone interested in the development of Stevenson's thought, art and character. The man who lived and wrote the experiences of *The Amateur Emigrant* cannot be fairly set down as a dilettante in life or as a writer of boys' books or as a pretty stylist in essays and travels. Of course it may be said that his steerage friends knew he was 'a gentleman' and so gave him intentionally or unintentionally a false impression of themselves. This Stevenson strenuously denies. Passengers and crew and officers all lacked the perspicacity of the Edinburgh and London police, and more nearly approached the obtuseness of the sleuth of Châtillon and the landladies who thought he and Sir Walter were peddlers. The sailors called him 'mate', the officers 'my man', and the steerage ranged him as anything from a mason to 'a practical engineer'. The experiences then were not 'contaminated' by the false relationship so hard to avoid in the contacts of different 'classes'. And such is snobbery that this merit and value of the book may have been among the reasons for which 'the friends' disliked and suppressed it. To be mistaken for a peddler by a French landlady in an obscure village easily passed as superior fun, especially since a baronet was included; but the genteel of 1880, who were very genteel, would very likely have felt there must be 'something not altogether nice in Mr. Stevenson' for him to be received so universally and unflatteringly as one more among those who, on his own showing, were idle, drunken and incompetent. The industry of his daily stint at writing was dismissed in stolid British fashion 'as a broad joke', nothing being more ridiculous to the *gros bovins* than 'pen-pushing', so that the purser out of sheer compassion offered to let Stevenson copy out the passenger-list 'for which you will be *paid*'. It was a prophetic glimpse of the Ant-hill State.

All this must have been far less entertaining for Stevenson to

W. E. Henley.

Edmund Gosse.

'Braemar'—the cottage where R.L.S. wrote *Treasure Island.*

[*To face p.* 112

R.L.S. as a youth.

R.L.S. aged 35.

R.L.S. aged 37

R.L.S. aged 43.

To face p. 113]

live than it is for us to read, and anyone can sympathize with his first impulse after he had found a cheap hotel in New York—which was to dine well for a change from ship's fare. He should have followed this up by at least a week's rest before starting for California. Unluckily for him he was booked to start on Monday evening (having landed on Sunday afternoon) and still more unluckily he had to spend the daylight hours of Monday walking to various places, ranging from banks to booksellers, in drenching rain. He was so completely soaked that he abandoned shoes, socks and trousers as unpackable, though an old soldier would have scrounged a sack. Here once again we have Stevenson the extravagant—knowing how little cash he had, and not knowing when he would get more, he eats at an expensive French restaurant and dumps wet clothes, as he threw away the leg of mutton and the bread in the Cevennes! Real bohemians can't afford such waste. On top of that he had a wet and tiring little trip across to Jersey City for the train, so again he was wet when the journey started. And he heard that Fanny had brain fever!

Strange to relate *Across the Plains* instead of being more is far less interesting than *The Emigrant*. This was certainly not because Stevenson made the average British supercilious approach to America. On the contrary; for as he himself says: 'America was to me a sort of promised land', but then it was rather a mirage than a true vision, built out of childhood story-books and American literature. Whitman's *Leaves of Grass* and Thoreau's *Walden* are great books, and of course are essentially American. But then Dickens's *Pickwick Papers* and Tennyson's poems are essentially English, yet not very safe guides to the ordinary ruck of life in the England of 1879. Stevenson sounds a little let down in this narrative, not unappreciative but 'unfulfilled', much as an educated American landing in Liverpool at the time might have felt wistful at failing to meet anyone as kindly as Mr. Pickwick, as amusing as Sam, or as nobly eloquent as the then Laureate. And then he started out tired and 'utterly dejected', and grew wearier as the interminable train journey ground on day and night. True, he managed to evade the worst fatigue of sleeping night after night sitting up, by hiring boards and a pillow, but he could not take off his clothes, washing was almost impossible, and there was no dining car.

'I can safely say, I have never been so dog-tired as that night in Chicago'—and it is a very long way from Chicago to San Francisco, especially in an emigrant train. By the time the train reached Laramie (Wyoming) Stevenson was really ill, and was more than a little staggered by what he thought the callous behaviour of the American emigrants—for there were few Europeans on the train. His mien as a sick man was greeted with laughter as something funny; and later on when another man had epileptic fits the only comment of a woman was: 'Oh, I hope he's not going to die! It would be terrible to have a dead body!' Stevenson was not 'destined' to annoy the lady with an undesirable corpse, but he was not far from it. In a letter written on the train to Henley he says:

> 'What it is to be ill on an emigrant train let those declare who know. I slept on till late in the morning, overcome with laudanum of which I had luckily a little bottle. All today I have eaten nothing, and only drunk two cups of tea, for each of which, on the pretext that the one was breakfast and the other dinner, I was charged fifty cents. . . . My illness is a subject of great mirth to some of my fellow-travellers, and I smile rather sickly at their jests.'

In spite of the fact that Fanny's cable must for ever remain unknown, Stevenson must somehow have learned that she was ill, and this must have been one of the motives if not the main motive of his desperate 'emigration'. A note to Baxter written the day before he sailed says that Fanny 'seems to be very ill', and adds enigmatically, 'at least I must try to get her to do one of two things'. But when the emigrant train at last set him down in San Francisco, he and not Fanny was 'very ill', and she had already become well enough to move south to Monterey. Thither by train he followed her. The apparition of a dejected, seriously ill, travel-bruised and indigent Louis who had managed once more to estrange himself from his father put Fanny 'on the spot', as they say. What was she going to decide? One serious problem had been solved for her, though not perhaps in the way she wanted. Belle had set her mother an example of unthrifty romance by marrying against Fanny's wishes a not very successful painter, Joe Strong. Some of the earlier narratives, in their desire for respectability, give the impression that Belle married only a few weeks before her mother re-married, thereby arousing a suspicion that the girl had sacrificed herself. It is a relief to find that this was not the case.

Though Belle was thus disposed of, Fanny's problems were not much lightened. She was living on Sam Osbourne's money, seeing him fairly often, endlessly discussing. If Louis had arrived looking brisk and as comparatively efficient as was possible with so feckless a person, with money in his pocket, his father's consent and an increased allowance, she might well have decided there and then on divorce and re-marriage. If, as some say, his friends had offered him money before leaving, he had been mighty foolish to refuse it. His precarious earnings as a writer were small re-assurance. Sam had a job and still supported her. What she and Louis said when they met at Monterey is now for ever lost, but she can hardly have been encouraging. Another note to Baxter (not printed by Colvin) and written only a few days after Stevenson reached Monterey announces that he is to 'go out camping', that he has no news, that he has 'the itch and a broken heart'. This does not sound like love's young dream fulfilled. On top of this he collapsed, and was picked up and nursed by 'an old bear-hunter' and 'a pilgrim' who was 'out under Fremont' at that time prosaically keeping Angora goats about eighteen miles from Monterey—so he had not got very far on his horse-and-buggy camping trip.

> 'I was pretty nearly slain; my spirit lay down and kicked for three days . . . I scarcely slept, or ate, or thought for four days. Two days I lay out under a tree in a sort of stupor, doing nothing but fetch water for myself and horse, light a fire and make coffee, and all night awake hearing the goat-bells ringing and the tree-frogs singing when each new noise was enough to set me mad. Then the bear-hunter came round, pronounced me "real sick", and ordered me up to the ranche.'

There, you would say, was a beaten man, whose only chance of remaining alive was to write his father for pardon and a promise of his allowance with a ticket home in exchange for a promise to give up Fanny. Possibly Mr. Thomas Stevenson would have been gratified by such a letter, which would represent his first real victory over Louis and his confounded obstinacy since the boy grew up. Well, Thomas Stevenson did not obtain that dismal satisfaction, and with no change in his fortunes except that he did not actually die Robert Louis had before long completely reversed the situation, at least so far as Fanny was concerned. How this was achieved is a mystery which tantalizes curiosity. True, *souvent femme varie*, and true again it is flattering to have a man almost die for her, but then Fanny was not twenty, she was nearly forty, and Louis's nearly dying of love for her (if that was the fact) did not change the situation in the least. Somehow he had got back to Monterey, where he lodged with a French doctor and took one of his meals at a French restaurant—'for the other two, I sponge', on Fanny, presumably. Another of these letters to Baxter claims, a little imaginatively, that Fanny was now better owing to him (Louis), that 'a private divorce' had been arranged for January 1880, and that he and Fanny would be married as soon after as was beseeming. He does not explain what 'a private divorce' is or how it differs from 'a public divorce', but as events showed, it was quite adequate to the purpose.

Stevenson remained three months in Monterey while Fanny went off to arrange the divorce proceedings. They were to meet in San Francisco. Sam Osbourne had been co-operative, offering no opposition to the divorce, and promising to keep Fanny and Lloyd until she re-married. Meanwhile, Stevenson struggled on in Monterey against ill health and poverty, over-working himself ('dibbs and speed are my mottoes') in trying to earn money by writing, finishing *The Pavilion on the Links*, *The Amateur Emigrant*, and plotting other work, some at least of which, as so often with him, was abandoned. In a letter, tentatively dated October 1879, he wishes Henley could suddenly be transported to Monterey, and thereby gives a sketch of his days there:

> 'That shall deposit you at Sanchez's saloon, where we take a drink; you are introduced to Bronson, the local editor ("I have no brain music," he says, "I am a mechanic, you see," but he's a nice fellow); to Adolpho Sanchez, who is delightful. Meantime I go to the P.O. for my mail; thence we walk up Alvarado Street together, you now floundering in the sand, now merrily stumping on the wooden side-walks; I call at Hadsell's for my paper; at length behold us installed in Simoneau's little whitewashed back room, round a dirty tablecloth, with Francois the baker, perhaps an Italian fisherman, perhaps Augustin Dutra, and Simoneau himself. Simoneau, Francois and I are the three sure cards; the others mere waifs. Then home to my great airy rooms with five windows opening on a balcony; I sleep on the floor in my camp blankets; you instal yourself abed; in the morning coffee with the little doctor and his little wife; we hire a waggon and make a day of it. . . .'

Incidentally, it is a touching tribute to Stevenson's friendly ways and to the kindness of poor Americans that these 'waifs' secretly subscribed two dollars a week for Bronson to pay him as an extra reporter.

But all Stevenson's charming vignettes of his life plus a hint that he hoped soon 'to have a greater burthen to support' made no appeal to Henley and had no effect on his selfish and prejudiced devotion. The devotion was genuine enough, but so too were the prejudices and the selfishness. Henley wanted Louis to be near him and collaborate in those unhandy plays; as a British imperialist he didn't like America; and very likely even at this early date he didn't like Fanny. So, as Louis began sending over his recent work, first from Monterey and then after Christmas 1879 from San Francisco, Henley persuaded himself (and apparently persuaded Colvin) that practically everything Stevenson had written since the *Devonia* took him out of the Clyde was poor stuff, and getting worse. What Louis ought to do was to leave America at once (presumably without waiting to marry Fanny) get back to the Savile Club and play-writing, and so save his soul alive. Henley and Colvin seem to have begun with a long silence of disapproval, and then in answer to Louis's appeals, began to write even more disapprovingly. Just at the moment when he needed encouragement they sent metaphorically douches of cold water by post. On Boxing Day he wrote Colvin that for four days he had spoken to nobody but the waiters 'and I must own the guts are a little knocked out of me,' He trusts something can be done with *The Emigrant* 'or, by God, I'll starve here'. The next letter to Henley pleads: 'Do not damp me about my work. . . . You know the wolf is at the door, and I have been seriously ill.'

Later in this letter he says: 'I have now £80 in the world and two houses to keep up in the world', for good-natured Sam had managed to lose his job, so that just when he needed to conserve his money Stevenson had to start keeping Fanny and Lloyd. He was cheered by the news that *The Cornhill* had bought *The Pavilion on the Links* through Henley, but then Colvin came in with a letter asserting that *The Emigrant* was dull, which it most certainly is not. But see the man's spirit. Though he had been counting on that piece of work for a little cash, which now seemed gone, he sat down and wrote twelve pages of *Across the Plains*, which news he defiantly tells Colvin, adding:

> 'Only, frankly, Colvin, do you think it is a good plan to be so eminently descriptive, and even eloquent in dispraise? You rolled such a lot of polysyllables over me that a better man than I might have been disheartened . . . everybody writes me sermons; it's good for me, but hardly the food necessary for a man who lives all alone on forty-five cents a day, and sometimes less, with quantities of hard work and many heavy thoughts.'

And in another letter he summed them up in a phrase: 'You and Henley both seem to think my work rather bosh nowadays.' It seems quite clear now that Henley, Colvin and even Gosse were in a conspiracy to force him back to England, though even Henley soon gave up hopes of avoiding Fanny. He refused to believe the perfectly true details of Stevenson's illnesses and genuine privations. Perhaps Stevenson did pile it on a little when writing to Baxter: 'It is today bitter cold, after weeks of lovely warm weather, and I am all in a chitter. I am about to issue for my little shilling and halfpenny meal, taken in the middle of the day, the poor man's hour; and I shall eat and drink to your prosperity.' There was a reason for this extra turn of pathos, for Louis knew perfectly well that if his father did not actually read his letters to Baxter, he had the substance of them from that excellent friend. He wrote Baxter that he had cut down to twenty-five cents a day for food, and asked that his books might be sold and the money sent to him. One or other of these letters did the trick. Mr. Stevenson relented and sent his son twenty pounds, which the Post Office failed to deliver, although earlier the family had tried to force him home by sending telegrams to say his father was dying! What is that story about George Washington and the hatchet?

Apropos hatchets—in his 'bosh' letter to Colvin, Stevenson gives an account of his life in San Francisco which ought to have made his trio of too officious friends ashamed of their schemes for 'saving' him by forcing him back to England. It was written only two weeks after the miserable Christmas he had spent in solitude, for it was impossible for Fanny over in Oakland to leave Sam and the children to come to him. Remember, he had been near to death and was before long to fight another round with that grim champion, was living in what for him was squalor and privation aggravated by skilfully administered literary discouragement from England. And yet he writes as gaily and wittily as if indeed all were for the best in this best of possible worlds. The extract is long, but is worth careful reading for all it gives us of the man, his real simplicity of living, his wit and laughter, his courage, and his 'flint-like' determination in sticking to work:

'Any time between eight and half-past nine in the morning, a slender gentleman in an ulster, with a volume buttoned into the breast of it, may be observed leaving No. 608 Bush and descending Powell with an active step. The gentleman is R.L.S.; the volume relates to Benjamin Franklin, on whom he meditates one of his charming essays. He descends Powell, crosses Market, and descends in Sixth on a branch of the original Pine Street Coffee House, no less; I believe he would be capable of going to the original itself, if he could only find it. In the branch he seats himself at a table covered with waxcloth, and a pampered menial, of High-Dutch extraction and, indeed, as yet only partially extracted, lays before him a cup of coffee, a roll and a pat of butter, all, to quote the deity, very good. A while ago and R.L.S. used to find the supply of butter insufficient; but he has now learned the art to exactitude, and butter and roll expire at the same moment. For this refection he pays ten cents, or fivepence sterling (£0 0s. 5d.).

'Half an hour later, the inhabitants of Bush Street observe the same slender gentleman armed, like George Washington, with his little hatchet, splitting kindling, and breaking coal for his fire. He does this quasi-publicly upon the window-sill; but this is not to be attributed to any love of notoriety, though he is indeed vain of his prowess with the hatchet (which he persists in calling an axe), and daily surprised at the perpetuation of his fingers. The reason is this: that the sill is a strong, supporting beam, and that blows of the same emphasis in other parts of his room might knock the entire shanty into hell. Thenceforth, for from three to four hours, he is engaged darkly with an ink bottle. Yet he is not blacking his boots, for the only pair that he possesses are innocent of lustre and wear the natural hue of the material turned up with caked and venerable slush. The youngest child of his landlady remarks several times a day, as this strange occupant enters or quits the house, "Dere's de author." Can it be that this bright-haired innocent has found the true clue to the mystery? The being in question is, at least, poor enough to belong to that honourable craft.

'His next appearance is at the restaurant of one Donadieu, in Bush Street, between Dupont and Kearney, where a copious meal, half a bottle of wine, coffee and brandy may be procured for the sum of four bits, *alias* fifty cents, £0 2s. 2d. sterling. The wine is put down in a whole bottleful, and it is strange and painful to observe the greed with which the gentleman in question seeks to secure the last drop of his allotted half, and the scrupulousness with which he seeks to avoid taking the first drop of the other. This is partly explained by the fact that if he were to go over the mark—bang would go a tenpence. He is again armed with a book, but his best friends will learn with pain that he seems to have deserted the more serious studies of the morning. When last observed, he was studying with apparent zest the exploits of one Rocambole by the late Viscomte Ponson de Terrail. This work, originally of prodigious dimensions, he had cut into liths or thicknesses apparently for convenience of carriage.

'Then the being walks, where is not certain. But by about half-past four, a light beams from the windows of 608 Bush, and he may be observed sometimes engaged in correspondence, sometimes once again plunged in the mysterious rites of the forenoon. About six he returns to the Branch Original, where he once more imbrues himself to the worth of fivepence in coffee and roll. The evening is devoted to writing and reading, and by eleven or half-past darkness closes over this weird and truculent existence.'

As that immediately precedes the 'bosh' remark it may have been written to remind Mr. Colvin that the writer could still use a pen more effectively than his English correspondents. Of course, the obvious criticism is that the show-piece is all about himself. Nobody could justly accuse Stevenson of neglecting that fascinating topic; but then, like charity, observation of mankind begins at home. A man who is only stupidly interested in himself will not be able to tell us anything worth hearing about the rest of mankind; which is perhaps one reason why in literature most of the world loves an egotist. As Dr. Johnson remarked (perhaps a little crudely for one who piqued himself on his politeness) if a man doesn't mind his own belly he probably won't mind anything else.

Naturally, this was too good a mood and, unfortunately, too prosperous a state to last. Stevenson's daily expenditure dropped to twenty-five cents, and even lower. In March he was emotionally distressed by a severe illness of his landlady's little son, and insisted on helping to nurse the child. He thought the child was dying, got into one of his 'states', and wrote a hysterical note to Colvin about it. The child did not die, but Louis Stevenson fell seriously ill, and remained so for several weeks. Indeed, if he had not had the luck to find an intelligent doctor (Dr. Bamford—'a name the Muse repels') and if Fanny had not had the good sense to defy convention and take him into her own cottage and the devotion to nurse him, he would have died. In addition to malaria, he had his first lung haemorrhage—tuberculosis had arrived:

> 'I have been very very sick; on the verge of a galloping consumption, cold sweats, prostrating attacks of cough, sinking fits in which I lost the power of speech, fever, and all the ugliest circumstances of the disease. . . .'

That may have been his 'destiny', but there was not much romance in it, especially since he was so ill that for weeks he was unable to do any work. It may sound like an anticlimax, but he was also in urgent need of dentistry. For Stevenson and Fanny to unite their respective poverties for a time looked almost insensate. Yet—how right Henley was!—he had no thought of abandoning the marriage which was the main reason for his painful travels. A letter to Gosse (16th April) refers to 'my wife that is to be' in complete confidence. Did he know all along that sooner or later he would fall on his feet and his father's legs as usual? At all events early in May he received what he described as 'a blessed business' in the form of a cable from Edinburgh: 'Count on 250 pounds annually'. How had this been achieved? Some say that Fanny 'made an appeal', but it seems much more likely that the real intermediary was that shrewd lawyer and excellent friend, Charles Baxter. Stevenson's letters to him must have been meant for his parents, and the instruction to sell his books and remit the money was an excellent stroke. One can easily imagine Mrs. Stevenson's tear-filled eyes gazing piteously at her husband as his fatherly love battled with outraged pride, wrath and respectability. The letter preceding the first draft of this allowance is said to have requested that the marriage be delayed as long as possible. If so, the request was disregarded, for these sorely-tried lovers were married on the 19th May, 1880. Nobody will be surprised to learn that the marriage was rather 'serious' than 'joyous'. After the fact that Fanny made the declaration that she was a widow, the most interesting episode recorded of this wedding is that Stevenson gave the clergyman a copy of his father's book in defence of Christianity. Was the irony wholly unintentional?

By upper-middle-class Edinburgh standards this wedding must

have appeared unconventional, although Stevenson had been shrewd enough to secure the services of a Presbyterian minister of Scottish descent. But what are we to say of the honeymoon? If it lacked some of the features of accepted romance, it united enough unusual circumstances to gratify even Stevenson. Here or there one or other of the recorded facts may doubtless have been duplicated, but there cannot have been many honeymoons where the bride was a divorcée ten years older than her new husband and accompanied by her twelve-year-old son, where the bridegroom was more in need of a sanatorium than a bride-chamber, and the place of their first home-making was a smashed and littered-up miners' doss-house standing derelict beside a worked-out mine, which the party took over and occupied by virtue of the use or abuse of squatters' rights. Such was the fact, and the story of *The Silverado Squatters* is the story of Louis, Fanny and Lloyd, on the honeymoon. The book was written in 1882, clearly based on a diary, and published in serial and book form at the end of the next year. Surprisingly Mr. Thomas Stevenson did not object, but by that time Stevenson had attained reputation and respectability as a writer of boys' books, and the persons criticized are nearly all Americans.

Too little has been written on the topic of: Honeymoons, and how to endure them. Suppose Fanny had been a girl of good family (money and ministers in the family) and the happy pair had left for the Continent (pursued by confetti and old shoes) in the usual style of the last century, what could we record but the disillusions of boredom and solitude? But in this case the bohemianism of Louis Stevenson was taken into due subordination by his American frontierswoman. Literary genius brings a man and his associates so near that we forget Fanny in her youth might have been scalped, and that she belonged to a generation of American women who had to be efficient in difficult situations or perish, and their families with them. Silverado! Stevenson is such a word-magician that he can make almost anything or anybody sound glamorous, and he has done all his virtuosity suggested to make Silverado look and sound attractive. The reality must have been gruesome. I have seen one or two of those Western mining settlements after they had been abandoned, but cleaned up. Silverado had not been cleaned up, and the mere ugliness of the desecrated mountain-side, the filth and litter left behind, the discomfort and difficulties and even dangers, are scarcely given sufficient emphasis in the genial pages of *The Silverado Squatters.*

Stevenson was seldom a humbug, he seldom really blinked the truth. He was an impressionist who most skilfully presented the truth in an 'arrangement'. Stevenson did tell the truth about Silverado, at least to the extent of not saying the thing that is not. He faithfully describes the neighbouring po' white trash (his portrait of Irvine Lovelands, the Caliban, the oaf, the loafer, is a masterly performance), the squalor, the litter, the discomfort, the danger of collapsing mine galleries. He passes far too lightly over the fact that the place was infested with rattlesnakes and the lesser but hideous menace of poison oak. Poison oak was growing through the floor of their ancient doss-house when they took possession, and Stevenson did physical exercises or sun-bathed in a small clearing to the menacing accompaniment of continual rattles, which he disregarded! The only sensible member of the party was the dog, which quite rightly refused to affront these terrors. Yet out of all this Stevenson in *The Silverado Squatters* has managed, by pure literary skill, to create an impression of—what shall we say?—adventure, remoteness, bohemian freedom, beauties of nature, amusing natives, and cheerfulness. Let us not doubt the cheerfulness and all the picturesque details, but not overlook this letter, which is not included in the official Colvin series:

> 'My dear, we have had a miserable time. We were six days in Silverado. The first night I had a cramp and was quite worn out after it; the second day Fanny mashed her thumb while carpentering, and had a nervous chill; the third day she had another from sleeplessness; the sixth day, she and Sam both began to have diphtheria. I got them down in an open cart; the cases are slight; Sam's especially, but Fanny has been pretty sick and a little light-headed for forty-eight hours. You may fancy if I am tired. I am homesick for Europe. . . .'

And so, we may reasonably assume, was Fanny. She naturally knew nothing of Edinburgh or the comforts of 17 Heriot Row, but—'anywhere, anywhere' out of this misery, must have been her unspoken but most earnest wish.

The advantages of this otherwise unattractive situation were its cheapness, its remoteness and its height above sea-level

(4,500 feet) so that Stevenson was protected from the 'poisonous sea fogs', whose invasion of the lowlands as seen from his rocky perch he has described so dramatically. The event of the day was the arrival of the two stage-coaches at the inn some distance from the squatters' 'home', bringing the mail and—somebody to talk to. Stevenson gives an indication of his sense of isolation by remembering the name of a traveller he talked with for a few minutes about 'Paris and London, theatres and wines'. From what he says the neighbours cannot have provided him with much beyond models for the exercise of his satirical verve. It was lucky for him that in those days neither the self-importance of insignificant people nor the law of libel had been developed to their present state of perfection. A new book containing so many frank (and true) statements about living persons, including a hotel-keeper, could not now be published. Consider, for instance, some of Stevenson's remarks about Irvine Lovelands, whom he affectionately introduces as 'an unmitigated Caliban', in itself a libel on this honest son of humble but proud parentage. Caliban chewed pine gum, and to Stevenson's 'annoyance, accompanied that simple pleasure with profuse expectoration'. Moreover:

> 'He had a tangle of shock hair, the colour of wool; his mouth was a grin; although as strong as a horse, he looked neither heavy nor yet adroit, only leggy, coltish, and in the road . . . he laughed frankly when we failed to accomplish anything we were about. . . . He prided himself on his intelligence. . . . He told us how a friend of his kept a school with a revolver, and chuckled mightily over that; his friend could teach school, he could. All the time he kept chewing gum and spitting. . . . A man, he told us, who bore a grudge against him had poisoned his dog. "That was a low thing for a man to do now, wasn't it? It wasn't like a man that, nohow. But I got even with him: I poisoned his dog." His clumsy utterance, his rude embarrassed manner, set a fresh value on the stupidity of his remarks. I do not think I ever appreciated the meaning of two words until I knew Irvine—the verb, loaf, and the noun, oaf; between them they complete his portrait.'

Stevenson goes on in this strain for two or three pages and then deals with other members of the family, but the brief passages quoted will suffice to show how this irresponsible and far from immaculate scribbler took on himself to bring into ridicule and contempt this not uncharacteristic product of life, liberty and the pursuit of happiness.

On the whole, though from previous experience he must have dreaded the long journey ahead, Stevenson (and especially Fanny who had to do most of the chores) must have been relieved when towards the end of July they said farewell for ever to Silverado. They did not travel 'emigrant' but first class from San Francisco to Liverpool, and it is safe to say that Louis could not have paid for their two and a half tickets—if Lloyd was entitled to a half—out of an income of five pounds a week. The obvious inference is that, as usual, his father paid.

8

THUS, Louis Stevenson's *Wanderjahre*, which was also his *Annus Mirabilis*, ended up happily like one of his early stories with a family reunion at Liverpool. 'Stevenson returned from America,' says one cynical critic, 'with some admirable travel sketches, a fading middle-aged woman and tuberculosis.' He forgot Lloyd, who was destined to play a succession of parts in the Stevenson saga, beginning as the indispensable boy playmate for battles with toy soldiers, passing to the inspirer and critic of world-famous adventure tales, and ending up as collaborator in less successful fiction until the day when he was chief mourner at the mountain burial. For the next seven years, until his father's death set him free to wander again, Stevenson lived the life of an invalid man of letters, moving between Scotland, London and Bournemouth, with Hyères and Davos as outlying resorts. The friends who deplored his visits to America ('that land of dollars and spew' as Henley elegantly described it) were too prejudiced to see that they inspired some of his best travel writing. His *Monterey* and *San Francisco* are among the best of his sketches, and more interesting to read now than his descriptions of Europe where, paradoxically, the changes have been less complete and dramatic in spite of the wars. They are part of the history of California.

Like the good friend he always was to Stevenson, Sidney Colvin took the trouble to journey as far as Liverpool, thinking that his presence would help to pass off a first interview which might have awkward moments. His anxiety was superfluous. Fanny had made up her very determined mind to end, if possible, the endless and wasteful disagreements between Louis and his parents. If she had not learned it from Louis before, she saw very quickly that the key to the situation was Thomas Stevenson—who was himself the key to the money-box. His mother would agree to practically anything 'Lou' liked to do, short of atheism, social misbehaviour and quarrelling with his father. The way to deal with the old man, who was in 1880 beginning to feel his age, was not to battle with him as Louis did, but to agree with him. To his surprise and pleasure Thomas Stevenson found that he and Fanny agreed about practically everything. She tried to please him even in trifles which exercised his prejudices. Thus, fashion had then recently ruled that women's stockings must be black, and not white as formerly; and when Thomas Stevenson objected to this harmless mutation, Fanny instantly returned to white. It must have been a pleasant change for him to be flattered, and he acknowledged her efforts with a very Scotch compliment—'I doot ye're a besom'.

The one person not particularly happy at the reunion was, strange to relate, Colvin. Though he afterwards loyally joined the 'happy as kings' chorus in praise of Fanny and her place in the R.L.S. myth, Colvin's first impression was anything but favourable. Indeed, like most of Stevenson's men friends in England he must rather have disliked her, though not of course so violently as Henley. At any rate he wrote off saying that of the two women Stevenson's mother looked 'the fresher'! And he went on to tell Henley that he doubted 'whether you and I will ever get reconciled to the little determined brown face and white teeth and grizzling (for that's what it's up to) grizzling hair, which we are to see beside him in future'. It is a tribute to her skill in party politics that she won Colvin over and used him against other friends of Louis's whom she disliked more.

A fellow passenger on the liner has recorded his memory of Stevenson's brilliant talk, but also his addiction to 'endless cigarettes' and sometimes 'a perilous cocktail', neither particularly indicated for a consumptive. When the Californian party arrived in England they must have been ill clothed. Until Vailima days Stevenson was pleasingly indifferent to clothes, and obviously had bought none for a year, while poor Fanny in her troubles must have been sadly straitened for herself and Lloyd. They probably looked like scarecrows to the respectable reception committee, who at once insisted on new ones under the tactful pretence of 'wedding clothes'. Pausing in Edinburgh on the way to the Highlands, Fanny relaxed in the solid comfort of Heriot Row, gladly accepting her mother-in-law's gifts of clothes and looking with astonishment at the rows of Louis's almost untouched suits. Perhaps she mentally determined that 'a time would come' when he would wear them. She could hardly fail to realize that, while the Grez stories of the Stevenson wealth were exaggerated, she had married into that solid middle-class security which has now vanished from Europe. Who will blame her for deciding that Louis must be prevented from further quarrels with their bread and butter? They could both be reckless with money, and it is obvious that their journeys, their doctors' bills, Lloyd's education, Louis's extravagances, could not be covered by his earnings and allowance of £250 a year. They must constantly have had to ask Mr. Thomas Stevenson for extra money. How little Stevenson made in those days may be judged from the fact that in 1879 he earned only £109. Ironically, during that period he was elected 'Laureate' of a club of his old school-fellows, and ground out a poem for them. A limited edition was published, and in the height of the Stevenson boom copies sold at from £180 to £250, far more than he had earned by a whole year's publication. Doubtless the machinations of Wise were behind those transactions, but they go to show how cynically willing the 'world' is to profit by writings as property while even more cynically willing to let the living author starve.

Perhaps by comparison with Silverado, Stevenson found the scenery of the Highlands enchanting, but the people at Strathpeffer 'a wholly bestial crowd'.

The Highlands were but a temporary perch for him to descant on the beauties of his country. Back in Edinburgh the family doctor—a Balfour, of course—sounded Robert Louis's chest and didn't like what he heard, suggested 'Davos', then the fashionable hope of consumptives with money. So to Davos they went. In London they went completely mad on recovering their freedom, and in a few days spent nearly fifty pounds in the Grosvenor Hotel. They met Louis's literary friends, and then was seen with what a strength and majesty the tight-lipped bride fights to keep what she has won:

> 'If we do not soon get away from London,' she wrote Louis's mother, 'I shall become an embittered woman. It is not good for my mind, or my body either, to sit smiling at Louis's friends until I feel like a hypocritical Cheshire cat, talking stiff nothings with one and another in order to let Louis have a chance with the one he cares the most for, and all the time furtively watching the clock and thirsting for their blood because they stay so late.'

Fanny Stevenson.

[*To face p. 128*

Lloyd Osbourne.

To face p. 129]

The situation is clearly stated in those plain words. Evidently a woman who knew her mind. And the fact is that she was, if not entirely right, far more right than Stevenson's friends. It seems to be the fact that she had foreseen the risk of tuberculosis long before she married him, and it is very much to her credit that fearing this she still linked herself with a sick man. From 1879 on tuberculosis had ceased to be a mere threat and had become active, and the only hope was to find the right climate which suited his particular case while avoiding irritations. We cannot possibly know what Fanny did or did not say privately to Stevenson's parents in his absence, but it does not sound improbable that she may have agreed to devote herself to trying to save their son's life while they agreed to a reasonable financial support. This cannot be proved, but seems likely. Now, Stevenson's friends were evidently well behind the times and Fanny in their ideas of how a man with active tuberculosis should behave. Late nights, excitement, continual talking, long dinners and burgundy, were certainly not indicated for a man who might at any moment by over-strain bring on another lung haemorrhage. Stevenson's friends seemed entirely unaware of this, and expected to continue their bohemian or scholarly vigils exactly as if this dreadful threat to life had never developed. Fanny was quite right to defend him. But, with such a woman—look at her arrogant face in the photographs!—love meant possessiveness; and, like so many wives, she was irrationally jealous of her husband's old friends. She wanted him all to herself—to save him, of course, but in her way. She was sensible about it. She saw that Baxter and Colvin were most valuable allies, but she discouraged and snubbed the mere literary men, above all the bohemian borrowers like Henley who resented her, took Louis's money, and could not be taught to respect his health. Among the innumerable 'recollections' of Stevenson's friends is one of a visit when he was discovered pacing up and down the room with a cigarette, in his usual overstrung way, while Henley with a heavy cold sat ridiculously by the hearth with a handkerchief over the lower part of his face. Of course, Stevenson caught the cold, and was seriously ill. Yet when Fanny made it an unbreakable rule that nobody with a cold might enter the house, this salutary measure was resented as silly female tyranny. Very likely, wife-like, she did want to get him away from his friends, but they put her in the right by their ignorance or stupidity in not seeing how carefully he should be treated.

So, from London they made their way by easy stages to Davos, accompanied by Lloyd and by an Aberdeen terrier, 'Woggs', thoughtfully bestowed on the nomads by Sir Walter Simpson. Somebody else gave them a Siamese cat, but they managed to get rid of it. Their first season at Davos occupied from November 1880 to the end of April 1881. The difficulty up there in the snow was not to protect Stevenson from too much talking and jollification with friends who did not understand the seriousness of his illness, but to see that he was comfortable, carried out Dr. Ruedi's orders, and was not too bored by the monotony. A difficulty was that Fanny Stevenson suffered from ill health, and seemed affected by the high cold altitudes the doctors prescribed for her husband. It is hardly an exaggeration to say that a considerable part of their lives was spent in trying to find a climate and dwelling where both could be comparatively well and at ease. Among the references to Stevenson in the letters of John Addington Symonds is one written at the beginning of Stevenson's second season (November 1881) when he had evidently been seriously ill:

> 'Stevenson is better. He is certainly not going to die yet. But I do not like his habit as an invalid. One thing is in his favour—his serenity of soul about what is called comfort. But the *défaut de cette qualité* is that he is, as a Bohemian, ever restless in mind.'

Symonds evidently thought that Louis Stevenson was too impatient and restless to carry out the strict rules of absolute rest and calm prescribed after a lung haemorrhage. When he was in comparative health Stevenson's nervous temperament kept him striding up and down the room, smoking and talking incessantly to friends, if he was not hard at work in solitude. Unfortunately, apart from the notes for his travel books, Stevenson had been through a barren period since his breakdown in California. Here once again the influence of Thomas Stevenson came into play. Not content with suppressing *The Amateur Emigrant* he joined with a Scotch professor in urging Robert Louis to a book about the history of the Scottish Highlands, from 1715. A sketch of the proposed book will be found in a letter to his father dated by Colvin the 12th December, 1880. Now, Louis Stevenson was certainly not disqualified from writing history, though one cannot say he had the scholar's and researcher's temperament. But a book involving so much preliminary work, not to say drudgery, was hardly indicated for a sick man; while Davos with its lack of a big public library was the last place to undertake researches into Scottish history. Symonds, who was a wealthy man, spent over a thousand gold pounds on buying books for his writings on the Renaissance, and yet lamented that he could not hope to achieve any original research in Davos. Moreover, a public which was thought to be too frivolous to accept *The Amateur Emigrant* could hardly be expected to enjoy toiling through the 'murky bog' of Scottish history. The inference is that Thomas Stevenson did not even then believe in his son's creative genius, and wanted to divert him from writing and publishing books that sounded 'unpleasant' and socially undesirable in Heriot Row. Scottish history was respectable and was locally acceptable and would moreover help to 'keep Lou out of mischief'. As he was quite dependent on his father, sensible Fanny doubtless advised at least a semblance of compliance. And Stevenson certainly did some preliminary work, for the letter mentions his having read about 900 pages of Wodrow's *Correspondence* 'with some improvement, but great fatigue'. He was clearly more interested in the 'Essays' (i.e. *Virginibus Puerisque*) then in the press which he expected for January or February 1881, though in fact they were not out until April.

The monotony of life in Davos makes a sameness about the two seasons, and it is perhaps mainly necessary to record that the climate and treatment did Stevenson a lot of good, which was undone each summer by the obligatory residence with his parents in the Highlands. Not until the autumn of 1882 did he and Fanny venture to rebel against Davos and to spend the winter in the Midi. Apart from the visit of one or two friends, such as Colvin, Stevenson's one real companion (apart of course from Fanny and Lloyd) was Addington Symonds, whose acquaintance he owed to Edmund Gosse. At first both were evidently pleased by this literary companionship in the midst of the commonplace hotel life. On the 17th November, 1880 Symonds wrote his friend Horatio Brown:

> 'There is a very interesting man come—Louis Stevenson—a friend of Lang and Leslie Stephen—really clever, and curious in matters of style. He is at the Belvedere. I find him a great acquisition.'

Stevenson, writing a little later, was not quite so enthusiastic but certainly not unappreciative:

> 'I like Symonds very well, though he is much, I think, of an invalid in mind and character. But his mind is interesting, with many beautiful corners, and his consumptive smile very winning to see.'

The strong homosexual tendency which complicated Symonds's life, although he was a married man with three daughters, may not have been known to Stevenson—it was most carefully hidden of course—but may have unconsciously caused a certain antagonism, though perhaps different views of life and different literary ideals would account for it. Stevenson offended Symonds by showing too openly his lack of esteem for Symonds's poems, in which Stevenson was right; but he made up for it later by praising some sonnets, and Symonds eventually dedicated to him the *Wine, Women and Song* translations from the Goliards. On the other hand, some of Symonds's judgments on Stevenson sound capricious. Thus while he found the *New Arabian Nights* 'light and brilliant'—which is true enough—he thought *Virginibus Puerisque* 'forced and flashy'. Symonds did not attempt fiction, so there was no rivalry; but his essays were his most popular work, and in comparison with Stevenson's they are either academic or too much a matter of word-painting. Of course Symonds *knew* much more than Stevenson, but then his essays tend to remain conventional both in thought and expression because he was so long under the Balliol yoke of having to write an essay every week—excellent training for potential parsons and their weekly sermons, but the wrong discipline altogether for a stylist. It is very curious to note how comparatively amateurish or even awkward the highly-trained Balliol Honours-man sometimes is in comparison with the self-trained, 'forced and flashy' bohemian Scot.

Fortunately for us, Stevenson that first season at Davos was not wholly barren. His working hours were much reduced by illness, and too many of them were wasted on the abortive Highland history, but he managed to write an essay on Pepys and another on *The Morality of the Profession of Letters*. Here again we find the supposedly irreligious Stevenson approaching a subject very near to him—his own profession!—from a moral point of view. Whether as a warning to himself and those about him or as a matter of fixed scruple Stevenson inveighs against James Payn who had written about the art simply from a money-making point of view. Stevenson foretold that this would lead to 'a slovenly, base, untrue, and empty literature', which has turned out to be a true prophecy of what happens under the régime of commercialized letters divorced from any other standard or ambition. He says:

> 'The copious Corinthian baseness of the American reporter and the Parisian *chroniqueur*, both so lightly readable, must exercise an incalculable influence for ill; they touch upon all subjects, and on all with the same ungenerous hand; they begin the consideration of all, in young and unprepared minds, in an unworthy spirit; on all, they supply some pungency for dull people to quote. The mere body of this ugly matter overwhelms the rarer utterances of good men; the sneering, the selfish, and the cowardly are scattered in broad sheets on every table, while the antidote, in small volumes, lies unread upon the shelf. I have spoken of the American and the French, not because they are so much baser, but so much more readable, than the English. . . ."

Except that they are aggravated, the present system and its results are much the same. Stevenson takes the view that 'it must always be foul to tell what is false, and it can never be safe to suppress what is true'. Whole areas, not merely of journalism, but of book publishing are based on an unacknowledged disregard for that elementary principle of literary morality. And he winds up with the general assertion that 'there is nothing that an honest man should fear more timorously than getting and spending more than he deserves'. But how is 'an honest man' to know what he is really worth, and whether 'the world' is paying him too much or too little? However, the general trend of his thought is perfectly clear and laudable—he is against propaganda, against all writing undertaken merely to flatter base propensities for the sake of money. Did Stevenson always live up to this ideal himself? It would make an interesting subject for debate.

Stevenson made use of his experiences at Davos to write four 'travel' sketches which appeared in the *Pall Mall Gazette* during February and March 1881. It is surely a tribute to the skill he had now attained as writer that these comparatively trifling pieces may still be read with pleasure. Yet it must be admitted that here at least Addington Symonds beats him, and for once Stevenson seems to be imitating his friend. Symonds knew the place far better, for his first 'season' there was in 1877, and he had determined to make the best he possibly could of this snow-bound place of exile. Where Stevenson gives us only personal impressions, underlying which is a perfectly comprehensible discontent with life in a remote village under snow, Symonds gives us a wider range of such impressions backed with a real knowledge of the people (he spoke German very well), and much interesting information on such topics as the Valtelline wines, the different kinds of avalanches, and the perils, thrills and rewards of winter travel. Most of what Stevenson learned about Davos came from Symonds, even to the tobogganing (at which Symonds was so good that he acted as one of the judges at the international contests) which Stevenson describes vividly, though less vividly than Symonds. *Alpine Diversions* refutes those who think that Stevenson was too ill to take any pleasure in tobogganing, especially at night; but a comparison shows Symonds the better informed and the more vivid writer. One of Symonds's notes on Stevenson runs thus:

> 'Meanwhile I have quite shelved *Vagabunduli Libellus*. I talked about it to Stevenson, who fell in love with the title, but who clearly does not believe I can write sonnets. If I don't take care, he will bag my title.'

The last sentence for long seemed to me gratuitous and rather offensive, but after those *Pall Mall* articles I can see that Symonds might well feel that Stevenson had been a little guilty of poaching. The happy-as-kings Stevenson myth-makers will always have him getting the best from everything in spite of tuberculosis. Now Symonds was worse hit than Stevenson was and ten years older, but compare Stevenson's description of an evening toboggan run with this of Symonds:

> 'We started late one February afternoon for a toboggan run to Klosters. The sun had set when we left Wolfgang; but all the sky was rosy with its after-glow; the peaks and snow-fields which surrounded us, shining in every hue of saffron and crimson. Then, as we rushed down the steep descent, there swam rapidly upon our sight from behind the vast bulk of a black mountain mass, the full moon, a huge transpicuous dew-pearl of intensest green, bathed in fiery colours of the glowing heavens. . . . Our swift motion beneath the celestial wonders, over the myriad-tinted snow-path, added

intoxicating glory to the vision. It was like flying through a sphere of irridescent beryl. But we soon passed downward from those airy heights, and plunged into the forest, where all the splendours of the sky and the path we sped upon were swallowed in chasms of black shadow.'

There are some, perhaps many, who will now disparage that kind of writing without being able to emulate it, but there can be no doubt that here Symonds was the master and Stevenson the imitator. Perhaps it should be noted that these were, with one exception, Stevenson's last travel sketches until he started to sail the Pacific as a harmless pirate of the picturesque. Did he realize that, so far as cultured Europe was concerned, Symonds was his master?

In the spring of 1881, the strangely assorted trio left Davos and made their way via Paris, Fontainebleau and St.-Germain-en-Laye, to Pitlochry. Whether urged by Fanny's good sense or his own, Stevenson then turned from plans of history he was not really competent to write and imitations of Symonds to more congenial fictions in which he honoured his wife with *Thrawn Janet* and Lloyd with *Treasure Island*. Fanny liked ghost stories, and Lloyd at that age liked pirate tales. Stevenson liked them all his life.

Meanwhile, just about the time they left Davos, *Virginibus Puerisque* was published, and this book which collected some of the thoughts and phases of Stevenson's bachelor days must at least be glanced at, especially since it is one of the books which long after he was dead still made him friends. It is a miscellany without structure, a collection without purpose, padded with one or two superfluous pieces which would never have been accepted from anyone but a popular myth, and yet full of interest and the authentic Stevenson charm. Perhaps I should admit a bias, and confess that it delighted me at eighteen—what, I wonder, can it mean to a boy of eighteen in the confused circumstances of the present age? I shall not attempt to guess, nor to summarize a book which is too fugitive and disconnected to admit of generalization; and limit myself to citing some of the wise saws or gnomic utterances which Stevenson affected in his pre-Fanny period, and which he owed to Montaigne.

Stevenson begins with a dubious statement, that except Falstaff all Shakespeare's characters are 'marrying men'. Was Timon married? Was Hamlet so keen on marriage? No matter, we soon reach an admirable aphorism:

'It is not taste that is plentiful, but courage that is rare.' 'Work upon that, now,' as Dekker says, for it is a great truth—or truism—and gives a clue to the tastes of every epoch. Speaking of 'Jesuits and Plymouth Brethren' and others divorced from him by prejudice and upbringing, he notes that: 'What was essential to them, seemed to me trivial or untrue'. Is this not still our reaction when meeting a real (not fairy) Communist or one who believes that Hitler was a much-injured man unjustly attacked by a militarist England? He provides the answer a little further on in another essay: 'There is nothing so monstrous but we can believe it of ourselves'—but, indeed, more readily of others. A line of superlative wisdom—'Man is a creature who lives not upon bread alone, but principally by catchwords'. A *vérité de La Palisse*, but did not Stevenson say it first?—unless indeed it is in Montaigne, as it well may be.

Changing to writing, he notes most cogently: 'The difficulty of literature is not to write, but to write what you mean'.

Readers of *Virginibus Puerisque* can collect many more of these admirable sayings for themselves. On the other hand we have to admit that some of these gnomic utterances are of rather dubious validity. For instance:

> 'Do you think it a hard thing to write poetry? Why, that is to write poetry, and of a high, if not the highest, order.'

We do not need to call the shade of A. E. Housman from the other world to realize that statement is 'nonsense'. Practically any barmaid, bootblack or prime minister will tell you it is hard if not impossible for them to write poetry—which doesn't make them poets.

'Letters are in vain for the purposes of intimacy. . . .' Is that true? Try to think so, after reading Héloïse, the Portuguese Nun and Mlle de Lespinasse! Had Stevenson read them when he wrote that 'epigram'? Perhaps he was merely recording or excusing his own failure to write to Fanny in those sad and bitter days of their separation.

The publication of *Virginibus Puerisque* (April 1881) was followed next year by *Familiar Studies in Men and Books*, though practically all if not all of the latter had been written by April 1881. They mark the end of an epoch in Stevenson's literary life, though the change must not be thought of as abrupt and complete. Just as a good deal of Stevenson the bohemian survived into the more decorous days of Stevenson the married man, so the poet and essayist did not abandon the career of the successful popular novelist. Moreover Stevenson had been making attempts at fiction since his beginnings as a writer, and had already achieved the 'marvellously brilliant and light' *New Arabian Nights* before Fanny's influence could have greatly affected him, though we do know she was present at the discussions with 'Bob' and encouraged the writing of the *Nights*. Fanny's 'influence' might mean that she deliberately used her power over Stevenson to urge him in the direction of writing which might be popular and profitable rather than 'disinterested' and of purely literary merit; or it might mean that Stevenson, acutely conscious of responsibility as he was, and under the still operative threat of being disinherited as an infidel, felt that now or never he must make every effort to earn money. Probably both are partly true. I am not aware that Stevenson ever thought he was being over-paid and returned his publishers some of his royalties; but on the other hand there is much evidence of his generosity, amounting to lavishness, which is more characteristic of the Scot than his alleged parsimony, which he mainly practises on himself.

At any rate that summer of 1881, at Pitlochry and later at Braemar, shows Stevenson hard at work on fiction, in some cases demonstrably influenced by Fanny and in another by his father and Lloyd. We also find him losing for a moment both his sense of reality and his admirable gift of laughter. He proposed in all seriousness to offer himself for the post of Professor of History and Constitutional Law at the University of Edinburgh, and made tremendous interest with his friends to secure testimonials which Graham Balfour describes as 'a tribute to the ingenuity of the human intellect'. The tributes of Professors Lewis Campbell, Meikeljohn, Sellar, Babington and Colvin, of Leslie Stephen, J. A. Symonds, Andrew Lang and Gosse, and five others, secured him nine votes, while the first two of the four candidates received 133 between them! The result must have been rather a shock to Robert Louis and to his family, an indication of how little he was then esteemed by respectable Edinburgh, which doubtless remembered the not so distant days of bohemian scandals and of being turned out of his own home. Henley, Baxter and Bob Stevenson, who knew Robert Louis's youthful pranks a good deal better than the eminent persons who sponsored him, must have been amused and a little scandalized by this bid for respectability and academic status on the part of one who had been somewhat irreverent on the topic of professors. No doubt, this aspect of the affair did not occur to his mind in the Highlands, and he was hypnotized by the thought of how pleasant it would be to have another £250 a year without much work.

This was a false step which had no ill consequences, and is worth mentioning only for its humorous side and for its evidence that Stevenson was trying very hard to make himself less dependent on his father's bounty. And while he was bedevilling himself with anxiety about this academic job he was all unconsciously making real progress towards eventual financial success by hard work at his own profession or trade. At Pitlochry he wrote *Thrawn Janet*, *The Body-Snatcher* and *The Merry Men*. Here we may reasonably see Fanny's influence, for she was interested in 'ghost stories' and in fact proposed to contribute to a joint book to be called *The Black Man and Other Tales*, containing eight stories. Only the three of Stevenson have survived, but two at least of them stand high in the esteem of readers.

The 'ghost story' is one of the lower grades of fiction, unless it happens to be genuine folk, and Stevenson was doubtless well advised to write the little tale in Scots which for a southerner helps to lift it by interposing a perfectly understandable but less familiar diction. He handles Scots so well that one regrets he did not more often make use of it except in his dialogue and in letters and verses, but of course he had to sacrifice to a 'public' which couldn't or wouldn't read Scots narrative. Stevenson criticizes his own story, saying he thinks it too Scottish to be understood out of his native land. This may be so, but the story has gone far beyond those limits. We may note that Stevenson called it a 'crawler', and that 'ghost story' is a little unfair to its merits. Demoniac possession is the theme, and the whole story and his treatment are again evidence of Stevenson's interest in and struggle with the religion of his fathers. To rank *Thrawn Janet* merely as a 'ghost story' or even a 'crawler' does it an injustice, for the tale is a psychological study of a gloomy religious temperament self-hypnotized into almost maniacal terror but facing that terror with a courage as profound as its uncomfortable faith.

It is strange that Colvin thinks *The Merry Men* was not written in the summer of 1881 when he himself dates a letter from Pitlochry as July 1881, in which Stevenson definitely says he is 'more than half through' the tale, and gives the sub-titles almost as we have them today! There are times when one feels Colvin may have delegated some of his editorial duty to someone else, while he whitewashed Stevenson unwisely and unnecessarily, by censoring the letters he published.

The *Body-Snatcher*, in spite of conventional opinion, is not a better and more appalling story than *Janet*. How much it owed to 'Cummy's' gruesome news of the underworld cannot be known—it may be one of her tales made vivid by a writer of genius; or it may not. But are such violations of our nerves to be considered art? Stevenson was surely pot-boiling here, and the lavish praise of these atrocities is the measure of his admirer's taste. The next step would be to photograph a decayed coffin and film a rape. Tragedy is terrific, not horrific; Shakespeare, not Harrison Ainsworth and Edgar Poe.

No such abatements of merit can by any reasonable standard be alleged against *The Merry Men*, which is genuinely tragic, and magnificently written from beginning to end. Before *The Merry Men* Stevenson had written things which, whatever may justly or unjustly be alleged against them, have endured for three parts of a century—near immortality as swift literary mortality goes. There, at one step, he went ahead of all his contemporaries in prose. Who that has read *The Merry Men* can forget that storm? It is true that 'the storm' has been hackneyed since Homer, and that following Stevenson we have had Conrad's *Typhoon* and Richard Hughes's *A High Wind in Jamaica*. Without disparaging any of them, let us give Stevenson his due—that storm in the Scottish Isles is a masterly achievement, and so too the mingled remorse, madness and religious frenzy of the old wrecker or, at any rate, murderous profiteer by a wreck. Once more the religious or superstitious Scottish belief must be grasped in order to understand the madness of Uncle Gordon and the 'judgment' of his death. The negro, the black man, is the 'muckle black deil' of *Thrawn Janet*, but here raised from a mere scare-fool to the status of Nemesis. If only we could all read Gaelic, in that language we should read this superb achievement. Appreciation of the story, its religious and even more powerful descriptive quality, may be taken as a touchstone of appreciation of the 'real' as contrasted with the 'successful' Stevenson, above all in the emotional religious symbolism of the tragical end. And as for eloquence, listen to this:

> 'The night, though we were so little past midsummer, was as dark as January. Intervals of a groping twilight alternated with spells of utter blackness; and it was impossible to trace the reason for these changes in the flying horror of the sky. The wind blew the breath out of a man's nostrils; all heaven seemed to thunder overhead like one huge sail; and when there fell a momentary lull on Aros, we could hear the gusts dismally sweeping in the distance. Over all the lowlands of the Ross the wind must have blown as fierce as on the open sea; and God only knows the uproar that was raging around the head of Ben Kyaw. Sheets of mingled spray and rain were driven in our faces. All round the isle of Aros the surf, with incessant, hammering thunder, beat upon the reefs and beaches. Now louder in one place, now lower in another, like the combinations of orchestral music, the constant mass of sound was hardly varied for a moment. And loud above all this hurly-burly I could hear the changeful voices of the Roost and the intermittent roaring of the Merry Men. At that hour, there flashed into my mind the reason of the name they were called. For the noise of them seemed almost mirthful, as it out-topped the other noises of the night; or if not mirthful, yet instinct with a portentous joviality. Nay, and it seemed even human. As when savage men have drunk away their reason, and, discarding speech, bawl together in their madness by the hour; so, to my ears, these deadly breakers shouted by Aros in the night.'

If Stevenson really did all the work on those three stories during June and July he could be well assured that neither tuberculosis nor marriage had in the least impaired his industry; and with an achievement such as *The Merry Men* (which he describes modestly in a letter as a 'Tip Top Tale') he could also be certain that the search for popularity and 'dibs' by way of 'crawlers' had in that case at least demonstrated his powers as a literary artist. It will always be a matter of debate, however, whether that can be so truly said of the book he wrote in the second part of the summer at Braemar. When in 1894 Stevenson wrote for Jerome K. Jerome's *The Idler* his contribution to a series by contemporary writers called *My First Book* he chose as his theme *Treasure Island*, although in fact it was his eighth book (Cassell, December 1883), and materials towards others were then in serial form. Apart from the fact that this was good business—in the sense that this was the book people wanted to hear about—it was also true to the extent that this book, after a hesitating start, was his first real popular success, and made his reputation with that great public which proudly boasts that it knows nothing about art but knows what it likes.

The story of the writing of *Treasure Island* has been so often told that it scarcely bears repetition. We may note that after having worked at 'crawlers' to please Fanny's taste Stevenson turned to a blood and thunder, pirate and treasure, story to please Lloyd and his own father. Lloyd at least comes out of it with flying colours, for his taste—to which Stevenson wisely submitted—proved to be that of all the other schoolboys from Mr. Gladstone downwards or upwards.

It is characteristic of Stevenson that he saw 'the finger of predestination' in the events which led to the production of this romance. There were Lloyd and days of (not unusual) heavy Highland rainfall and Lloyd's attempts to amuse himself by painting, in which he was joined from time to time by Stevenson. Stevenson invented the map of an island, and in his imagination peopled it with characters—no doubt from his own and his father's collection of bed-time self-told tales—and sketched out chapters:

> 'It was to be a story for boys; no need of psychology or fine writing; and I had a boy at hand to be a touchstone. Women were excluded.'

He had found the formula for success in the English-speaking world. Supposing Flaubert had been asked how he came to write *Madame Bovary* might he not have answered?:

> 'It was to be a story for adults; the interest would be mainly in the psychology and at the same time would need the most careful and beautiful writing I could furnish. I had only my reverence for the greatest literature and my own literary conscience as a touchstone. Women were to be as important to the story as men.'

Perhaps it is merely the difference of two cultures, but the fact is that the English *en masse* have always hated *Madame Bovary* and tried to pretend it is 'dull', while the French are bored by *Treasure Island* and genuinely perplexed that anyone but a child should read it. With us it is different, and great rewards, perhaps the greatest, go to the writer who can produce a children's book which adults will enjoy reading aloud to the offspring. In *Treasure Island* Stevenson found the key to open the money chest of peter-pannery, perhaps not on the scale of *Alice in Wonderland* and *Winnie the Pooh*, but well enough to leave us admiring the romance of destiny:

> 'My father caught fire at once with all the romance and childishness of his original nature. His own stories, that every night of his life he put himself to sleep with, dealt perpetually with ships, roadside inns, robbers, old sailors, and commercial travellers before the era of steam. . . .'

The Wardour Street *crème de la crème*. Mr. Thomas Stevenson spent the better part of a day making an inventory of what ought to be found in Billy Bones's chest, and Robert Louis most wisely took it over intact. Thus, the fortunate author had in his own home experts to advise him on what would please the young boys and the old boys. And then, when the exciting tale was only partly written, the 'finger of predestination' produced Dr. Japp as a visitor. Dr. Japp was one of those persons who are immensely concerned to correct writers on points of fact of no particular importance or relevance. He was in fact a Scotch pedant, and came to Braemar to correct Stevenson on some alleged errors in the Thoreau essay. But—and here 'the finger of predestination' is again manifest—all unknown to Stevenson Dr. Japp had been entrusted by its editor with the task of finding serials for *Young Folks*. The early chapters of *The Sea Cook* (as *Treasure Island* was first called) were carried off by Dr. Japp, and in due course the whole story (with a Prologue afterwards cancelled) appeared in *Young Folks* and earned the disapprobation of its youthful readers and £34 7s. 6d.

A main source of disagreement about *Treasure Island*, and of injustice to Stevenson, is that people argue about it as 'a novel' without considering what sort of a novel or doing the author the elementary justice of finding out his intentions and standards. The book cannot be compared with such a novel as *Madame Bovary* since its object and standards are exactly opposite. If *Treasure Island* does not belong to the adult 'art' novels, neither does it belong to the fairly common type of adult book which happens to please children. It is unfair to Stevenson to compare

Treasure Island, as is usually done, with *Gulliver's Travels* because the adult reader of Swift is constantly aware of the moral and intellectual satire which passes over the inexperience of a child absorbed in the wondrous tale. An adult can get nothing more from *Treasure Island* than a boy does, except that the adult must suspend his knowledge and ask no questions about probability, motive, and character. The boy is not shocked by improbabilities and grows impatient with character—it is possible that the first serial readers were 'put off' by the excellent study of Billy Bones at the opening of *Treasure Island.* This lasted too long for their impatience, and is too good for the *genre*. The boy is content with a few elementary motives, enjoys violence for its own sake, and those scenes of fighting which, as Symonds said, 'Stevenson does with a turn of the wrist and a large daub of blood'. We can only do justice to *Treasure Island* by accepting the fact that it belongs to a special *genre*—the boy's adventure story—in which of course it stands very high.

The violence of Stevenson's letter to Henley against those who wanted him to go on writing 'refined, high-toned, bejay-bedamn masterpieces' seems to indicate an uneasy consciousness that he had in fact betrayed the standards he had before so loftily defended. *My First Book* makes clear that he wrote only in the hope of getting money, and prettily admits his conscious and unconscious plagiarisms, which after all are almost an essential of the *genre*—'the mixture as before with different names and another setting' might be the formula. There was certainly 'more coin in it than in any amount of crawlers' as he prophetically wrote Henley, for though the book started slowly, within less than fifteen years it is said to have sold 75,000 copies.

Treasure Island was not finished at Braemar or when Stevenson went to England, in spite of the pleasure he took in writing the novel, 'a chapter a day' he says in *My First Book.* There he says that he broke down at the sixteenth chapter, but a contemporary letter to Henley says he had reached the nineteenth—probably writing later he deducted the cancelled prologue. At any rate, although the serialization had started before he left England, Stevenson finished the book in the *Chalet am Stein* which he and Mrs. Stevenson had taken at Davos for the winter. They arrived at Davos on October 18th, 1881, and in *My First Book* Stevenson says that there he 'sat down one morning to the unfinished tale' and 'in a second tide of delighted industry' completed it again at the rate of a chapter a day. He paid a heavy price for his ardent industry, for writing to Horatio Brown on the 2nd November, Symonds says that he had seen Stevenson that day, and continues:

> 'He was lying, ghastly, in bed—purple cheek-bones, yellow cheeks, bloodless lips—fever all over him—without appetite—and all about him so utterly forlorn. "Woggs" squealing. Mrs. Stevenson doing her best to make things comfortable.'

This must have been the 'very bad cold' which later got worse, mentioned in a letter to his father. Symonds's little vignette looks dismal, but we must remember that he was a wealthy man accustomed to luxury, and saw squalor where Stevenson probably found none. Yet the winter was a harsh one for him, since Fanny fell ill ('drain poisoning', according to Stevenson but really a gall-stone) and early in December she left to consult doctors in Berne, taking Lloyd with her, so that Stevenson was left alone in the chalet, and didn't like it. On Christmas Day he went to meet them on their return, and has described with his usual verve a most uncomfortable seven hours' journey in an open sleigh:

> 'The cold was beyond belief. I have often suffered less at a dentist's . . . my courage disappeared, and I made the rest of the stage in the same dumb wretchedness as the others. My only terror was lest Fanny should ask for brandy, or laudanum, or something. So awful was the idea of putting my hands out, that I half thought I would refuse.'

In view of all this and the fact that Fanny had relapses one hardly can agree with those who think this Davos season was 'happier and more fruitful than the first', especially since when they left the Stevensons seemingly made up their minds they would never return. Moreover, Symonds's laconic phrase 'Woggs squealing' refers to the fact that the dog developed a very painful infection or canker, about which the Stevensons seem at first to have been as helpless as they were concerned. Two invalids and a dog howling with pain don't sound very cheerful. On the other hand, in November 1881 Symonds twice reports that Stevenson was better ('but he lost blood a few nights since') and evidently maintained or regained his courage and spirits:

'I wish to goodness we were all like Stevenson! To be reasonably and justly self-satisfied about one's style, to take life smoothly, and have a cheerful conscience! oh, what bliss!'

Nor did the dismals of his and Fanny's health situation stop him from writing. By April 1882 he could inform his mother that during this second Davos 'season' he had completed *Treasure Island* and had written *The Silverado Squatters*, ninety pages 'of magazine work' and the preface to *Familiar Studies*. The magazine work included *Talk and Talkers* and *A Gossip on Romance*. Time was spent on preliminary work for a life of Hazlitt, which was never written, and on poems for *A Child's Garden of Verses* (he called them 'penny whistles') begun at Braemar. By way of recreation he and Lloyd played elaborate war games with tin soldiers in the attic, and turned out poems and woodcuts on the boy's toy printing press. Nobody can say Stevenson did not work hard that winter. Fortunately Stevenson could justly claim that he had worked well also, for while *Treasure Island* is one of the best if not the best of boys' books, the other work mentioned is all of high quality. Yet here and there one detects a sign of haste, even in the famous style which Symonds so rightly praises. The italics in the following passage are mine, and the quotation comes from the preface to *Familiar Studies*:

'Had *it* been possible to rewrite some of these papers, I hope I should have had the courage to attempt *it*. But *it* is not possible. Short studies are, or should be, things woven like a carpet, from which *it* is impossible to detach a strand. What is perverted has *its* place there for ever, as a part of the technical means by which what is right has been presented. *It* is only possible to write another study, and then, with a new "point of view", would follow new perversions and perhaps a fresh caricature. Hence, *it* will be, at least honest to offer . . . &c.'

And there is still one more 'it' before the paragraph ends. *It* seems unfortunate that none of those numerous literary advisers Mrs. Stevenson wrote about so bitterly noticed that there for once the hand of the master of style shook.

As must happen with almost any collection of 'occasional papers' there is not much to bring them into a coherent whole except that they illustrate phases of the writer's literary interests and help to an understanding of his personality. We have Burns and Thoreau, Villon and John Knox, Whitman and Charles d'Orléans, Pepys and the Japanese nationalist Yoshida-Torajiro. But, then, each essay is complete in itself and some are of high quality, while in detail Stevenson, as always, is interesting and acute. Courage as well as discernment were required of a Scot who, on the morrow of Carlyle's death could write:

> 'But the "point of view" was imposed by Carlyle on the men he judged of in his writings with an austerity not only cruel but almost stupid. They are too often broken outright on the Procrustean bed; they are probably always disfigured. The rhetorical artifice of Macaulay is easily spied; it will take longer to appreciate the moral bias of Carlyle.'

The novels of Victor Hugo are now mostly (let us except *Notre-Dame*) stranded sea-monsters which can hardly be re-launched, and Stevenson's choice of them as a subject seems to show less prescience than his note on Carlyle, but he hits on a real and permanent distinction in literature when he speaks of 'that sort of brutality, that useless insufferable violence to the feelings, which is the last distinction between melodrama and true tragedy'. From this condemnation he strangely exempts *Les Misérables*, as if the pages where the young mother sells her hair and her teeth to get money for her starving child are not 'insufferable violence to the feelings'! And there is plenty of other melodrama in *Les Misérables*.

The *Burns* has already been mentioned because of the vindictive nationalist abuse it received when published in a periodical. Perhaps this essay is not the best thing that has been written about Burns, but it is sensible, clear-sighted, intelligent and honest, which cannot be said of some Burns 'literature'. If we may judge from a letter to his father, Stevenson wanted to omit the essays on Knox and finally yielded to his father's views, though the book would be better without them. At the same time Thomas Stevenson wanted to omit the essay on sinful Mr. Pepys, and luckily did not succeed. To be lively about John Knox is even more difficult than to be dull about Pepys if you quote him enough. Stevenson is so widely read and echoed that it seems worth while to point out how completely mistaken he was in thinking that Pepys intended his diary to be read. Stevenson is amazed that Pepys bought 'an idle, rogueish French book' and was ashamed of doing it; and yet recorded the fact; and again amazed that after destroying the harsh letter from his wife 'down goes the whole story with unsparing truth and in the cruellest detail'. Stevenson asks in bewilderment 'to whom was he posing in the Diary, and what, in the name of astonishment, was the nature of the pose?'. This misses the whole point. Pepys was not writing for others, but only for himself, in a cipher based on 'Shelton's system of tachygraphy' which he further complicated in the hope of ensuring complete secrecy. Of course, he was an egotist—who isn't?—but he was not in the least the inexplicable and silly exhibitionist Stevenson imagines. Without announcing so much Puritan smugness he wrote the diary to try to keep himself up to living a better life. It is obvious from the fines he put on himself for drinking and going to the theatre instead of working (and Pepys was a super-worker who puts us all to shame) and the careful way he records backslidings and new vows of abstinence; as also in the accounts of his affairs with women and the dismal quarrels with his wife in consequence. The whole 'Deb' episode is related with all the details of humiliating reality Pepys would never have recorded if he had intended anyone else to read his diary. Stevenson is wrong. It is by accident that we have this unique record of a man's daily life set down, not only utterly without 'pose', but with dogged sincerity and regard for truth.

The French and American authors reviewed in *Familiar Studies* are records of old literary allegiances. Stevenson owed much to American writers, though he exaggerated when he said that he had never written ten lines since reading Thoreau without showing his influence. Nevertheless that influence was great, as was that of Whitman, and we can only regret that Stevenson did not also give us essays on Hawthorne and Melville, but he may not have met with Melville until later. It is nice to know from a letter that Melville was 'a howling cheese' but expansion and clarification of that praise would have been gratifying. After *Familiar Studies* Stevenson published no more essays on authors and their works apart from such purely personal notes as *Books Which Have Influenced Me*, and the 'gossip' about Dumas *père*.

The steady output of literary work which, in spite of all the illness, had made the winter memorable, stopped when the Stevensons left Davos (for ever) in April 1882, to spend the summer with his parents in Scotland. Apart from *The Treasure of Franchard* he wrote very little that summer. On the good side of these visits we may place the reunion with his parents and friends, and familiarity with Scottish scenes and traditions which he afterwards used in some of his best works of fiction. On the bad side we have to admit that the winds, cold and rain which so often intervene in a Scottish summer damaged his health. It was so in 1882. After a short time in England (where he saw Meredith again) and a month in Edinburgh, Stevenson went to Peeblesshire with his family. Within a fortnight he fell ill and was ordered north to Inverness-shire, and then early in September, after another haemorrhage, was back in London consulting Sir Andrew Clark. Since Fanny was also seriously ill, this must have been a miserable time for them. The good that came of this crisis was Clark's agreement that Stevenson should not return to Davos but go to the South of France, and the abandonment of these fatal Scottish sojourns. With Fanny a casualty, Bob Stevenson went with him to help find a place where he could keep alive if not live.

Even in those years of plenty, 'finding a place' with a limited income was not so easy. He first tried Montpellier in Languedoc, which one would have thought would have been just right for him, since the *mistral* there is comparatively mild, while the town is a great medical centre and was for centuries renowned as a resort for foreigners with lung troubles. In the eighteenth century part of London was called 'Montpelier, (as it is still misspelled) because it was supposed to be so healthy. Unluckily in Stevenson's case a slight haemorrhage started soon after his arrival, and the specialist advised him not to settle in Montpellier. Bob Stevenson had to leave, and Stevenson went on alone to Marseille where Fanny joined him about the middle of October.

In spite of Fanny's reputation for being 'practical', the events of the next few months show that she did not always succeed in directing her husband's less prudent impulses. Within three days Stevenson discovered and fell in love with a house called Campagne Defli (not 'de bug' he hoped) at St. Marcel, a suburb to the east of Marseille. Apparently without stopping to make inquiries or to consult a doctor, they took the place. *Mistral* blows often in the neighbourhood of Marseille (up to 175 days in the year) and that might account for the fact that Stevenson was never well there and had several haemorrhages. This was discouraging enough, especially since he was hoping for better health and spirits by keeping away from Davos and Scotland. On top of this discouragement there arrived an outbreak of typhoid about Christmas time, and rather hastily the decision was made for Louis to go to Nice where Fanny would join him as soon as money arrived. Unfortunately whatever arrangements they made for keeping in touch were ineffective; Fanny became more and more agitated at receiving no news and made useless excursions to Marseille and Toulon looking for a man who was in Nice. It is rather hard to believe that the whole postal and telegraph system between Nice and Marseille broke down for at least a week. A telegram from Stevenson to St. Marcel would have solved the whole difficulty. Fanny's account shows her usual exaggeration and inaccuracy. Nice and another doctor set him up again, and after spending a couple of months between Nice and Marseille (getting rid of Campagne 'de bug') these babes in the wicked wood of the Midi are discovered in March 1883 at the Hotel des Iles d'Or at Hyères. They moved to the Châlet la Solitude up on the hillside, where, according to Stevenson, he spent some of the happiest days of his life. There they remained until May 1884 when Stevenson had a very bad haemorrhage.

Although this Swiss chalet, so incongruously erected in the Midi, had seven rooms including a kitchen, they were small, too small. The reason is that it was a 'model' bought by the owner at an *exposition*, and of course intended to be enlarged to scale for actual building. The small rooms would not matter to a French family using it as a summer-house, and taking their meals in the garden. This garden was evidently a pleasure to Stevenson, as much for the views it commanded as for itself, and in his letters he is lyrical, perhaps a little too lyrical, about his great possession. On the practical side Fanny made a more permanent acquisition by finding Valentine Roch, the ideal maidservant, who remained with them and shared their fortunes for six years until, like all good servants, she fell a casualty to matrimony. There was other good news on the earning front. Through Gosse a serial sale of *The Silverado Squatters* was made to Mr. Gilder, editor of *Century Magazine*, for £40, which seems rather small pay from a periodical so opulent, but Stevenson was delighted. He was even more delighted when Cassells gave him an advance of £100 for the book rights of *Treasure Island*. According to a note of Sir Graham Balfour this book in the seventeen years between its publication and 1901 had earned over £2,000. This again seems small for a book of such unique power and merit in its own class and so great a public, but then it was pirated in America and doubtless in other countries. The sale to Cassell which pleased him so much was arranged by Henley, who for some years acted as Stevenson's unofficial agent. In new work during this year or less at Hyères Stevenson wrote some of his poems, added to the *Child's Garden*, worked on *Prince Otto*, and wrote another serial for *Young Folks* called *The Black Arrow*. It is one of the ironies of Stevenson's destiny that this book which is unquestionably inferior pleased the readers of *Young Folks* as much as *Treasure Island* had bored them. In this case Lloyd proved to be a far more discerning critic than the English schoolboys of his age.

That summer (1883) there was no journey to England, but at Hyères Stevensons met the parents at Royat for a couple of months. Royat is a small 'spa' in Auvergne with a number of hotels, casino and so forth, about 1,400 feet above sea-level, and with a resident population even now of less than 3,500; but as it is practically a suburb of Clermont-Ferrand it has the advantages of a fair-sized town. The choice turned out happily—Stevenson did not fall sick, and the relations with the parents were pleasant. The long battle between father and son was now dying down, partly no doubt because of Fanny's influence, but mainly because the balance between the two men was slowly shifting in Stevenson's favour. First, by the mere passage of time. Although Robert Louis still had to ask his father for money the need was getting less (this was the year he could boast of earning £465) and as the older man aged and his health failed, the son, with amazement and some remorse and grief, found that he was becoming the man while his father became the child. Robert Louis had infinitely vexed and disappointed his father from adolescence, but had in turn been treated with a most strange mixture of tenderness and tyranny, good will and misunderstanding. The paradox is that Thomas Stevenson subsidized his son's literary career while bitterly opposing it. We have noted his anger at the mere suggestion that Robert Louis might one day earn as much as his father, which did in fact happen though not until after his father's death. Stevenson's material success as a writer was not absolutely certain until the publication of *Dr. Jekyll* and *Kidnapped* in 1886, just as he was never fairly paid until he went to America in 1887, but by the summer of 1883 even an obstinate and affectionate Scottish father could not any longer deny that his son was gifted as a writer, that considering his bad health he was amazingly hard-working and fertile, and that his gifts were slowly being rewarded. Each had something to reproach himself with, each something to forgive; and during those sunny weeks at Royat there was at last peace between them. This, however, was not the perfect and henceforth cloudless relation of reciprocal affection and understanding represented by over-hopeful adherents. There were still disagreements and clashes of will—how should there not be between men at once so different and so similar, especially in that 'core of flint'? In the year before his father died Stevenson (living with him at Bournemouth) wrote of him to his mother in these terms:

> '. . . my father, I am sorry to say, gave me a full dose of Hyde this morning. He began about breakfast as usual; and then to prove himself in the right and that he did well to be angry, carried on a long time (obviously on purpose) about the moon. I was very severe with him, and refused to speak again until he was quiet; after which he admitted he had been silly; and yet when I, to let him down gently, took the thing humorously, he began to start it again. He is certainly hard to manage.'

Why it was an offence for the old gentleman to talk about the moon escapes me, unless he referred to his son's (entirely unimportant) mistakes about our satellite in his novels; but evidently until the last little clashes occurred.

Peacefulness did not long survive the return to Hyères, for soon after his return Stevenson heard of the death of his friend Walter Ferrier, a loss which hit him the more severely since it was the first among the half-dozen or so of his old and really intimate friends. Soon he was ruefully writing to Bob Stevenson that he had 'been decading in several steps', and specified: 'Toothache; fever; Ferrier's death; lung', with the news that he was leaving for Nice 'penniless' to see the lung specialist. All of which did not prevent him from working on steadily, culminating at the end of the year in the triumphant letter already quoted about his increased earnings.

Early in 1884 the romance of destiny (and possibly a small subsidy to Henley) brought him and Charles Baxter to Hyères and very nearly killed Stevenson. Fanny's mistrust of or even dislike for some of Robert Louis's friends had in no wise abated, and if she disliked one more than the rest that one was probably Henley, who certainly seems to have made no effort to placate her. Henley was a crock like his friend, but his weakness was in the leg, not in the lungs; and when he drank and shouted and rolled out his laughter and sat up late he did himself no injury, while failing to perceive that these were exactly the excesses counter-indicated for a frail, excitable, over-sensitive consumptive. Fanny did well to object, but then Henley was certainly Stevenson's most congenial literary friend, and he was far from being the envious and treacherous person of Fanny's imagination. True, even as early as 1884 he must have begun to resent and probably to oppose what he thought was Louis's backsliding to respectability and the Shorter Catechism under the influence of the alien Fanny. But Fanny's own son Lloyd has left us a glimpse of Henley's vitality from which we can easily infer how he would delight and dominate Stevenson:

> 'He was the first man I had ever called by his surname;* the first friend I had ever sought and won, a great, glowing, massive-shouldered fellow with a big red beard and a crutch; jovial, astoundingly clever, and with a laugh that rolled out like music. Never was there such another as William Ernest Henley; he had an unimaginable fire and vitality; he swept one off one's feet. There are no words that can describe the quality he had of exalting those about him; of communicating his own rousing self-confidence and belief in himself. . . .'

That was the gift which D. H. Lawrence gave so lavishly to the few who knew him at all intimately, though of course being a consumptive like Stevenson he lacked Henley's massive energy and Jove-like hilarity. One can easily understand why Fanny dreaded him both as a danger to Louis's health and a danger to her power over him. If Louis had acquired an energetic and matronly mother-in-law who doted on Fanny and thought him rather an unfortunate acquisition he would have felt towards her much as Fanny felt towards Henley. And, with excellent logic, she resented the small sums Louis lent or gave him, quite forgetting that Henley helped Louis to increase his income by

* He means 'Christian name'.

acting as his unpaid agent—the hundred pounds advance on *Treasure Island* is a case in point.

Anyone can see that this burly colossus added to a fair-sized Writer to the Signet would make the model-sized rooms of La Solitude seem like a doll's house. Whoever made the suggestion Fanny would not unreasonably think that the real cause was Henley—the three men decided to go to Nice. Fanny was a pessimist—people who live with an optimist usually are—and in her wifely anxiety to aid her husband she over-estimated her powers of successfully digesting or rejecting the numerous medical fads reported in *The Lancet*, discovering for instance that salt hardens the arteries and salads may carry tape-worms. But she was perfectly right in isolating him from people with colds and in thinking that in his state of health he should not go junketing to Nice with two hearty talkers and drinkers. Very soon they had to admit that Louis was 'down' with a bad lung and kidney infection—the latter perhaps due to too much Anglo-Scottish festivity. When the two 'culprits'—if they were culprits—departed, Fanny was left alone with her sick husband in Nice, only to be warned by the English doctor that Louis might be dying. Anyone can see the impact which such gloomy news would make on her sensational and pessimistic temperament, especially as it was accompanied by the grim advice to send for some man friend to help with the funeral and similar troubles. Fanny never forgave Henley for his share in this ill-fated spree, was furious with Sir Walter Simpson for not rushing instantly to her aid, and records deep gratitude to Bob who did come.

This might be called the second major breakdown of Stevenson's health, if we count the California illness as the first. When he was well enough—or rather not too ill—to return to Hyères, he had to lie with his right arm strapped to his side, and under strict orders not to talk. On top of which he then developed sciatica, rheumatism and ophthalmia, so that in addition to being speechless he could not read or play any game or indeed do anything but lie drearily sleepless until drugged. They relate stories of Stevenson's courage and wit in these and similar dreadful trials of sickness which may be the usual biographical apocrypha of unknown origin, or may be true. One is that after the diagnosis of ophthalmia Fanny said to him sarcastically: 'I suppose this is the best thing that could have happened!' and he just managed to scrawl the answer: 'How odd! Just what I was going to say myself'. This, if not true, ought to be; and so too the other occasion when a friend deplored that he had been condemned to silence for so much of his time, whereupon Stevenson wrote: ''Tis my vocation, Hal'. Some of the poems in the *Child's Garden* are said to have been written with his left hand at Hyères during this time.

On the 9th March, 1884 Stevenson wrote Colvin:

> 'I am today, thanks to a pure heaven and a beneficent loud-making, antiseptic mistral, on the high places as to health and spirits. Money holds out wonderfully. Fanny has gone for a drive to certain meadows which are now one sheet of jonquils. . . .'

The letters and no doubt literary work started up again as he recovered, but not for long. One night early in May he suddenly coughed and as suddenly was choked with a flow of blood. Fanny was too shaken to be able to measure out the ergotin for him, and he did it for himself, having previously written the message: 'Don't be frightened. If this is death, it is quite easy'. What was far less easy was for the patient to maintain such cool courage and the sense of laughter at such a bitter crisis. So dangerous was the crisis that a doctor was sent out from England, and though less pessimistic than his colleague at Nice gave stringently restrictive orders for the next two years:

> 'He must be perfectly tranquil, trouble about nothing, have no shocks or surprises, not even pleasant ones; must not eat too much, drink too much, laugh too much; may write a little, but not too much; talk *very* little, and walk no more than can be helped.'

Some of these forbiddings might have been aimed direct at certain junketing and exuberant friends, and show how right Fanny had been. But the romance of destiny did not allow him to vegetate the weeks and years away in his Solitude. The 1883–87 epidemic of cholera reached Hyères, and Fanny, with her nose in *The Lancet*, grew seriously alarmed—not without cause—and insisted that they must leave. With the aid of Walter Ferrier's sister and an invalid valet ('I got him cheap, second-hand') Stevenson was moved to Marseille and thence to Royat, on the way to England to which he was thus again beaten back.

9

'Wensleydale, Bournemouth
Sunday, 28th September, 1884.

My dear People.

I keep better, and am today downstairs for the first time. I find the lockers entirely empty; not a cent to the front. Will you pray send us some? It blows an equinoctial gale, and has blown for nearly a week. Nimbus Britannicus; piping wind, lashing rain; the sea is a fine colour, and wind-bound ships lie at anchor under the Old Harry rocks, to make one glad to be ashore.

The Henleys are gone, and two plays practically done. I hope they may produce some of the ready.

I am, ever affectionate son,
R.L.S.'

THIS perfunctory begging letter, with hardly a trace of the verve, wit and good spirits of Stevenson's letters, is an indication of how much his energy had been reduced by illness. At the same time the letter, for all it is so brief, touches the main points of the monotonous life he led at Bournemouth. He was ill and recovered only to fall ill again; the weather was often unfavourable to so sensitive an invalid; he was often worried about money; he worked hard whenever he could, and it seems that he was able to write in states when other people would just give up; and friends came to see him from London, not always to Fanny's delight especially if she caught them sniffling. Naturally life was not always so uninspiring as that sounds. There were changes, spells of better health, good news on the book front, to compensate for disappointments. A great alleviation came in the spring of 1885 when they were able to give up the furnished house they had been living in and move to another, a real home, given to Fanny by Thomas Stevenson together with £500 to furnish.

Most women enjoy the work of decorating and furnishing a new home, and as a rule American women excel in both energy and efficiency. Fanny seems to have been exceptionally vigorous and more than one description has been left of her work at

Skerryvore (as Stevenson called the house in compliment to his father) though perhaps none is quite so pleasant as the refined approval of a biographer who states:

> '. . . all the comforts and modern elegancies, in which good taste and limited means combined to prevent a vulgar profusion, marked and embellished the new possession.'

A fine sense of discrimination might be exercised in defining the exact line where good taste reinforced limited means in avoiding vulgar profusion, but unfortunately this is left unrecorded. What we do know is that Fanny's energy was not limited to indoors and that she herself worked to re-model the garden, in which she introduced flowers grown from American seeds. It is said that in fine weather Stevenson would stroll about the paths shaded by a red parasol to watch his wife at work. This, if true, is a remarkable contrast to the physical activity Stevenson displayed after he had recovered health in the Pacific. In any case, these Bournemouth years were dominated by invalidism in Stevenson and the approach of death for his rapidly ageing father. The journeys he made were few and the longest was only to Paris with Henley to see Rodin. He stayed with Colvin in London, went to Matlock and Exeter, and almost always had cause to regret even such modest excursions. Inevitably then, such a life would be nothing but a record of relapses and recoveries but for the visits of friends and the writing and publication of books.

The question is sometimes asked: why, after the not too satisfactory early months, did the Stevensons remain at Bournmouth and then allow themselves to be anchored there by ownership of a house? One reason may be that the cholera epidemic lasted until 1887 and that in those days England was better organized against it than most Continental countries, which facts would not be overlooked by the amateur medical authority in the family. In the truce that had at last halted the long battle between father and son, Stevenson knew well enough that his father had not long to live, and that opportunity to see his son meant everything to him. Fanny spoke French badly and they saw few friends at Hyères, and at any rate Bournemouth spoke English and friends came calling. It seems likely as well as most reasonable that she would have preferred to spend at least part of the time in her own country. There was talk of the health resorts in Colorado (Symonds mentions this) and as soon as Mr. Stevenson died and they got some money they did go to America—and Robert Louis never returned. Meanwhile Bournemouth was no doubt the least objectionable compromise, but even with the home and their friends (nearly all his friends, by the way) this cannot have been a lively time for either of them.

The letter just quoted refers to the visit of the Henleys and the attempt to make money by collaborating together on plays. Those referred to in the letter must be *Admiral Guinea* and *Beau Austin*, which were preceded by *Deacon Brodie* and followed by the deplorable farce, *Macaire*. The impulse towards the composition of these unprofitable failures came from Henley who was convinced that they would succeed and make money. Stevenson was far more sceptical, and showed his good sense on at least one occasion by writing Henley that he was too hard-up to be able to spare time for such speculative work. No doubt this irritated the exuberant and over-optimistic Henley, but events proved Stevenson was right. The only one which had even a modest success was *Deacon Brodie*—in its way a distant forerunner of *Dr. Jekyll*—and Henley's actor brother failed when he tried them out on a tour in America. How ruthlessly strict the requirements of the stage are may be seen from the fact that even two such widely-known names as Stevenson and Henley have never secured a run for these plays. For a long time the belief was that Fanny disapproved of these speculative productions, and that her opposition to them was one of the main causes of the dislike between her and Henley. But, as a matter of fact, she was as keen about them as Henley himself, and for a long time took an active part in the discussions, fully believing that here was the way to make money. She may have felt vexed with Henley when time showed how he had over-estimated their chances, but the causes of dislike were human and not literary. For once let it be recorded that pessimistic Fanny, whose husband said she could extract dismalness from a sunbeam, fell a victim to unfounded optimism over these plays.

The main advantage of living in Bournemouth was unquestionably its accessibility. His father and mother stayed there near him in 1884, and it is a fair inference that the gift of the house to Fanny (Stevenson, by the way, wrote: 'I shall call *my* house

Skerryvore . . .') was intended by the parents to link him closer to them. They certainly stayed with him. Along with the Henleys or rather after them came other old friends—Bob and his wife and sister, Katherine de Mattos; Colvin and Baxter; and Professor Jenkin, not long before his death. Symonds, who saw Stevenson there for the last time just before he left for America noted:

> 'I spent a day at Bournemouth with the Stevensons. He has gone down hill terribly. They are all off to Colorado next month. I expect his father's death will have made his circumstances easier. But he is still nervous about money. *Dr. Jekyll* has been worth £350 to him, he says. I should have thought he would have got more for it.'

That 'gone down hill terribly' gives a hint of how much Stevenson had suffered in health between leaving Davos (in 1882) and Symonds's visit in 1887. Yet during these Bournemouth years, in spite of the desperate struggle against illness, he managed to make and keep new friends. Some of these were elderly and perhaps more decorative than intrinsically stimulating. Shelley's son, Sir Percy Florence, took unflattering photographs of Stevenson; while Lady Shelley, a fanatical worshipper of Percy Bysshe, insisted that Stevenson resembled the great lyrist and by some mystical trick claimed him as a son. Another was Sir Henry Taylor, one of those senior civil servants who obtain a spurious temporary reputation as poets because of their influential friends. Among Sir Henry's friends was that Mrs. Cameron who persecuted Victorian celebrities with her camera, and if she were still alive in 1885 it is a wonder she did not include Stevenson among her victims. She could also have introduced him to the Prinseps and G. F. Watts and the Tennyson circle. Seemingly Stevenson never got any nearer that than an invitation to stay with the Master of Balliol—very likely arranged by Symonds, an old and critical friend of Jowett's. The parents also were to come, and as Jowett was a theologian (in hot water at one time) this might have been awkward. Either Stevenson was really ill or he funked a week-end of Balliol culture, for he evaded the invitation by alleging the fear of a breakdown and haemorrhage—and it is a fact that most of his few excursions ended that way at this period.

Among the more lively new friends were Henry James, who had not then reached the hippopotamus-trying-to-pick-up-a-pea stage, and Sargent who (judging from the unreliable basis of photographs) painted two of the best portraits of Robert Louis. Another new friend, if he ever really became a friend, was William Archer whose acquaintance was made through a critical article on Stevenson which both directly and ironically questioned the sincerity of his optimism and adventure-worship. Archer really got under his skin if we may judge from this reply in one of the several letters Stevenson wrote him about the article:

> 'If you knew I was a chronic invalid, why say that my philosophy was unsuitable to such a case? My call for facts is not so general as yours, but an essential fact should not be put the other way about.'

It was of course done ironically to underline what Archer considered the factitious side of a pre-conceived optimism which attained the object of popular applause by evading the facts of his own life in particular and the universe in general. Happiness is not our 'great task', it is a by-product of life; and to write that we should all be 'as happy as kings' when lying in bed after a haemorrhage, half-blind, with one arm bound down, probably sounded to Archer a pose contaminated with humbug. Stevenson realized this, as the next words in his letter show:

> 'The fact is, consciously or not, you doubt my honesty; you think I am making faces, and at heart disbelieve my utterances. . . . Is it quite fair . . . to keep your face so steadily on my most light-hearted works, and then say I recognize no evil? Yet in the paper on Burns, for instance, I show myself alive to some sorts of evil. But then, perhaps, they are not your sorts.'

Archer was the first to hint a criticism of Stevenson which became more precise and vehement after the collapse of Victorian money prosperity and ignoring of facts in the calamity of 1914, from which neither England nor optimism has yet recovered. Archer's argument, I take it, would be that the private 'evil', if it was evil, wrought by a boozer and womanizer (to put it at its uncomplimentary crudest) such as Burns, is nothing compared with the collective evil wrought by a bogus financier who ruins thousands of little people, an ambitious politician who wades through blood and injustice to a dictatorship, a newspaper proprietor who deliberately provokes or prolongs a war to serve his own interests, the scientist who irresponsibly hands a lethal discovery to persons with the passions of savages and the self-control of children.

Whether Archer's challenge was responsible for it or not, this existence of what we call 'evil' is recognized in the most successful book Stevenson wrote at Bournemouth. *The Strange Case of Dr. Jekyll and Mr. Hyde* seems as if it might have grown consciously or unconsciously out of this debate with Archer, though it is also related to the Deacon Brodie story. Like all books *Dr. Jekyll* is open to criticism, even if that was limited to the 'defects of its qualities', as Symonds would have said. But this short novel definitely marked the permanent success of Stevenson as a writer, particularly in the United States. It is a startling and original plot, suggested to Stevenson by a nightmare from which Fanny to his annoyance prematurely woke him, or by the dramatic functioning of the 'little people' of his dreams. It has not much 'style' to speak of, so the average reader was not disturbed by literary intrusions. Above all it stated the drama of human 'good' and 'evil' in obvious pulpit terms no one could miss. The book belongs no doubt to the category of 'crawlers', and owes something to Poe and perhaps a little to Dickens. But it is original, and by sheer power of dramatic interest and hard writing *Dr. Jekyll* has kept a genuine popularity for eighty years. In no idle spirit of superfluous praise one may add that *Dr. Jekyll* is almost the ideal Hollywood script, and has actually caused one of the very few films which inspire a genuine sensation of horror.

According to Lloyd Osbourne, the draft of this story, which in its present form is over 25,000 words (grossly over-estimated by Fanny as 60,000), was written in three days. Fanny Stevenson criticized this draft, in which (we are told) Jekyll was from the beginning an evil man, like Deacon Brodie, and the change into Hyde was undertaken merely 'for the purpose of a disguise'. She is said to have pointed out that he ought not to make it just another crime story such as his *Markheim* (written in 1884) but an allegory of the 'good' and 'evil' in human nature. This was excellent advice, though not altogether palatable to an author who has just laboured to produce what he hopes is a masterpiece. Either from pique or because he did not want to be influenced by this draft, Stevenson burned it, and re-wrote the story in its present form. Again we are told that he did this in three days. Now, for a healthy person in good spirits and full of his subject, 5,000 words a day for three days is hard work. 8,000 a day for a chronic invalid, even one of Stevenson's undoubted energy, courage and fertility, is a tall story. The mere writing down would take from eight to ten hours, and that for a man whose average writing day was from three to five; and at the time 'had lately had a haemorrhage, and was strictly forbidden all discussion and excitement'. The two most authentic of these literary marathons are *Rasselas* and *Guy Mannering*; the former of these (about 35,000) was written in a week or rather more than 5,000 a day, and the latter (about 160,000) in six weeks, or about 4,000 a day. Scott's achievement is the most remarkable since he maintained that average so long. Stevenson himself gives *Dr. Jekyll* about ten weeks!

However, even if we may justly suspect Lloyd and Fanny of making a good story too good, there can be no doubt that *Dr. Jekyll* was written at a high speed and with fiery concentration, which helps to account for the story's readability and the grip it instantly takes and holds on the reader's attention. The ancient *clichés* 'not a dull moment in it' and 'I could not put it down until I had finished it' are literally true here; and if there are any negligences of style one doesn't notice them, as is sometimes the case in Stevenson's far more carefully laboured and 'styled' books.

Some of the objections made to the story seem unfounded. Thus, the complaint is made that in his own way Jekyll is as bad as Hyde, if not worse. No doubt this is true from the point of view of a sceptical modern intellectual, but it was not true for Stevenson's audience who would consider the prosperous, fashionable, luxurious and rather smug doctor a fulfilment of their ideals of respectability. Again, there is the objection that the potion which causes the physical changes of Jekyll and Hyde is medically impossible. Of course it is. But just as in most adventure stories, including *Treasure Island*, the reader must accept improbabilities and even absurdities for the sake of the action, so in these tales of fantasy we must accept impossible causes of remarkable effects. Dr. Jekyll's magic potion is not so incredible as the suspension of Mr. Valdemar's dissolution by hypnosis. Besides, Stevenson had dreamed the potion, and rightly accepted the gift of his phantom 'little people'. Indeed if we are looking for subsidiary allegories here we might find one in the ultimate failure of the potion—symbolizing the ultimate failure of Science either to resolve Man's destiny or to alleviate his lot. There are minor points of more validity. Thus, at the time of publication Frederick Myers wrote Stevenson and noted several, including the now famous one where Hyde, about to drink the potion in Lanyon's presence, conjures him to silence 'under the seal of *our* profession'. Obviously Dr. Lanyon's instant and indignant answer would have been: 'You're not a doctor!'. Even the change to 'your profession' would bring the retort: 'You're not my patient!' Stevenson could easily have corrected this, but did not; and after all what do such trifles matter? I should guess that on a first reading ninety-nine people out of a hundred never notice them.

Perhaps a more cogent objection is that raised on the lines of William Archer's criticism of Stevenson's evasion of 'evil' or rather his limited idea of what constitutes 'evil'. We are not told anything much of Hyde's wicked ways except that he was an incarnation of fiendish malevolence, as exemplified by trampling the child and the murder of Sir Danvers Carew. These are purely individual acts, dreadful of course, but of strictly limited scope. Suppose, for instance, that in his fiendish malice Hyde had used Jekyll's medical knowledge to contaminate London's drinking water with cholera? That would be a crime on the grand scale, and a splendid irony might have been introduced by making Jekyll win tremendous newspaper applause and a knighthood for his devoted care of the stricken victims. Or he might have come nearer Deacon Brodie, and have made Hyde the head of a gang of West End burglars, making use of Dr. Jekyll's knowledge of wealthy homes in order to rob them. With Stevenson's great powers of invention there is no knowing where he might have gone on such lines, but clearly Hyde's wickedness like Jekyll's goodness is meant to be symbolical and personal only. Such complications would have taken up too much room and have overloaded the neat swiftly moving tale Stevenson planned and carried out so skilfully.

Other minor objections raised are that the police inquiries into the murder of Sir Danvers would certainly have connected Hyde with Jekyll, and the doctor would have had to answer some very embarrassing questions. Symonds, after reproaching Louis for being too harsh (not so long after Archer had done just the opposite!) thought Jekyll should have handed Hyde over to the police—which would have caused a fearful legal imbroglio if he kept enough of the potion to change back to Jekyll during the trial. It was useless for Jekyll to destroy Hyde's cheque book—Stevenson forgot that earlier in the story Hyde had been able to write a perfectly valid cheque in Jekyll's name. And surely the fiendishly malicious Hyde would hardly have committed suicide so tamely. He would certainly have been armed, and would have shot Utterson and Poole before killing himself. He might even have dashed out and shot a policeman before doing himself justice.

The answer to all such objections is that the story achieved its aim of interesting readers. Graham Balfour says that 40,000 copies were sold in England in six months; and he estimates that the authorized edition and numerous piracies in the United States must have accounted for a quarter of a million. Moreover the story had a distinct influence on younger writers so different as Oscar Wilde in *Dorian Gray* and Conan Doyle in the Holmes stories. If Doyle might have handled the themes of some of the *New Arabian Nights* more effectively than their author, he derived from Stevenson that 'atmosphere' of foggy London which is so essential to a real Holmes melodrama. True, the fog probably derived from Dickens's *Bleak House*, as Mr. Utterson seems a more lax and genial Mr. Tulkinghorne, but neither Dickens nor Doyle could better this as 'atmosphere':

> 'It was by this time about nine in the morning, and the first fog of the season. A great chocolate-coloured pall lowered over heaven, but the wind was continually changing and routing these embattled vapours; so that as the cab crawled from street to street, Mr. Utterson beheld a marvellous number of degrees and hues of twilight; for here it would be dark like the back-end of evening; and there would be a glow of a rich, lurid brown, like the light of some strange conflagration; and here, for a moment, the fog would be quite broken up, and a haggard shaft of daylight would glance in between the swirling wreaths. The dismal quarter of Soho seen under these changing glimpses, with its muddy ways, and slatternly passengers, and its lamps, which had never been extinguished or had been kindled afresh to combat this mournful re-invasion of darkness, seemed, in the lawyer's eyes, like a district of some city in a nightmare.'

Surely the next sentence will be: 'Come along, Watson! Here's our man's address!'

Dr. Jekyll was a great public success—*the* success for which Stevenson had been working and hoping to clinch the delayed but certain success of *Treasure Island*. However well founded were the objections we have noted from such intellectuals as Symonds and Myers, they were irrelevant so far as popular success was concerned, for the 'public' does not read books with the care and attention to detail of critics but runs through them for the sensation or emotion contained—and if this can be combined with a 'moral' lesson, so much the better. The encouragement came just in time to reassure Stevenson. As we have seen, he was still worried about money when Symonds visited him in 1887, and at the end of 1885 his anxiety was acute. He was then thirty-five, and in a wretched state of health, knowing that he was still dependent on an ailing father who had not long to live, while Stevenson himself had never acquiesced in his father's religious prejudices by which he was virtually disinherited. In contrast to his letters to William Archer and to the optimistic sentiments expressed in his essays we have a long letter addressed to Edmund Gosse and dated the 2nd January, 1886—the month in which *Dr. Jekyll* was published but before the book was actually a success, for at first the response was hesitant. Stevenson was chilled by the reception of *Prince Otto* (which ran as a serial in *Longman's Magazine* and appeared in book form in November 1885) of which he could only report that the book had 'done fairly well in spite of the reviews, which have been bad'. This rather Meredithian story had been 'well slated' in *The Saturday Review*, while others had intelligently described it as 'a child's story' or 'a Gilbert comedy'! Stevenson then turns to the 'public' and says:

> 'What the public likes is work (of any kind) a little loosely executed; so long as it is a little wordy, a little slack, a little dim and knotless, the dear public likes it; it should (if possible) be a little dull into the bargain.'

Perhaps one may interject that none of this is true of *Treasure Island* or *Dr. Jekyll* or indeed of Stevenson's work in general, and as he was on the verge of becoming one of the most popular authors of his time this poor opinion of public taste was exaggerated—but remember that one of the most gifted British authors of his time had then been continuously before 'the public' for eleven years and still could not earn an adequate living.

He goes on, more hopefully, to say he knows good work sometimes 'hits' but firmly believes it is by accident; he also 'knows' that good work must eventually succeed 'but that is not the doing of the public; they are only shamed into silence or affectation'. Stevenson denies that he writes for 'the public'; he writes for money 'a nobler deity' and 'most of all for myself . . . both more intelligent and nearer home'. And then:

> 'Let us tell each other sad stories of the bestiality of the beast whom we feed. What he likes is the newspaper; and to me the press is the mouth of a sewer, where lying is professed as from an university chair, and everything prurient, and ignoble, and essentially dull, finds its abode and pulpit. I do not like mankind; but men, and not all of these—and fewer women. As for respecting the race, and, above all, that fatuous rabble of burgesses called "the public", God save me from such irreligion!— that way lies disgrace and dishonour. There must be something wrong in me, or I would not be popular.'

This is very engaging, coming from Stevenson, who only a short time before had been denouncing the Shakespeare of *Timon* as 'atrabilious'; but it was lucky for him, if these were really his permanent views and not merely the result of a fit of the blues, that he put them on record only in a private letter. Even if he had put them into an article, Fanny and Colvin would never have allowed him to publish it, just as they restrained him from publishing his violent political views about such public events as Majuba and General Gordon. Like many other people Stevenson enjoyed that severely moral and idealistic patriotism which has no information more exact than the newspapers and public gossip, which, being free from the responsibilities of power, feels itself called on to censure those who are struggling with the dangers and difficulties of reality. In the fluid realm of ideas there is no stubbornness of facts and of men to overcome. He would have been taken aback if Mr. Gladstone had suddenly called on him to apply to the art of literature those quixotic standards he demanded in the far more difficult art of politics!

The statement in this letter to Gosse that he likes fewer women than men is worth noting. Even if it was true in 1886 had it always been true? Lloyd Osbourne, whose loyalty to his stepfather is not to be questioned, mentions the 'many women' who came into Stevenson's early life. But it is the fact that as a writer

Stevenson avoided women characters as much as possible and was not always successful with the few he did attempt. By Lloyd's request there are no women in *Treasure Island* (except the boy's mother) and there are none but servants in *Dr. Jekyll.* He has nothing to set against Meredith's gallery of women or such a masterpiece of observation and creation as the Miriam of *Sons and Lovers.* Stevenson shared the Anglo-Saxon view of females, which wavers between sentimentality and mistrust. He could be rapturous about them as little girls, contented with or even submissive to them as mothers and motherly bodies, but as women in their flower—no. In Stevenson's case the comparative absence of women and the almost complete ignoring of sex were a great asset. It was considered meritorious and 'masculine', and was doubtless a solid factor in his popularity.

The importance of *Dr. Jekyll* in Stevenson's career and in his struggle for financial independence has naturally led us to concentrate on that book to the exclusion of others which preceded and accompanied it during the Bournemouth period, September 1884 to August 1887. They include *The Black Arrow* (serial in 1883), *Prince Otto*, *More New Arabian Nights* (with Fanny Stevenson), *A Child's Garden of Verses*, *Kidnapped*, *Memories and Portraits*, *Underwoods*, such stories as *Markheim* and *Olalla* and a number of essays. Taking them at the lowest estimate, nobody can refuse Stevenson admiration and praise for his industry, his fertility and his versatility. The versatility is especially notable, not only because it is rare for any writer to excel in so many different ways, but because that bugbear 'the public' is usually supposed to mistrust and dislike it. They are supposed to insist that a favourite painter shall all his life paint variations on the same picture—so that his 'style' may be instantly recognized—while a popular writer should stick to one type of novel, which again can be instantly recognized. At any rate, Stevenson is a striking example of a writer attaining great contemporary success while remaining extremely versatile. Of course, some if not much of this work had been in hand for a long time—the idea of *Prince Otto* dated from very early days—but there cannot be many writers who in the space of four or five years have published so much that is good in so many different *genres.*

The Black Arrow does not really come into the 'Bournemouth period' since it appeared as a serial in *Young Folks* in 1883, and was not published in book form until 1888. Like *Treasure Island*, it was signed 'Captain George North', but its fate was exactly contrary—it pleased the young folks and has never been liked by the Stevensonians, beginning with Fanny who said she could not even read it. Indeed the Wars of the Roses are a confused turbulent epoch and not very interesting to civilized foreigners. Stevenson himself did not attach much importance to it, but then he had not thought much of *Treasure Island*, since he considered it not really worth the one hundred pounds advance he received for the book rights. Travelling about as he wrote the serial he forgot to what point he had brought his characters, and as the book drew to its end the magazine 'reader' had to remind the author that he had forgotten to dispose of the fourth black arrow and the villain. Stevenson's reply is pleasingly candid:

> 'To the contrary I thank you most cordially; indeed, the story having changed and run away from me in the course of writing, the dread fate I had already designed for Sir Oliver became impossible, and I had, I blush to say, clean forgot him.
>
> 'Thanks to you, Sir, he shall die the death. I enclose tonight slips 49, 50, 51; and tomorrow or next day, after having butchered the priest, shall despatch the rest.'

The adventures of young Shelton come thick and fast in much the same happy-go-lucky fashion. There is a heroine this time, Joan Sedley, but the circumstance is extenuated by disguising her as a boy during much of the time she is on the stage, whereafter she is a mere symbol in the background. It would be an interesting study in literary market research to discover why *The Black Arrow* and *Treasure Island* have had such totally different fates, for the difference cannot be accounted for merely by a dislike for women. There is in *The Black Arrow* no such striking character as Long John Silver (founded on Henley, by the way!) but Lawless is a brawny swashbuckler out of Scott, and the sketch of young Richard Crookback remarkable in its skill. The adventures show a Stevensonian disregard for expense in the matter of bloodshed and hanging, and there are such striking episodes as the encounter with Sir Daniel disguised as a leper, and the stealing and navigation of the *Good Hope*. Perhaps a main difference is that *Treasure Island* is a fantasia of the subconscious in terms of pirates and pieces of eight, while *The Black Arrow* is a historical novel (based to some extent on the Paston letters); and by

Stevenson's time the historical novel was becoming the costume novel because it lacked ideas. Scott had loyalty to the lawful king, Kingsley the struggle of Protestant and Catholic, but what has *The Black Arrow*? In spite of which, many of the hard things said about *The Black Arrow* are not really justified, and its lack of popularity is not due to any of the faults alleged but to the subject and period, both unfamiliar and unattractive to the average reader. What remains inexplicable is that anyone who has taken part in a real battle should be interested by Stevenson's facile and dilettante bloodshed.

Prince Otto is so different that apart from its great literary skill (an important exception!) it might be by another author. Stevenson had worked on it at intervals since 1879, and even then its theme was rescued from an early tragedy, while its title had passed from *The Forest State* to *The Greenwood State* to that we now have. Mildly Ruritanian and set in an imaginary old-time German principate, the book shares with *The Black Arrow* the disadvantage that it is neither fantasy nor history, but a mixture—which may account for its unpopularity. Henley had warned the author that it would not win him new readers, but Meredith praised warmly, not necessarily because it was the work of a disciple but because he recognized the care and thought given both to construction and to style. Edmund Gosse like *The Saturday* reviewer protested against 'the false style' of Seraphina's flight as 'a wilful and monstrous sacrifice on the altar of George Meredith'. Indeed the chapter 'Princess Cinderella' does read like an emulation of one of Meredith's prose-poetry chapters, such as the meeting of Richard and Lucy in *Feveral*, executed with much taste and feeling. Yet Steuart says this chapter first convinced him of Stevenson's genius. Unluckily Stevenson's faulty natural history introduced a note of bathos in the midst of his most polished and tremulous periods when he wrote:

> '. . . in the small dis-shaped houses in the fork of giant arms, where they had lain all night, lover by lover, warmly pressed, the bright-eyed, big-hearted singers began to awaken for the day.'

Fortunately not too much of *More New Arabian Nights* (or *The Dynamiter*) need be credited to or blamed on Louis. He wrote the sections in which Prince Florizel reappears, fallen from his high rank to the keeper of a cigar shop—a tribute perhaps to democracy—and *Zero's Tale of the Explosive Bomb*, which Stevenson hoped would make the nihilists' dynamiting 'ridiculous, if he could not make it horrible'. Everybody was against it anyway except the actual perpetrators; and did he expect these lugubrious fanatics to read his tale and say: 'Stevenson has made dynamiting ridiculous—we must give it up'? At all events the book is dedicated to the police. For the rest we come on the usual conflicting statements, some saying that the stories were invented by Fanny to entertain her husband when he was so ill at Hyères, others that she supplied 'only two' of them. Whatever she supplied Stevenson presumably reconstructed or at any rate 'put style on'.

Which brings up, perhaps prematurely, the subject of Stevenson's collaboration with his wife and stepson. Fanny's assumption of omniscience and authority in criticizing, altering and even vetoing her husband's work would arouse more indignation and alarm if we did not know that Stevenson at times ignored her. Yet one of her countrymen has described her contributions to *The Dynamiter* as 'curiously vulgar', and the question whether her influence was good or bad might be debated indefinitely. Perhaps it would boil down to the question: was his object to be a literary artist or a popular and financial success? Fanny was not capable of furthering the higher ideal, but for the other she did much. Stevenson's fault—or one of his faults—as a popular writer was that he was too literary, remembered too nostalgically his aesthetic youth—as in the *Princess Cinderella* chapter just quoted. He had yearnings towards biography and history, confidently planned a life of Wellington before he had even looked at the majestic series of *Dispatches* and *Despatches*, and even in the Pacific worried Fanny extremely by projecting a history of Oceania instead of saleable travel notes and stories. She won, and on the whole she was right.

A Child's Garden of Verses! Here again is proof of Stevenson's versatility—there is Voltaire, but he never wrote about his childhood in verse, it would have been considered indecent in the eighteenth century. Indeed, one of the greatest geniuses who has ever infested our island not so long ago issued a ukase to the effect that 'we must always suspect' those who write well about childhood. What we must suspect them of was not stated—possibly, human sympathy. At any rate Stevenson certainly deserves whatever suspicions do attach to those who write well about childhood. But there is more than one way of doing this. A. A. Milne, for example, wrote about childhood in such a style as to please multitudes of children, and also their parents. Stevenson, like Anatole France in *Le Petit Pierre*, writes about his own childhood for grown-ups; but while France remembers the little person he had been with adult detachment and irony, Stevenson tries to re-live his childhood and to write in the way he thinks that child would have written verse if he could. Inevitably there is something a little factitious about this. The verses of young children are invariably feeble and absurd, touching perhaps because of some accidentally just naïveté. What child, however gifted, could command such octosyllables as these:

'Where are forests, hot as fire,
Wide as England, tall as a spire,
Full of apes and cocoa-nuts
And the negro hunters' huts;—
Where the knotty crocodile
Lies and blinks in the Nile,
And the red flamingo flies
Hunting fish before his eyes. . . .'

only a child who had read Milton and Blake, and had not learned that flamingoes don't eat fish. The charm of that, as of all these *Child's Garden* poems, is sophisticated—the master touching up the child's drawing—and perhaps for that reason they do not please small children as Milne and Carroll do. On the other hand we have here a literary skill approaching the *tour de force*, and a collection of wholly personal rhymes which have stubbornly kept alive through an epoch of war and revolution and wilfully perverse changes in aesthetic fashions.

Dr. Jekyll, which we have already discussed, appeared in January 1886, and was followed by another *Young Folks* serial in May–July, with book publication in July. Stevenson was better inspired here than with *The Black Arrow*, and came far nearer to a successful compromise between the boy's paper serial and the historical novel, the pot-boiler and the genuine novel. The period, 1751, was near enough to the last Jacobite rebellion for it to seem familiar to the still innumerable readers of Scott. And he kept to his own people and his own country and the seas about it, so was writing within his own experience. He had sailed parts of David Balfour's uncomfortable voyage, knew the island of Earraid on which he wrecked the ship, and had visited the country where the lad wanders and meets adventure with Alan Breck. The letters from Bournemouth to his father, and his cousin David, show how meticulous Stevenson was in getting his hero's land and sea wanderings topographically correct. Yet, as always, he could be careless about other details or at least not hanker after verisimilitude when his purpose was better suited by ignoring it. I cannot think that even in the Scots law of 1750 forcible abduction of a minor with intent to sell him into slavery and defraud him of his heritage could have been anything short of felony; yet Stevenson shows us a canny Scots lawyer cheerfully compounding it, to bring the tale to a prosperous end. Nobody seems to have queried this, so I may be wrong.

Even a determined anti-Stevensonian—if any such exists—could not withhold admiration for the real modesty and self-control which enabled a man of his literary gifts to work for a trashy production such as *Young Folks*, and to use it not merely to boil a scanty pot or two but to continue learning his craft as a novelist. *Treasure Island* was a lucky hit of genius, but an unsuccessful serial; *The Black Arrow* was a good serial but with all its merits an unsuccessful novel; *Kidnapped* which Stevenson began as a pot-boiler and with distaste suddenly became alive, and made both a good serial and a good novel. If it has much of Scott, it has more of Defoe, and Stevenson, assimilating both ancestors, made the book wholly his. The book publication, only six months after *Dr. Jekyll*, was well received and certainly spread his fame, especially in the United States. What is amazing is that his work was still so poorly paid, that for the serial rights he received only thirty shillings a thousand words.

Leaving *Underwoods*, *Memories and Portraits* and the memoir of Professor Jenkin for later notice, we still have to consider the short stories published serially in 1885. Both might come into the category of 'crawlers'. In the various forms of the story of how Fanny secured the re-writing of *Dr. Jekyll*, as an allegory, she is always said to have cited *Markheim* as a mere story, whereas in its own slighter way *Markheim* also is an allegory—of the awakening conscience. The visitor so startlingly intruding on the scene of the crime is the 'devil' but is also Jesus, and is an allegory of the conflict 'good-evil' in Markheim's soul. What disconcerts the reader a little, as so often in moral tales, is that someone has to be foully murdered in order that the sinner may repent. Stevenson can hardly have reflected that when the maid-servant came home after her brief Christmas outing to be met by a strange man 'with something like a smile' and the remark: 'You had better go for the police, I have killed your master', the poor girl would certainly have let out a terrified scream and probably have fainted—which is not the 'note' on which he meant to leave us. Moreover, though it is a little thing, Stevenson had not yet learned that a phrase may be over-wrought and that ingenious evasion of a commonplace may be worse than the commonplace itself. The phrase from *Markheim* has often been quoted, where, wishing to say that he had stopped the old man's life as a clockmaker stops a clock, Stevenson writes:

> '. . . and now, and by his act, that piece of life had been arrested, as the horologist, with interjected finger, arrests the beating of the clock.'

Olalla is more ambitious. Like *Dr. Jekyll* it came to Stevenson in his sleep from 'the little people' or at least the central part of the story, 'the court, the mother, the mother's niche, Olalla, Olalla's chamber, the meetings on the stair, the broken window, the ugly scene of the bite'. There are derivations to be noticed which must unconsciously have influenced Stevenson's dream. His work on Wellington may have suggested the setting in Spain during the Peninsular War; the episode of the boy torturing the squirrel is said to derive from Lytton's *Strange Story* (which if I have read I have entirely forgotten), and there is a touch of Balzac's *El Verdugo* in the tragic family destiny. The sadism in the boy Felipe might be, if we follow the hints, 'vampirism' in the mother. Olalla, entirely free from this, is a sacrifice to the family taint, and will not allow her love for the English stranger to carry her away to the extent of perhaps passing it on to her children. The story is too imaginative and wildly romantic for many readers, who brush it aside as a failure. Of course it is a failure but it is far finer than many successes; and it is mainly the feeble ending which is responsible for that. Stevenson clearly did not know what to do with the situation he had dreamed, and it was quite above Fanny's level. Perhaps the real ending would have been the natural one of Olalla's flying from the horror of her mother, living rapturously happy in her marriage, and then having to share with her husband the even greater horror and misery of seeing the trait reappear in their child—but his readers would never have tolerated that and Fanny would have put in her veto! If Stevenson had put it aside unfinished, dreamed over it again, he would certainly have found the right and dramatic ending.

Of course the books we have been discussing were not all written during the Bournemouth period, and in the case of *Prince Otto*, for example, all but the last two chapters had been completed at Hyères. And, of course, Stevenson started or worked at other books in those years, but these additions only increase admiration for his industry and versatility. He had different types of literary gift and generously used them all, and it was not his fault if the contemporary audience preferred him in his less distinguished moods and phases. Time is needed to sort out these merits, and again it is not Stevenson's fault if commentators still tend to equate his success as an artist with sales. On the other hand while we praise Stevenson's continuous output we must not think of him as a *forçat de la plume* like Balzac, or even like Scott, though Scott with all his immense literary production still managed to live a very full life. Stevenson may at times have overworked as writers sometimes must, but on the whole he seems to have behaved most sensibly, accepting the medical restrictions and periods of rest imposed on him, and making such amusements as he could. If he wrote a great deal one main reason is that a permanent invalid confined generally to the house has a great deal of leisure for writing. It may be true that Fanny imposed on him at Bournemouth some of her own nervous valetudinarian fears and habits, but after all she was just as closely at his side in all the activities of Samoa. There must have been moments during those interminable hours of bed and silence when his laughter-loving spirit saw the dismal humour of a situation where the champion of cheerfulness, the open road and the adventure of pirates found himself imprisoned in bed, in Bournemouth—in Bournemouth!—not even able to sing: 'Yo, ho, ho, and a bottle of milk!' However much we attribute to 'destiny' and the efforts and influence of those about him, it was the man's indomitable spirit which saved him from what must have begun to seem another Heine's 'mattress grave'. The more so since, as we have noted, the few excursions he did make nearly always ended up with yet another haemorrhage.

However devotedly and, perhaps, domineeringly Fanny tried to protect her husband from the assaults of the outer world, there were some blows she could not parry. On the 12th June, 1885, Fleeming Jenkin died. His death, we are told, distressed Stevenson nearly as much as that of Walter Ferrier, and by way of a memorial Stevenson planned and eventually completed a biography of Jenkin. In a letter to Colvin written from Honolulu in March 1889 Stevenson wrote:

> 'My dear Colvin, I owe you and Fleeming Jenkin, the two older men who took the trouble, and knew how to make a friend of me, everything that I have or am. . . .'

This is large praise, but it was part of the generosity of Stevenson's nature that he loved to acknowledge publicly his human obligations if only by a dedication. Some may think—and Stevenson was probably among them—that in many ways 'Cummy's' treatment of his childhood was injudicious and even harmful, but the strength and truth of her devotion are not to be questioned, and those only Stevenson chose to remember in his letters to her and in his dedication of his *Child's Garden*. In much the same spirit Stevenson undertook the life of the Edinburgh Professor of Engineering, and his principles of selection may be seen from the following remark in the published biography:

> 'The very day before this (to me) distasteful letter, he had written to Miss Bell of Manchester in a sweeter strain; I do not quote the one, I quote the other; fair things are the best.'

No doubt, but the fairness of a biographer consists in setting down the facts as fairly as possible without bias one way or the other, avoiding the *suppressio veri* as much as the *suggestio falsi*. This is a counsel of perfection which nobody attains, but Stevenson's frank admission of his bias implies what the book itself proves—that if not a downright eulogy it is an 'official' biography with all that that implies. How could he do otherwise? Mrs. Jenkin has put on record in her emotional way how Stevenson made notes of her recollections, arranged them and at their next interview read them over to her, making constant corrections in order to get down precisely what she wished to say. Here, of course, we see the practised writer and lifelong stylist who knew that it is easy to say something, but that the great difficulty is to know exactly what you wish to say and to say it so that the reader will understand just that and nothing more or less. This is another counsel of perfection but that he always strove for it is among his high merits as a writer. In this case, however, the method had its drawbacks, for he could not disappoint the mourning widow by printing anything that happened to turn up in the way of evidence suggesting a less admirable protagonist.

By undertaking this biography (which was not published until January 1888) Stevenson unconsciously demonstrated his versatility once more. The *Memoir of Fleeming Jenkin* has been differently estimated, usually passed over rather casually, while it can never have been anything but a dead weight on his popular reputation. As a biography the *Memoir* has considerable merits although, as the custom then was, page after page of undigested material from letters is given, with no attempt to weave them into the narrative. Stevenson was far too neat a workman to produce one of those higgledy-piggledy Victorian books which are not really biographies but collections of materials for biography, but though he selected he did not thoroughly incorporate. The fatal objection to the book is not to be found in the author's methods—which are a matter of opinion and may please some readers—but in the inescapable fact that not even Stevenson's brilliancy can make Professor Jenkin very interesting to those of another age who would never have heard of him but for his friendship with his biographer. Stevenson does his best, and is particularly good on Jenkin's parents and grandparents, and on such little traits as the family's getting 'so used to revolutions' during their 1848 travels on the Continent. But he leaves in Jenkin's own words the description of his experiences in laying ocean cables, and they do not interest like Robert Stevenson on his lighthouse. And in touching on his own relations with his subject Stevenson states rather than creates his character, and in the end leaves us pondering on the possible monstrosity of a person who was at one and the same time 'a Greek sophist, and a British schoolboy'. The mind boggles at so unprosperous a crasis, a contribution to the mythology of monsters which leaves Chimera in the realm of commonplace. 'The art of narrative,' says Stevenson very justly, 'in fact, is the same, whether it is applied to the selection and illustration of a real series of events or of an imaginary scene'; but neither, I think, has room for British schoolboys who are Greek sophists.

I take this quotation from *A Humble Remonstrance*, which was written at Bournemouth in answer to essays on fiction by Walter Besant and Henry James. Some of Stevenson's remarks reveal much more about him than about the art of fiction or child psychology. Talking of *Treasure Island* James had written (ironically) that he could not criticize the book because though he had been a child he had never been on a quest for buried treasure. On this Stevenson takes him up sharply:

> 'There has never been a child (unless Master James) but has hunted gold, and been a pirate, and a military commander, and a bandit of the mountains; but has fought, and suffered shipwreck and prison, and imbrued its little hands in gore, and gallantly retrieved the lost battle, and triumphantly protected innocence and beauty.'

While that statement is certainly true of Master Stevenson, it is quite untrue of children in general, at least of those whose education and early reading are supervised by persons of taste and judgment. The child Henry James—and quantities of other children—did not have a father who delighted in telling bedtime tales of blood and thunder, nor did he have a nurse who allowed him to revel in penny-dreadfuls, and cultivated his infant mind with pleasing fables of ghosts, corpses, body-snatchers, bloody martyrdoms and the like. Stevenson imagines that the exceptional (and censurable) circumstances of his own childhood were common to all children—a most gratuitous assumption. No doubt what he says is true of children as badly brought up as he was, but it is equally certain that James is right and it was not true of the children of the middle class in England and in New England. And again Stevenson is making a personal statement and hardly a valid generalization when he says:

> '. . . I believe, in a majority of cases, that the artist writes with more gusto and effect of those things he has only wished to do, than of those which he has done.'

This essay, with its defence of Stevenson's literary views and methods, was included in *Memories and Portraits* which together with *The Merry Men* and *Underwoods* made up his publications in book form during 1887. Before looking at them we must mention one of Stevenson's most remarkable and thoughtful essays which appeared in the *Contemporary Review* for April 1887

Robert Louis Stevenson and Fanny Stevenson (third from left. front) in Samoa with a group of Chiefs and their families.

[*To face p. 176*

Robert Louis Stevenson, his stepson, Lloyd Osbourne and McPherson.

John Poor—Postmaster, Mrs. Joe Strong, R.L.S., Lloyd Osbourne, Fanny Stevenson.

To face p. 177]

under the title *The Day After Tomorrow*, and never appeared in book form until after his death. Its theme was one rather popular towards the end of the nineteenth century, namely, a speculation as to the future of the world under the conditions of the obviously approaching Socialism. William Morris's *News from Nowhere* is a wish-fulfilment dream of a gifted poet-craftsman and aesthete who was passionately in love with a quite imaginary Middle Ages and deeply influenced by Marx as well as by Ruskin. There would be no machinery and no factories, everybody would be 'free' to work at what pleased him, there would be no money, everything you needed would be gratis, and the main object of society would be to get rid of ugly capitalist buildings and put up lovely Socialist ones of a pre-Raphaelite kind. There would be no war, and everyone would be happy. Oscar Wilde did rather better with his *Soul of Man under Socialism,* though his main theme is that Socialism far from making people drably similar and boringly equal would cause an immense outburst of individualism. In fact his Socialism would make the world the perfect habitat for Oscar Wildes just as Morris's Socialism would for William Morrises. Only in Wilde's Socialist world there is a great deal of machinery:

> '. . . so while Humanity will be amusing itself, or enjoying cultivated leisure—which, and not labour, is the aim of man—or making beautiful things, or simply contemplating the world with admiration and delight, machinery will be doing all the necessary and unpleasant work. . . . Scientific men . . . will have delightful leisure in which to devise wonderful and marvellous things for their own joy and the joy of every one else . . .'

. . . such as robots, mechanical memories, H-bombs, supersonic planes and radio-guided missiles capable of destroying and maiming hundreds of thousands at one blast.

Of course Morris and Wilde were quite right to denounce the evils of *laissez faire* industrialism and its slaves. Stevenson agrees over that:

> 'Freedom, to be desirable, involves kindness, wisdom and all the virtues of the free; but the free man as we have seen him in action has been, as of yore, only the master of many helots; and the slaves are still ill-fed, ill-clad, ill-taught, ill-housed, insolently treated, and driven to their mines and workshops by the lash of famine.'

This state of affairs is lamentable, says Stevenson, and will have to go—it is going, 'we are all becoming Socialists without knowing it'. He does not look for a bloody revolution in England—'we may rather look to see a peaceable and blindfold evolution, the work of dull men immersed in political tactics and dead to political results'. The change in fact will be made by Parliament which will make a 'new waggon-load of laws' . . . 'designed and administered (to put it courteously) with something short of inspiration'. And what will happen then?

> 'Well, this golden age of which we are speaking will be the golden age of officials. In all our concerns it will be their beloved duty to meddle, with what tact, with what obliging words, analogy will aid us to imagine. . . . The laws they will have to administer will be no clearer than those we know today, and the body that is to regulate their administration no wiser than the British Parliament. So that upon all hands we may look for a form of servitude most galling to the blood—servitude to many and changing masters, and for all the slights that accompany the rule of jack-in-office.'

Compared with Wilde's and Morris's foolish anticipations those sentences of Stevenson's reveal a sensible man with a statesman-like ability to foresee the inevitable results of Socialist legislation. What he shudders at as a dreadful threat is the state of affairs under which we live. Of course England is not yet so bad as the totalitarian Socialist states but it is moving that way with all the delightful inevitability of gradualness. Stevenson then goes on to consider what these officials will have to do or try to do:

> 'Man is an idle animal. He is at least as intelligent as the ant; but generations of advisers have in vain recommended him the ants' example. Of those found truly indefatigable in business, some are misers; some are the practisers of delightful industries, like gardening; some are students, artists, inventors, or discoverers, men lured forward by successive hopes; and the rest are those who live by games of skill or hazard—financiers, billiard-players, gamblers, and the like. But in unloved toils, even under the prick of necessity, no man is continually sedulous. Once eliminate the fear of starvation, once eliminate or bound the hope of riches, and we shall see plenty of skulking and malingering. Society will then be something not wholly unlike a cotton plantation in the old days; with cheerful, careless, demoralized slaves, with elected overseers, and, instead of the planter, a chaotic popular assembly.'

A more admirable description of France under a Socialist government could hardly be devised. It is exact, except that the 'careless, demoralized slaves' are always grumbling and seeking more carelessness and demoralization, by means of strikes and underhand political action. But Stevenson foresaw that too, for on a later page he says:

> 'Bread we suppose to be given amply; the cry for circuses will be the louder, and if the life of our descendants be such as we have conceived, there are two beloved pleasures on which they will be likely to fall back: the pleasures of intrigue and of sedition.'

Stevenson goes off the mark when he imagines that a system of communes (or soviets) would lead to a resumption of local warfare; but that is because he still unconsciously retained freedom and had not envisaged the immense tyranny of centralized Socialism. Yet his last words again have an awful ring of truth when he says that such a state of affairs 'irresistibly suggests the growth of military powers and the foundation of new empires'. Which is exactly what has happened—at the expense of the old empires. Certainly there are errors in this forecast, but the amazing thing is that seventy years ago Stevenson should have foreseen so much so clearly. After reading that article nobody can justly say that Stevenson was superficial or lacking a sense of reality. We must not exaggerate the importance of an article, but we may legitimately link the Stevenson who wrote it with the clear-sighted author of *The Amateur Emigrant* and the disreputable bohemian getting into conversation with characters in the streets and in 'howffs' and learning from such frequentations.

The Socialism article had only just been published when Stevenson was again upset by a death. For some years his father had been losing hold on life, and his mind wavered as physical energy failed. Outbreaks of irritation, such as the 'Hyde mood' referred to in Stevenson's letter to his mother, alternated with periods of pathetic almost submissive gentleness. At times he was the child and Robert Louis the man; and then, without losing this second childishness, Thomas Stevenson would treat his son as if he were a little boy again—anxious lest he should fall when he stood on a seat in the theatre, and comforting him with a good-night kiss and the promise 'you will see me in the morning, dearie'. After the weary years of fierce antagonism and battle between father and son such touching little scenes as these must have cut Robert Louis to the heart. It was dreadful to realize the tragedy that they had hurt each other so much simply because the love between them was so real. Stevenson was not a homosexual, but he had played about so much with women in his youth that he could not give himself entirely to a woman, and kept some of the best of himself for men. His relation to Fanny shows that, as Mr. Furnas most justly points out, it was more like a symbiosis than a marriage; and there are times when one stands a little aghast at suspecting that he really loved Lloyd more than Fanny. I doubt if even 'Cummy' and his mother meant as much to this rather feminine man as his father, and Henley, to whom he transferred some of his son-love when the older man's bigotry drove him penniless from shelter, in his poverty took the fugitive and nursed him.

In April, 1887, Stevenson's parents were with him in Bournemouth, but by a bitter irony of the romance of destiny the son was too sick to minister to the sicker father. As the dying often do, Thomas Stevenson longed to return to his own home, and was taken to Edinburgh on the 21st April in a special railway ambulance. A telegram brought Robert Louis and Fanny to Scotland on the 7th May, and the next day Thomas Stevenson died, still 'on his feet' but mentally so decayed that he did not recognize his own son. This would be a shock to any son, but particularly to one so self-centred as Stevenson who for so long had taken for granted that whether in good or ill repute he was chief in his father's heart and thoughts. He was horrified by the change:

> 'If we could have had my father, that would have been a different thing. But to keep that changeling—suffering changeling—any longer, could better none and nothing. Now he rests. . . .'

That is from a letter to Colvin, and later in the same letter Stevenson says:

> 'My favourite words in literature, my favourite scene—"O let him pass", Kent and Lear—was played for me here in the first moment of my return. I believe Shakespeare saw it with his own father. I had no words; but it was shocking to see.'

Robert Louis fell sick in Edinburgh and was not present at his father's grave, though he received the mourners as they came to Heriot Row for the funeral. Before *Memories and Portraits* went to press Stevenson had added to it a sketch of his father, a little in the style of Lamb, from which we may select these lines:

> 'He was a man of a somewhat antique strain; with a blended sternness and softness that was wholly Scottish, and at first somewhat bewildering; with a profound essential melancholy of disposition and (what often accompanies it) the most humorous geniality in company; shrewd and childish; passionately attached, passionately prejudiced; a man of many extremes, many faults of temper, and no very stable foothold for himself among life's troubles. Yet he was a wise adviser; many men, and these not inconsiderable, took counsel with him habitually.'

In so solemn a requiem Stevenson could not quote a remarkable instance of his father's unconquerable pessimism. He had had jaundice and insomnia, and kept his wife awake to share his miseries. At last one night both fell asleep, to her infinite relief no doubt; but she was speedily awakened to hear this awful communication: 'My dear, the end is now come; I have lost the power of speech.'

10

THE death of Thomas Stevenson broke the link which for so long had held Robert Louis almost imprisoned as an invalid in Bournemouth. If Fanny's (by no means wholly unfounded) dread of cholera had brought them back from the Continent, Louis's continued dependence on his father forced them to remain within the old man's orbit. Stevenson was now free to look for adventure, if he could only get well enough to enjoy it when he found it. He was not wholly disinherited as he so long expected, for Thomas Stevenson added a codicil to his will in 1883 which safeguarded Robert Louis's eventual rights. Thomas Stevenson was not anything like so wealthy as people believed. He left about £26,000; and about £3,000 went to Stevenson at once under his mother's marriage settlement, while she had a life interest in the estate. If he had continued to need money she would obviously have helped as generously as his father, but in fact Stevenson was able to offer to lend her £100, while with £3,000 to back him he should have felt free at last from financial worry. It is perhaps worth recording that one of the most admired and popular English authors of England's most prosperous epoch had to be subsidized until he was nearly thirty-seven.

Where was health, if not adventure, to be sought? At Edinburgh in the days following Thomas Stevenson's funeral, coincidence, if not the romance of destiny, came into action. Stevenson's doctor uncle, George Balfour, was not one of those who disapproved of the marriage to Fanny. 'I married a besom myself,' he told his nephew, 'and never regretted it.' Presumably that experience made him tactful in dealing with Fanny, whose hypochondriacal alarms he managed to sooth without offending her feelings. Probably he saw that Fanny wanted to return to America—at any rate, one of the places he advised for Louis's health was Colorado. Nearly seven years had passed since she had left her country and though her marriage had presumably made her officially a British subject, Lloyd was still an American citizen and was now nineteen—it was high time for him to see his native land again. At all events, a winter trip to Colorado at the expense of Stevenson's mother was planned for them all, and at her son's request she agreed to go with them.

Fanny was responsible for the practical arrangements of transport from London to New York, and had an eye to the picturesque but not much common sense; for after the party of Mrs. Stevenson, Fanny, Louis and Lloyd and the French maid got on board they discovered that the ship was to carry a cargo of 'monkeys, stallions, cows, matches, hay'. The ship rolled as abominably as it smelt. Poor Fanny! Not thus had that sociable but social climber envisaged her return home. Yet all the others enjoyed this singular trip, and Stevenson especially was cheerful, happy, and comparatively well until he caught a bad cold on the Newfoundland Banks. When the *Ludgate Hill* reached New York harbour it was boarded by enthusiastic adventurers, shouting: 'Stevenson ahoy!' In a flash the startled and now almost semi-professional emigrant was surrounded by reporters who learned with gratification—it was the silliest season of September—that the visiting fireman had an American wife and stepson, to both of whom he was sincerely devoted, and what is more had brought with him his own dear old 'Mom' complete with widow's cap. This was a welcome change from degenerate Continental authors who were usually accompanied by someone else's wife; and in a flash the intellectual public was put in possession of the most important facts. The correct pronunciation of 'Jekyll' is 'Jeekyl' and 'Mr. Stevenson has a classic head from which proceeds a hacking cough'. On landing the classic Mr. Stevenson went to bed, and refused all further interviewers except the inevitable Edinburgh Scot. 'My reception here was idiotic to the last degree,' Stevenson reported to Colvin, but confessed that 'the poor interviewer lads pleased' him.

And well they might, for the remarks Stevenson chose to regard as 'idiotic' were doing him real financial service. America might and did steal his books—it is always a pleasure to rob an artist—but was willing to make up for it and even to over-pay him if he would consent to become a magazine writer. For the first time in his life Louis Stevenson was offered more than adequate payment for writing. The *New York World* offered him 10,000 dollars for 52 weekly articles; McClure offered 8,000 dollars for the serial rights of his next book; and Scribner

3,500 dollars for twelve monthly articles. It is not strictly true to say that the Americans 'discovered' Stevenson as a writer, but they were certainly the first to offer to pay him handsomely. A compromise was effected, and Stevenson accepted the milder discipline of Scribner, but, most unfortunately, lacking the help of Baxter or Henley, did the unpardonable thing of promising his next serial rights to two publishers. Fortunately both were good fellows, and accepted his explanation that it was a blunder due to lack of practical experience.

On a visit to his friend, Fairchild, at Newport (R.I.) Stevenson again caught cold and spent most of his time in bed, though actually without a haemorrhage. This may account for the fact that the well-known bas-relief by Saint-Gaudens shows Stevenson smoking in bed, though it contrives to give him that air of dignified respectability which Henley afterwards so much deplored. But the family did not go on to Colorado for the winter as planned. An interesting letter to Bob Stevenson shows that the notion of a yachting cruise had seized Stevenson following the cattle-boat voyage which evidently had delighted him:

> 'I was so happy on board that ship, I could not have believed it possible. . . . I had literally forgotten what happiness was, and the full mind—full of external and physical things, not of cares and labours and rot about a fellow's behaviour. My heart literally sang. . . .'

Colvin dates that letter October 1887, and it was written, not from a sea port, but from the tuberculosis health resort of Saranac Lake in the Adirondacks. The idea of a yacht was not abandoned, but postponed under stress of ill health. Saranac is now quite a large place, very popular in summer as in winter, but its vogue started in 1882 when Dr. Trudeau started his famous sanatorium there. In 1887 it was still a small and rather primitive place and although Stevenson was under the care of this specialist the little house he lived in was not as comfortable as a Davos hotel. In the early part of his stay Stevenson had only Lloyd and Valentine Roch with him, as Fanny had gone to Indianapolis to see her family and Mrs. Stevenson went off on her own to view Niagara Falls. Saranac is only about 1,600 feet above sea-level (Davos is 5,200) but the intense winter cold later made Fanny ill and she had to leave.

Meanwhile the post from England brought Gleeson White's

anthology of ballades and rondeaux, with its warm dedication to R.L.S., and the reviews of his own *Underwoods*. Considering that Henley's contributions to the anthology number thirty and are the best poems in it, Stevenson's judgment that it is 'a ridiculous volume' was not very kindly or tactful, especially since he had tacitly admitted his inability to handle these complicated and delicate old forms with success by destroying his own efforts. *Underwoods* more than made up for this slip by bringing together the poems Stevenson had been writing and publishing in periodicals for years. Still, if you want to note the difference between a really accomplished master of verse and one less gifted, compare any of Henley's poems in ballade form with Stevenson's *To H. F. Brown*, which superficially looks like a ballade but is not, as Stevenson avoids all the real difficulties of the exact form. Even so, in comparison with Henley's work it is almost amateurish. The over-ardent Stevensonians who think of Henley as a blatant vulgarian and journalist forget that as a poet his work is far superior to Stevenson's.

Which is not to say that Stevenson's verse is without merit. Any man who has written even two or three poems worthy to stand in the English Anthology is more certain of qualified 'immortality' than the author of fifty novels and biographies. And Stevenson has done that. One of the best of his poems is not in *Underwoods*, and appeared as 'xv' in *Songs of Travel* (1895):

'In the highlands, in the country places,
Where the old plain men have rosy faces,
And the fair young maidens
Quiet eyes;
Where essential silence cheers and blesses,
And for ever in the hill-recesses
Her more lovely music
Broods and dies.

O to mount again where erst I haunted
Where the old red hills are bird-enchanted,
And the low green meadows
Bright with sward;
And when even dies, the million-tinted
And the night has come, and planets glinted
Lo, the valley hollow
Lamp-bestarred!

O to dream, O to awake and wander
There, and with delight to take and render,
Through the trance of silence,
Quiet breath;
Lo; for there, among the flowers and grasses
Only the mightier movement sounds and passes;
Only winds and rivers.
Life and death.

Once again it is Scotland remembered from far overseas, but a man who can write as good a poem as that on top of all the good work Stevenson did in other forms is entitled to praise. The later *Ballads*, which Stevenson himself liked so much, as authors often do like their weaker work, miss the elusive charm of his best lyrics and have little of his often superb narrative powers. On the other hand in *Underwoods* he announces Housman with such a quatrain as this:

It is the season now to go
About the country high and low,
Among the lilacs hand in hand
And two by two in fairyland.

Housman did it better, no doubt, but the tune is already there. *Requiem* and *The Celestial Surgeon* have been over-quoted and over-praised, and are rather evidence of the uncertainty of popular taste than of Stevenson's genius. Both are a little factitious, a little insincere. Stevenson himself has refuted the 'great task of happiness' fallacy both in his letters and in his essay on Socialism. On the other hand the truth, the good humour and sly satire of the neglected Scots pieces, such as *The Scotsman's Return* and *A Lowden Sabbath Morn*, are admirable and in Stevenson's best vein:

'The lasses, clean frae tap to taes,
Are busked in crunklin' underclaes;
The gartered hose, the weel-filled stays,
    The nakit shift,
A' bleached on bonny greens for days,
    An' white's the drift.

An' noo to face the kirkward mile:
The guidman's hat o' dacent style,
The blackit shoon we noo maun fyle
    As white's the miller:
A waefu' peety tae, to spile
    The warth o' siller.

Our Marg'et, aye sae keen to crack,
Douce-stappin' in the stoury track,
Her emeralt goun a' kiltit back
    Frae snawy coats,
White-ankled, leads the kirkward pack
    Wi' Dauvit Groats.

A thocht ahint, in runkled breeks,
A' spiled wi' lyin' by for weeks,
The guidman follows close, an' cleiks
    The sonsie missis;
His sarious face at aince bespeaks
    The day that this is.'

Burns showed him the way to do it, but to a Southron the whole poem seems a happy exercise in the great man's style. The English poems are often less successful when, to use his own phrase, he 'tootles on the sentimental flute', and most attractive when unabashed he takes the world as it is—witness these lines written at Hyères, a little in Marvell's vein, *To a Gardener*:

'Friend, in my mountain-side demesne,
My plain-beholding, rosy, green
And linnet-haunted garden-ground,
Let still the esculents abound.
Let first the onion flourish there,
Rose among roots, the maiden-fair,
Wine-scented and poetic soul
Of the capacious salad-bowl.
Let thyme the mountaineer (to dress
The tinier birds) and wading cress,
The lover of the shallow brook,
From all my plots and borders look.
Nor crisp and ruddy radish, nor
Pease-cods for the child's pinafore
Be lacking; nor of salad clan

The last and least that ever ran
About great nature's garden-beds.
Nor thence be missed the speary heads
Of artichoke; nor thence the bean
That gathered innocent and green
Outsavours the belauded pea.

In justice to the poet's gastronomic merits let it be recorded that these 'directions to a gardener' end with the pious but comfortable vignette:

And I, being provided thus,
Shall, with superb asparagus,
A book, a taper, and a cup
Of country wine, divinely sup.

It is not always recognized that to succeed in his art a poet must have either the temperament of a martyr or a secure and comfortable private income—if he cannot be Verlaine he may at least be Swinburne. Stevenson had neither, though the money his father spent in succouring fallen women in a Magdalen Home (in expiation perhaps of his son's little failings?) might have been more sympathetically dedicated to the Muse. As it was, Stevenson could only 'meditate the thankless Muse' in such brief respites as were allowed him by tuberculosis and the endless slogging at marketable prose. But he was right to do the best he could with the limited gift he had—we should be the poorer without these poems.

How did those poems sound to the writer if he read them in autumn sunlight or early snow up in that uncomfortable shack of the Adirondacks? Would it might have protected him from falling, mainly through sheer affection for Lloyd, into collaborating with the lad in a farce called eventually *The Wrong Box*. It was very much to the credit of Stevenson's heart that he gave the prestige of his name and reputation to try to launch his stepson as an author, though he himself described the tale as 'so silly, so gay, so absurd, in spots (to my partial eyes) so humorous. . . .' Alas, it is rather facetious than humorous, and rather crude than gay. The pro-Lloyd Stevensonians conceal the facts that McClure advised Stevenson (to his annoyance) not to let his name appear on it; while the editor of *Scribner* refused to buy it. It is amazing to find that there are 'critics' who depreciate *Olalla* and praise

The Wrong Box! Fortunately for us, Stevenson was better occupied during that winter, making his magazine articles into literature, and beating out the first scenes of *The Master of Ballantrae*. And every writer, especially a master writer, is to be judged on his achievements, not on his failures. Stevenson is not responsible for *The Wrong Box*. It was Lloyd's youthful indiscretion, and Stevenson wanted to help him and make it saleable by lending the book some of his style and his name.

Towards the end of this long winter at Saranac Lake Stevenson received a letter from Henley (dated 9th March, 1888) which caused him the most acute distress and virtually put an end to the deep friendship between them. It is a curious fact in Stevenson's life that he, who was far indeed from being a quarrelsome man, should have suffered so much from the two men he most loved—his father and Henley. But then it is those we love most who have most power to hurt us, and neither of those two men was sufficiently scrupulous in sparing Robert Louis's almost feminine susceptibility. Under stress of emotion, and particularly of a hurt from either of those two, the hysteria of his childhood, which Cummy's injudicious treatment had inflamed and Fanny's valetudinarian discipline had not lessened, could and did break out with most lamentable pain to him.

Is it possible, even now, to discuss this quarrel impartially? Three people mainly are involved, Stevenson, Henley and Fanny—for Katherine de Mattos was a mere pretext for war—and reading over the narratives, even the most recent, one cannot but be struck by the bias, mostly unconscious no doubt, for or against one or other of the parties involved. Amazing how much can be suggested by omission or by stress, by hinting motives and by half concealing testimony.

To begin with, we must recognize once again the antagonism between Henley and Fanny. As we have seen, this did not extend to Lloyd, who worshipped Henley next to Louis himself and was quite aware of his mother's faults. Henley resented, and not wholly without justification, what he considered the presumption and arrogance with which this 'semi-educated woman' imposed her censorship on his beloved Louis and his writings. Jestingly and affectionately Robert Louis himself called her in a dedication 'The Critic on the Hearth', but the question is whether by temperament, talent and culture she was really qualified for the task she discharged with such absence of misgiving? Henley thought not, and with growing irritation he watched his best friend yielding to Fanny's censorship with what Henley thought a subservience Stevenson had never yielded his intellectual peers. Nationalism came into it, and the imperialist jingo in Henley resented the American woman as he resented Louis's expatriation to America. This feeling was not limited to Henley, as McClure found when he visited England and naïvely complained of the 'jealousy of America' in Stevenson's friends—as if any country shows more jealousy of its expatriates than America, any country more tolerance than England! But undoubtedly in this case the prejudice was there. And it was not all prejudice. Stevenson had made many concessions in England for the sake of money, and his exultant accounts of the large sums he had been offered for journalism in America caused apprehension that he might be betraying his talent. Henley resented his beloved Louis being held 3,000 miles away with the strong possibility that the distance might be doubled. He wanted Louis to be within reach, and like most intellectuals in or near a metropolis thought that creative literature had not much chance beyond the outer suburbs of his own town. Fanny, on the other hand, resented Henley's influence over her husband and used fair and unfair means to discredit it. She was right in thinking that Henley's exuberance endangered Louis's health; she was wrong in thinking that he did not give more than he received in loyal devotion to his friend's literary and material interests. She contrived to forget when Henley drew on Louis for money that for years he had acted as unofficial agent, and in their necessity had given the two of them what money he had.

The actual *casus belli* derives from a lamentable small affair, of which one can only say that Fanny might have done otherwise and have done better. Bob Stevenson's sister, and Louis's cousin and playmate since childhood, Katherine de Mattos, was poor—and incidentally recommended to Louis's care in his father's will. She had some small literary gift, about as good as Fanny's—such people always tend to write when they are in the ambiance of a great author. She wrote a story about a meeting in a train with a girl who had escaped from a lunatic asylum. Fanny heard the story discussed and suggested the girl should be made a 'nixie', a water spirit; which Katherine rejected. In Henley's presence

Fanny suggested that as he had failed to place the story, she (Fanny) should take it and rewrite it; to which Katherine verbally agreed with a reluctance which both she and Henley evidently took to mean a more or less polite 'No'. In her domineering way Fanny took it to mean 'Yes', rewrote the tale using much of Katherine's original material, and had not much difficulty in selling it to *Scribner's* (March 1888)—to which her husband had just become a valued contributor on a salary! The unfairness is obvious, but might have been overlooked if Fanny had made some acknowledgement of her source and had sent Katherine half the money. She did neither.

Then, the romance of destiny so arranged affairs that Henley was in a particularly depressed and resentful state of mind when he read *Scribner's* with *The Nixie* by Fanny van de Grift Stevenson. On top of all this, he had lately heard that Stevenson and Lloyd had done the housework at Saranac Lake while Fanny and Valentine were ill in bed. He wrote a letter, marked 'Private and Confidential' which started thus:

> 'Dear Boy,
>
> If you will wash dishes and haunt back-kitchens in the lovely climate of the Eastern States, you must put up with the consequences. Very angry I was with you when I heard of it, and very glad I am to know that you got off so cheaply. That attack of *The Newcombes* is a distressing sympton, it is true, but no doubt you'll get over it in time. But no more dishes, meanwhile. 'Tis gay, 'tis romantic, 'tis bohemian, 'tis even useful and cleanly, but 'tis too desperate a delight to be often yours.'

After some joking about Stevenson's success and his taking out his M.A., Henley went on to say that he 'felt out of key' and quoted R.L.S. himself to the effect that life is 'uncommonly like rot'. 'Have you only just begun to find that out, O Poet of the *Counterblast*?' he asks, referring to one of the Scots poems in *Underwoods*, and proceeds:

> 'These three years past I've been entertaining the idea and it promises to master me. I've work in hand; I owe not more than a hundred pounds; I am beginning to make a reputation; my verse is printing, and promises well enough; other joys are in store, I believe; and I'd give the whole lot ten times over for—*enfin!* Life is un-common like rot. *C'est convenu.* If it weren't that I am a sort of

centre for a number of feebler folk than myself, I think I'd be shut of it dam soon.'

The letter goes on to speak of Henley's literary work which he felt had suffered because of the time he had to give up to journalism. Then came the passage about the *Nixie* story:

'I read *The Nixie* with considerable amazement. It's Katherine's; surely it's Katherine's? The situation, the environment, the principal figure—*voyons!* There are even reminiscences of phrase and imagery, parallel incidents—*que sais-je?* It is all better focused, no doubt; but I think it has lost as much (at least) as it has gained; and why there wasn't a double signature is what I've not been able to understand.'

He then turned to their play, *Deacon Brodie*, which Henley's actor-brother had put on in New York:

...'as you say, if the play has failed in New York, there's an end of it.

Lewis, dear lad, I am dam tired. The Châtelaine's away. The spring is spring no more. I am thirty-nine this year. I am dam, dam tired. What I want is the wings of a dove—a soiled dove, even!—that I might flee away and be at rest.

Don't show this to *anybody*, and when you write, don't do more than note it in a general way, if at all. By the time you *do* write, you will have forgot all about it, no doubt. But if you haven't, deal vaguely with my malady. I wish you were nearer. Why the devil do you go and bury yourself in that bloody country of dollars and spew? And you don't even get better. *C'est trop raide.* And you are 4,000 miles from your friends! *C'est vraiment trop fort.* However, I suppose you must be forgiven, for you have loved me much. Let us go on so till the end. You and I and Charles—D'A., and Porthos, and *le nommé* Aramis. 'Twas a blessed hour for all of us, that day 13 years syne, when old Stephen brought you into my back-kitchen, wasn't it? *Enfin—!* We have lived, we have loved, we have suffered; and the end is the best of all. Life is uncommon like rot; but it has been uncommon like something else, and that it will be so again—once again, dear!—is certain. Forgive this babble, and take care of yourself, and *burn this letter*. Your friend, W.E.H.'

The reference to the Nixie story must not be read quite apart from the rest of the letter, which is the writing of a tired, overwrought man out of spirits and depressed by the absence of his wife. It is affectionate in tone and unquestionably sincere. The arrival of *Scribner's* in London just as Henley was about to work off a fit of the dismals on his old friend was an evil little trick on

Robert Louis Stevenson at Vailima shortly before his death.

[*To face p. 192*

Vailima.

The inscription on the grave at the summit of Mount Vaea. In 1915 the ashes of Fanny Stevenson were brought from California and laid beside those of her husband.

To face p. 193]

the part of the romance of destiny. The 'Private and Confidential' obviously applies to the bulk of the letter confessing Henley's troubles and not merely to the Nixie. But why mention the Nixie at all? Well, he had just read it, and the thing was on his mind; and it is a matter of opinion whether the reference was meant merely to record what Henley thought a fact, or whether it was meant as a malicious stab at Stevenson through his wife. The Henley-Katherine version of the 'permission' given to Fanny always differed from that of the Stevensons. In other words, whatever they might say, Katherine's 'reluctant consent' was not meant to authorize and did not authorize Fanny to swipe the story, alter it a bit, and sell it as her own. At this date I should say it is quite impossible to determine who was right and who wrong—probably they were all a bit in the wrong, Fanny for acting in a high-handed, patronizing way, and Katherine and Henley for resenting it at the expense of the innocent Louis. And the plea in other parts of the letter might be paraphrased: 'For heaven's sake, why do you allow Fanny to boss you so completely, even to the extent of taking you from your friends and country, and shutting you away from the world in a dismal snow-bound village while you write journalism for her?' I should judge that gave quite as much offence as the Nixie reference.

Unfortunately, Henley was not the only man of letters who was sometimes over-worked and nervous, while such solitude as that of Saranac Lake was just the situation needed to inflame the susceptibilities of an over-sensitive man. What Henley in London looked on as just another example of Fanny's 'presumption and arrogance' struck Stevenson as a charge of theft of money and reputation. He had theoretically a very high ideal of honour, and at that time he must have been still feeling unhappy about his mistake in selling the same rights to two publishers, an error which might have been severely judged by men less generous and kindly than the two Americans. And then he went to Fanny, who was ill in bed, and very unwisely told her what Henley had written about the story. Her fury and resentment may be guessed from the absurdly pompous letter Stevenson was forced to write Henley in order to pacify her, beginning:

'My dear Henley,

I write with indescribable difficulty; and if not with perfect temper, you are to remember how very rarely a husband is expected to receive such accusations against his wife.'

And so forth. The letter is addressed to Henley but was meant for Fanny, and so perhaps Henley guessed. Unfortunately, a routine business letter from Henley's assistant editor of the *Art Journal*, written before Henley received Stevenson's letter, was interpreted as a slight, though in writing about that Stevenson added: 'I will say no more on any other matter; indeed I now somewhat regret my last.' What he wanted, of course, was to keep his old friend and persuade him through Baxter to write some kind of apologetic retraction which would appease Fanny. Henley was ready to be conciliatory, affectionate, and even apologetic, but he would not retract or tell what he thought a lie, as emerges from his letter of the 7th May, 1888:

'My dear Lad,

Your letter is heart-breaking; and I do not know how to reply to it, for it convicts me (I now see) of a piece of real unkindness, unworthy of myself and our old true friendship. You may blame me in the bitterest terms you will for the cruel blunder I made in opening my mind to you; and I shall not complain, for I deserve them all. I should, I know now, have said nothing; and I shall never cease from regretting that I gave you this useless, this unnecessary pain.

You must not believe, though, that I struck to hurt. I did not, I thought the matter one of little consequence. It seemed right that you should know how it looked to myself, and that there might well be the end of it. I was elbows deep in the business from the first, and I had (I thought) a right to make remarks. It was surely as well (I reasoned) that you should hear of certain coincidences from me as from another quarter. That I had any feeling of unfriendliness is what I want now explicitly to deny.'

On this letter Stevenson wrote in pencil:

'His original position carefully saved throughout; and yet (1) I gave him my word as to certain matters of fact; (2) and yet the letter (in consequence of this) can never be shown to my wife; (3) and yet, even if he still thinks as he did, I think a kind spirit would have even lied. R.L.S.'

The pathos of that is touching, and one cannot but pity the sufferings of the poor man torn between moral wild horses—the stern rectitude of Shepherd's Bush and the implacable wrath of Indianapolis. At that epoch Stevenson might have remembered the suffering caused when he himself refused as a matter of principle to lie to his father about his religious beliefs. And could Henley 'lie' sufficiently to satisfy Fanny without basely betraying Katherine de Mattos? There are some temperately worded but quite definite sentences in a letter from her to Stevenson showing that she did not accept his and Fanny's version of the affair:

> 'As Mr. Henley's very natural but unfortunate letter was written without my wish or knowledge, I have refused to let him go further in the matter. He had a perfect right to be astonished but his having said so has nothing to do with me. If Fanny thinks she has a right to the idea of the story I am far from wishing to reclaim or to criticize her in any way. . . . It is of course very unfortunate that my story was written first and read by people and if they express their astonishment it is a natural consequence and no fault of mine or any one else. . . . I trust this matter is not making you feel as ill as all of us.'

Short of a positive statement there could hardly be a more definite repudiation of the assertion that she had given Fanny permission to rewrite the story and to sell it as her own. To this Stevenson replied with a sermon which must have been hard to bear, ending up: 'I counsel you if you wish peace of mind, to do the right thing and to do it now', i.e. to admit that Fanny is right! In spite of which Katherine replied, like Touchstone, with an 'if':

> 'If I have failed to understand anything said to me at Bournemouth, or put a wrong construction on things, I am more grieved than ever, but I *cannot* say it has been intentional.'

It remained a deadlock, and unfortunately the person who suffered most acutely was Louis Stevenson.

Meanwhile, Fanny had recovered sufficiently to travel to San Francisco where she was occupied in trying to make arrangements for the proposed yacht voyage, while Stevenson and Lloyd moved down from the Adirondacks to Manasquan (N.J.) where he worked at his *Scribner* essays and at his share of *The Wrong Box*. His letters to her at this time are full of affection for her and of distress about Henley. What Fanny's mood and temper were may be judged by two extracts from her letters to Baxter from San Francisco. The first concerns some alterations to Louis

Stevenson's will by which Henley and Katherine were omitted but (Baxter's advice) an annuity was to be arranged for Katherine's child, while a little money (five pounds a month) was to be conveyed to Henley as coming from someone else. Fanny did not want an annuity to be paid from Thomas Stevenson's money to the daughter of Thomas Stevenson's niece; she was against 'new-fangled annuities' and thought money had best be doled out as she thought fit. She wrote:

'Already the hands that dealt me the cruellest blow are held out to be filled. . . . I am not likely to change in my feelings of resentment. The wrong can never be condoned, nor do I ever wish to see England again. It is most probable that I never shall. Every penny that goes to them, any of them, goes with my bitterest ill will.'

By this time six lines about Fanny's use or misuse of the Nixie story had become an international episode, and so it remained with a little touch of injured pathos in a letter written by her on the 29th May, 1888:

'As it is, they have nearly, perhaps quite, murdered him. It is very hard for me to keep on living! I may not be able to, but I must try to, for my dear Louis's sake. If I cannot, I leave my curse upon the murderers and slanderers. . . . I think it is almost better that we both out of such a world. I never go to bed now but I am tempted sorely by the morphia and the arsenic that stands by my bed.

. . . If it so happens that I must go back to perfidious Albion, I shall learn to be false. While they eat their bread from my hand—and, oh, they will do that—I shall smile, and wish it were poison that might wither their bodies as they have my heart.'

That is from the last letter in Charles Baxter's neatly kept dossier of this affair, and seems to need no comment. But to give Fanny the last word, as is only fair, we should remember what she wrote as late as the 20th July, 1893 (when she had forgotten all about the Nixie), in the diary which has lately been published (1956) under the title *Our Samoan Adventure*:

'I wish I were able to write a little tale that I might save some money of my own. I know that people speak about my [*eight words missing*]. I don't mind that so much, for there is such a blessing and pleasure in sharing anything in the [*about six words missing*]. All the money I have earned [*about eight words missing*] away to other people. Of the last I got twenty-five dollars out of a hundred and fifty, which I sent to my dying brother-in-law. I wonder what would become of a man, and to what he would degenerate, if his life was that of a woman's: to get the "run of her teeth" and presents of her clothes, and supposed to be always under bonds of the deepest gratitude for any further sums. I would work very hard to earn a couple of pounds a month, and I could easily earn much more, but there is my position as Louis's wife, therefore I cannot.'

II

On the 31st May, 1888, Stevenson, accompanied like a Highland chief with a 'tail' consisting of his mother, Lloyd and Valentine Roch again started on the trans-Continental train journey from New York to San Francisco, but this time not as an amateur emigrant but comfortable by Pullman. That was a good day in his life when he was able to turn his back on such petty disagreeables as this Nixie affair, which would not be worth discussing if it had not accidentally released such electric storms of emotion and, above all, so bedevilled the over-sensitive and innocent Stevenson. One could not say truthfully that his life thereafter was free from worries and annoyances, but those extra thousands of miles and then the thousands of Pacific miles did shelter him from importunities and jealousies, if only because sailing about the Pacific and working on his land at Vailima kept him in touch with realities more elemental and satisfying than the Savile Club and Henley's magazines. And seldom was the wisdom of a reckless act more justified than when Stevenson decided to spend two of the three thousand pounds he had inherited on hiring the yacht *Casco* for a seven months' voyage. Again, one could not say truthfully that his health thereafter was immune from sickness and haemorrhages, but the improvement was so great and the haemorrhages so few (mainly in Hawaii and Sydney) that the decision to risk his money on the cruise brought him back from semi-death to life. The statement in his letter about the voyage to America on the cattle-boat, that he had 'forgotten what happiness was', gives some measure of the release these last years were after the prison years of Bournemouth. Only against that background of suffering and deprivation can we realize the poignant gratitude and exultation of the words he wrote during his Pacific wanderings:

> 'It is like a fairy-story that I should have recovered liberty and strength, and should go round again among my fellow-men, boating, riding, bathing, toiling hard with a wood-knife in the forest.'

Contrast that with the vignette of the Stevenson of Skerryvore prudently watching his energetic wife gardening while he sheltered under a red parasol!

The comparative value of Stevenson's different books is naturally a matter mainly of personal opinion, so that one can hardly state categorically that this improvement in health and enjoyment of life was accompanied by a similar improvement in his writing. Some think so, and others do not. We may at least note that these last years produced *The Master of Ballantrae*, which was started at Saranac Lake; *Catriona*, the sequel to *Kidnapped*; the unfinished *Weir of Hermiston*, which many enthusiastic readers of Stevenson think his best book; *Island Nights' Entertainment*, which includes the *Beach of Falesà* and *The Bottle Imp*; many of the *Songs of Travel* which some judges rate as about the best of his poems; and such inspired pot-boilers as *St. Ives*, *The Wrecker* and *The Ebb Tide*. *The Wrecker* achieved its object so successfully that Stevenson and Lloyd received 15,000 dollars for the American serial rights. And on top of all that we have the various writings which came out of his voyages and residence 'in the South Seas', including the many letters to his friends. Taking into account all the varied work Stevenson had achieved before he set sail in the *Casco* nobody can deny that this is a very impressive record. Oscar Wilde's jest that 'genius revolves in a cycle of masterpieces' is unfortunately not true, as his own work shows. And Stevenson combined amazing fertility of invention with a restlessness and change of purpose which sometimes led him astray. I don't mean that he lacked the grit and perseverance to stick at a long book, because he most undeniably did finish long books. But he often dropped one piece of work for another, took it up again and then once more dropped it. He was not a slow worker, in the sense of turning out very little during each day's stint, but he was very fastidious, scrapped, and rewrote continually. Of course we cannot know what we lost through his sudden and comparatively early death. Such fragmentary pieces as *The Young Chevalier* and *Heathercoat* might have been put aside for years, then once more taken up, totally reconstructed and re-created and made into masterpieces, as had happened with other work. It is a very lucky or rather very gifted writer who can turn out two such world successes as *Treasure Island* and *Dr. Jekyll* with comparatively so little time lost on false trails.

While fully realizing the great improvement in Stevenson's life resulting from this change, we must be careful not to make the error of supposing that it was all cheerfulness and rapturous discovery and 'success'. By the time when the Stevenson party sailed from San Francisco in the *Casco* he had already a large 'public' of readers. The 'public' always tend to idealize a writer who has managed to please them, and they generally do this by insisting that he is very much like what they erroneously imagine themselves to be—a rather gallant and faultless person of singular merit liable to strange neglect but on the whole bound to succeed and be happy ever after in the long run. Through no fault of his own the excellent Stevenson unconsciously fitted himself for the part of embodying the frustrated hopes and desires of a sedentary and sentimental population. In those days very few people knew anything at first hand about the Pacific islands, and the fact that they were then inaccessible to ordinary persons strengthened the myth that they were so many earthly paradises inhabited by delightful 'natives', who were so grateful for a little notice from their white superiors that the women eagerly huddled into decorous and becoming mother hubbards and the men transformed themselves into industrious household 'boys'. Some of these idealists who happened to have more money than was good for them followed in the great artist's wake, and produced those 'With Stevenson . . .' books of which Fanny complains so bitterly. As Edmund Gosse wrote:

> 'Since Byron was in Greece, nothing has appealed to the ordinary literary man so much as that you should be living in the South Seas.'

By 'literary man' Sir Edmund almost certainly meant 'reader', but whether he did or did not, such was the fact. But why sailing about the Pacific in a yacht and trading-schooners and building a home at Vailima should have been thought in any way comparable to dying for Greece at Missolonghi would be a complete mystery, if we did not know the curious process by which a hero's admirers admit him to their private Valhalla.

At all events, even the first and very expensive (2,000 pounds) cruise on the *Casco* had its little rubs and troubles, and some which might have been very big ones. Rightly or wrongly Stevenson thought the *Casco*, which had been used as a racing yacht, 'was over-rigged and over-sparred' which her skipper,

Captain Otis, at a later date strongly denied. Obviously Stevenson was not an expert, though he had sailed in yachts in the dangerous Scottish seas, and nobody will deny that the Americans are supremely skilful in the building and sailing of yachts. (Ask the shade of Thomas Lipton!) But the fact that Stevenson had this misgiving must have detracted greatly from his enjoyment after he found out that the 'South Seas' are embittered by ferocious squalls and that navigation among ill-charted islands and coral reefs was the reverse of comfortable.

These innocents abroad must have taken on trust the sea-worthiness of the yacht, since it is impossible that an examination by Lloyd's agent would have failed to disclose that the *Casco*'s masts were affected by dry-rot! This was luckily discovered by Captain Otis in time, but obviously the yacht and all hands would have been lost if one of the masts had snapped when they were on a lee-shore or in the flurry of a bad squall.

Captain Otis started the voyage with a complete contempt for his passengers and employers, which seems to have been not uncommon among maritime gentlemen. Logan Pearsall Smith has recorded a Mediterranean voyage he made on a yacht belonging to his distinguished countrywoman, Edith Wharton. The skipper of this yacht had such a contempt for his employer and her friends that whenever they wanted to land he sent them off in a shore boat! Stevenson of course knew too much about the sea and had too much spirit to endure such a deadly insult from any skipper, but he had difficulties. Fanny and Valentine were bad sailors. Dead-lights were left open, and the yacht shipped water in squalls. Then Fanny had a fit of 'democracy' which consisted in breaking an elementary law of ship's discipline by talking to the steersman on duty. This brought down on her a scathing sarcasm from Otis, under which even she cringed and retired. Only Stevenson and his mother got their sea-legs, and the old lady kept the red duster flying by beating the Captain at whist. Later, it is said, they became good friends. Let us hope so. But all these trifles must have been flies in the ointment of Stevenson's bliss especially in the early days of at last sailing in his own yacht on the high seas in quest of adventure.

One result of the immense popularity of these Pacific experiences is that we have a quite overwhelming amount of literary material about them, more, I should say, that for all the rest of

Stevenson's life in spite of the fact that Scottish clannishness has collected every available scrap of relevant and irrelevant reminiscence about his early life. Hagiography is a ruthless pseudo-science. Stevenson himself has left a disproportionately large amount of writing on the period. *In The South Seas* deals with the Marquesas, the Paumotus and the Gilberts, yet the book must be about 120,000 words—on top of which we have *A Footnote to History*, the political letters to London periodicals, the Damien pamphlet, and all the letters including of course the Vailima letters to Colvin. I haven't worked it out, but I should guess they must have run to about a quarter of a million words. We have two volumes of letter-journals from Stevenson's mother ('Aunt Maggie' as she was called in the family); Fanny's certainly expurgated *Cruise of the 'Janet Nichol'* and fortunately restored-from-expurgation diary of life at Vailima. There are Lloyd Osbourne's notes, Graham Balfour's first-hand reminiscences in the official 'Life', Belle's 'memories' (in collaboration with her brother) and even a *Reader's Digest* 'unforgettable character' by Austin Strong who was still a schoolboy when R.L.S. died. As to the host of 'With Stevenson' books, I think personally that by the American trader, H. J. Moors, is the most honest and interesting, in spite of some minor errors and a possible bias against Fanny and Belle. It is quite impossible in a short book to digest all that into a few pages—the detail cannot be summarized. Those who want to study those years in anything like fullness must go to the originals.

They were thirty days out from San Francisco when they made their first landfall at Nuka-hiva in the Marquesas on the 28th July, 1888. That simple statement brings up another drawback, not merely to the *Casco*'s but to all these ocean cruises. In addition to being a bad sailor Fanny, so she wrote Mrs. Sitwell, feared and hated the sea and was in addition bored by ship life. Here was another unavoidable incompatibility of physique and temperament in this ménage, for the snow mountains and particularly the sea which were life to Stevenson were a misery to his wife. Possibly the 'hating and fearing the sea' belongs to Fanny's store of energetic over-statements, but references in her husband's letters show that she was always the least contented of the party until they reached land. Stevenson fancifully explained that his love of sailing and the health it brought him were 'inherited' from his grandfather, whereas the love of the sea at any rate much more probably came from hearing so much about it as a child and from being taken on the lighthouse yachts. Fanny, on the other hand, had spent her early life inland and knew and cared nothing about the sea. She was, as her husband told her, 'a peasant', and the fact that her outraged vanity could not forget this wound for days is some indication of its truth. The settling in Samoa was clearly a compromise between the seaman and the peasant.

Stevenson opens his *In The South Seas* with the now famous description of this landfall which shows him all agog to become 'one of the bondslaves of the isles of Vivien', though in fact this was one of the only two places where they were received with hostility in all their voyagings—and that surely arose from a misunderstanding, for the Marquesans knew nothing of pleasure yachts, and were offended when the *Casco* had no trade to offer. In spite of the hostility they went ashore and remained until the 22nd of August. The 'Stevenson charm' came into action, and friendship was soon established. When they moved on to the neighbouring island of Hiva-hoa they went through the ceremony of being adopted into a native family. Stevenson's method of getting on terms and extracting information about beliefs and customs is too characteristic to pass over. From what he had read about the Islands before sailing he assumed that they were in somewhat the same state as his own Scottish Highlands in the eighteenth century, and to draw the information he wanted he would begin by telling them some tale of his own country: 'Michael Scott, Lord Derwentwater's head, the second-sight, the Walter Kelpie, each of these I found to be a killing bait'. Who but Stevenson would have had the imagination to fish for Oceanic folk-lore with bait from the Hebrides or have the rare but necessary skill in telling tales? Hearers have testified that Stevenson's telling of a story was even more fascinating than his writing of it, and this is doubtless one of the marks of the born novelist, as distinct from the man of letters who can turn out novels. The latter are almost certainly doomed to extinction, for the story must live before style can preserve it.

When they left Taahauku for the Paumotus on the 4th September Stevenson already was filling notebooks with 'serious observations' on every aspect of island life. They spent two weeks at Fakarava and then proceeded to Tahiti, where the newly-gained health was suddenly attacked by cough and a 'fever'. He became so ill that he had to be moved to Taravao and then to Tautira, where they were succoured by that princess Moë who has been celebrated by Pierre Loti. It was now that Captain Otis found that the *Casco*'s masts were attacked by dry-rot, and the Stevenson party were practically marooned for weeks while they were repaired. Fortunately, with his amazing resilience, Stevenson soon recovered, and so well that he bathed in the sea nearly every day and almost completed *The Master of Ballantrae*. They lodged with a local chief, Ori, who exchanged names with his guest, Stevenson becoming Teriitera, and Ori 'Rui' the nearest to 'Louis' the island speech could compass. This was a happy time, though the long absence of the *Casco* reduced them to penury, which might have meant famine but for 'Rui' who fed them and took a hazardous sea trip to bring them supplies and money. When at last the *Casco* turned up it was Christmas, so nearly three months of the yacht's use had been lost; and their voyage north to Hawaii was so unprosperous that they were posted as overdue, and people in Honolulu ceased to mention the ship's name to Mrs. Strong, Belle, Fanny's daughter, who was expecting them. They did not come into port until the end of January, and they remained in Honolulu until June.

When Stevenson had time to reflect after paying-off the *Casco* he began to see that the venture had been recklessly extravagant. Two thousand pounds for seven months' use of a yacht, which was out of commission with rotten masts for three of them, was a very stiff price even though it included the services of a surly captain and a crew of sea-lawyers. I should say that Stevenson was taken for a ride by the owner. True, he recovered health, he was able to go ashore where he wanted for the first three months, and he collected material for his work. But surely all this could have been done less dangerously and far less expensively by shipping on trading schooners? Stevenson wrote to his publisher E. L. Burlinghame:

> 'As far as regards interests and material, the fortune has been admirable; as far as regards times, money, and impediments of all kinds, from squalls and calms to rotten masts and sprung spars, simply detestable.'

As late as the 6th October, 1888, a letter in Scots to Baxter shows that he was still at that time unhappy about captain and crew, and he only saw them again on the voyage up to Honolulu. And in February 1889 he wrote his cousin Bob:

> 'But, second (what I own I never considered till too late), there was the danger of collisions, of damages, and heavy repairs, of disablement, towing, and salvage; indeed, the cruise might have turned round and cost me double. Nor will this danger be quite over till I hear the yacht is in San Francisco. . . .'

If Fanny ever was 'a good manager' she certainly did not show it in this transaction; and, as we shall see, a similar reckless extravagance prevailed in the building of Vailima. On the other hand, in spite of various quibblings about the terms in which she made her protest, Fanny was quite right to oppose Stevenson over the matter and manner of the 'Letters' he was to write for McClure and the *New York Sun*—letters which were mainly intended to replace as much as possible of the capital spent on the *Casco* and subsequent voyages. Here is what she wrote to Colvin from Honolulu on the 21st May, 1889:

> 'He has taken into his Scotch Stevenson head, that a stern duty lies before him, and that his book must be a sort of scientific and historical impersonal thing, comparing the different languages (of which he knows nothing, really) and the different peoples, the object being to settle the question as to whether they are of common Malay origin or not. . . . Think of a small treatise on the Polynesian races being offered to a people who are dying to hear about Ori a Ori, the making of brothers with cannibals, the strange stories they told, and the extraordinary adventures that befell us. . . .'

Now, this programme (which, by the way, was also to include a perilous comparison of Protestant and Catholic missions) might indeed have produced a valuable book of a serious kind, supposing Stevenson possessed the full and accurate knowledge necessary to write it, which at that epoch seems a little doubtful. But this sort of thing was not what the readers of even a high-class newspaper like the *New York Sun* wanted to hear about from Stevenson. They wanted to hear of his adventures, not of his theories:

> '. . . of most disastrous chances,
> Of moving accidents by flood and field,

> Of hair-breadth 'scapes i' the imminent deadly breach,
> Of being taken by the insolent foe,
> And sold to slavery, of my redemption thence,
> And portance in my travels' history:
> Wherein of antres vast and deserts idle,
> Rough quarries, rocks, and hills whose heads touch heaven . . .
> And of the Cannibals that each other eat,
> The Anthropophagi, and men whose heads
> Do grow beneath their shoulders.'

It was a strange perversity in Stevenson to want to play the sober historian when the reading world was longing to hear the traveller's tales he alone could furnish with such incomparable zest and charm. Would *Treasure Island* have delighted the world if he had made it a scientific history of buccaneers and the slave trade? *A Footnote to History* is proof that Stevenson could write a valid book on such a theme as the contemporary history of Samoa. But he didn't hope to run it as a serial in a newspaper. Unluckily, the joint influences of Fanny and Colvin resulted in a hybrid book, and *In The South Seas* for all its fine qualities fails to be either a serious work of observation or a fascinating travel book. After thirty-four numbers, the *Sun* refused to continue publication. Too late Stevenson wrote the fascinating chapters on Apemama and its king, which stand high among his many great achievements. In her letter Fanny twice regrets that he is being 'impersonal'. By that she meant no attack on 'objectivity', but that Louis's 'Letters' should deal with persons and not with abstractions, politics and religious sects. Even more far-fetched is the inference that since she had not objected earlier to his attempts on the history of the Highlands, her objection to the history of Pacific Isles implies that Stevenson had now reached a maturity which took him out of her orbit. In each case it was a matter of common sense and cash. The Highland history pleased Thomas Stevenson who was then the provider. The romance of destiny and not history was needed to please the new and generous paymaster, the Public. It is not at all hard to agree with Fanny here that trying to deal with a man of genius is like managing an overbred horse.

One extraordinary result of all this is that Fanny's diary and even Mrs. Stevenson's placid old-lady letters sometimes have more readable news and gossip of a human kind in them than many parts of *In The South Seas*, though of course the master-scribe's hand is visible in every paragraph. If that sounds 'daft', as Stevenson would say, I can only suggest that the reader makes the comparison; and in any case this does not apply to the two sections on the Gilbert Islands which are so absorbing that one can understand why Conrad preferred them to *Treasure Island*.

In May 1889 Stevenson made his visit to the settlement of segregated lepers at Molokai. Why did he make this visit which caused him acute mental suffering, since, as he wrote his wife, his 'horror of the horrible' was about his 'weakest point'? I do not think it was mere reporter's quest for copy. We have to admit that Stevenson was rather egocentric, that he did frequently dramatize himself, and that he did consciously seek experiences in order to use them in his writings. I should say that is characteristic of many writers, particularly of the 'subjective-romantic' kind. What is far less characteristic is Stevenson's compassion and generosity, his pity for helpless suffering and instant impulse to give help. In April Stevenson had visited the Kona Coast of Hawaii, and had been overwhelmed by the sight of a leper girl under arrest waiting to be deported to Molokai along with the mother who volunteered to go with her but without any certainty of being allowed to remain. Stevenson could do nothing to change this situation, but he could and did give money in the hope of alleviating it. What made the separation so agonizing was the extreme family love of the Hawaiians which, like that of southern Europeans, puts the family and even friends above respect for the law or the interests of the State. We, who are somewhat over-furnished with Roman fathers and Spartan mothers, may reprehend but cannot remain unmoved. Stevenson was deeply moved by the collective grief and lamentation at the partings, though he tries to jest it off by saying: 'we miss in our modern life these operatic consolations of the past'. Having seen and suffered the departure he would not spare himself the distress and upset of the settlement, where he spent a week 'hag-ridden by horrid sights, but really inspired with the sight of so much goodness in the helpless and so much courage and unconsciousness in the sick'.

From the Sisters and others in the island settlement Stevenson heard about the Belgian, Father Damien, who had died the previous April from leprosy contracted while tending the sick. He wrote to Colvin:

'Of old Damien, whose weaknesses and worse perhaps I heard fully, I think only the more. It was a European peasant: dirty, bigoted, untruthful, unwise, tricky, but superb with generosity, residual candour and fundamental good humour . . . a man, with all the grime and paltriness of mankind, but a saint and hero all the more for that.'

Here was a character after Stevenson's own heart, and it is one more lovable trait in him that he became for all his life a fanatical supporter of Damien's memory, though he knew nothing about him at first-hand. And in February, 1890, when Stevenson was in Sydney, he read in the *Presbyterian* a letter about Damien written by the Rev. C. M. Hyde (predestined name!) who said that the Catholic was: 'a coarse, dirty man, headstrong and bigoted. He was not sent to Molokai, but went there without orders. . . . He was not a pure man in his relations with women, and the leprosy of which he died should be attributed to his vices and carelessness. Others have done much for the lepers, our own ministers, the government physicians and so forth, but never with the Catholic idea of meriting eternal life.'

This, on the face of it, does not look so unlike what Stevenson himself had written in his letters, particularly since his remarks had included these words:

'. . . my sympathies flow never with so much difficulty as towards Catholic virtues. The passbook kept with heaven stirs me to anger and laughter. One of the Sisters calls the place "the ticket-office to heaven".'

Why then the tremendous moral indignation and invective of Stevenson's famous pamphlet? Well, among Stevenson's endearing traits is a streak of the Knight of La Mancha's character which shows itself in a propensity to become inflamed with chivalrous emotions about matters of public interest. Fired by moral indignation and patriotism Stevenson had wished to publish pamphlets on such topics as Majuba Hill and the death of General Gordon, about which he knew nothing but what he read in newspapers. In 1887 he had planned to rent and inhabit with his family an Irish farm which was under boycott, as a protest against the violence of the Moonlighters. By doing this he imagined he would be courting martyrdom for himself and the heroic family who had accompanied him, but as his biographer J. A. Steuart says drily:

'I lived five years in Ireland, and from actual observation knew something of the matters which agitated Stevenson. His presence in Kerry in the character of martyr would have provoked nothing deadlier than derision.'

The fury over Dr. Hyde's letter seems the more curious since many of its phrases and those in Stevenson's own letters might be interchanged. It is said that Stevenson feared that Dr. Hyde's letter would prevent the setting up of a public memorial to Damien. The fact is that for some reason Don Luis Roberto de la Mancha was ready for another attack on windmills, and thirsting for martyrdom. He knew his sizzling pamphlet was libellous, and once again, as over the Irish farm, Fanny and Lloyd professed their willingness to die—or least pay heavy damages—with him. Stevenson later admitted that his pamphlet was 'barbarously harsh' and again that 'it was virtuous to defend Damien; but it was harsh to strike so hard at Dr. Hyde'. Indeed. The fact is that Dr. Hyde's letter, however unjust and bigoted, was a private one and never intended by him for publication. In the event Stevenson upset himself more than his antagonist, since he passed several agitated months awaiting a suit for libel which he would certainly have lost; and Dr. Hyde 'contented himself with the remark that his assailant was a 'bohemian crank', a 'negligible person whose opinion signified nothing'. This was not true either, but once again the romance of destiny rescued Stevenson from a situation which might have been both unpleasant and crippling—a verdict in Hyde's favour would have turned against Stevenson the power of the whole venal and gutter presses. But, after all, Damien died in trying to minister to the lepers, while, if Stevenson is right, his Presbyterian critic never saw the leper island and lived most comfortably in Honolulu.

Perhaps we may note here a little fact which is usually overlooked. The editor who took the risk of publishing the Damien pamphlet in England, within a few weeks of its private publication in Sydney, was that bad friend and feckless Micawber, W. E. Henley (*Scots Observer*, 3rd and 10th May, 1890). Prosecution would have ruined him.

Meanwhile, on the 24th of June, 1889, the party sailed on a second cruise, in the American trading schooner, *Equator*; but it was a party reduced in numbers. Mrs. Stevenson, who seemingly had greatly enjoyed her life in Honolulu, went off to Scotland in

May; and Valentine Roch left them to go to California where she married. Their vacant places were filled by Ah Fu, a Chinese cook, and Joe Strong, the husband of Belle who was sent to Sydney with her child to wait for them. The main object of the cruise from Stevenson's point of view was to increase his knowledge of the Pacific islands by visiting the Gilberts and Samoa, of which last he had heard much in Honolulu. In the Gilberts he was moving out of Polynesia and making acquaintance with Micronesians. The first experience was not altogether reassuring, and at Butaritari on Makin Island the party were in much greater danger than at Nuka-hiva. It is a pure coincidence that hostility in each island group occurred only at the first contact. This was not due to any ignorance or clumsiness on the part of the visitors. Butaritari was much under American influence though not under responsible American administration—the missionaries, and the traders keeping stores, were mostly American. On the 4th of July the local king, Tebureimoa, had unwisely lifted the taboo on alcohol, and when the Stevenson party arrived they found that most of the islanders including the king had been drunk for ten days, while the king refused to restore the taboo. The situation certainly looked threatening, especially since a good many of the inhabitants had fire-arms and Stevenson on two occasions was narrowly missed by large stones thrown as he sat on the veranda at dusk. By way of a counter demonstration they practised ostentatiously revolver shooting at bottles on the beach. This unpleasant state of affairs lasted another ten days, with the king refusing the taboo, the rival traders unwilling to stop making money, and drunkards firing shots at night. At last a deputation, headed by one of the traders' wives as speaker, threatened the king with a British warship to avenge any insult or injury to Queen Victoria's son, Mr. Stevenson, the taboo was restored, and 'din' and 'peranti' ceased to be on sale.

In his public-spirited way Stevenson helped to draw up a petition to the United States government for 'a law against the liquor trade in the Gilberts', adding a signed personal report on what had happened. This early lobby for local prohibition was neither acknowledged nor acted on.

Here was good copy for his Pacific Letters, and Stevenson handled it admirably, but unfortunately the serial publication was discontinued before he got to this point. He did still better with his next stopping place, Apemama, and its tyrant king, Tembinoka, who took a fancy to Stevenson which was quite reciprocated. A dictator who took to himself the whole copra trade of the kingdom, who summoned his subjects to work by firing his rifle in the air and if any dared to disobey instantly fired at the culprit to kill, who robbed his own wives by cheating them at cards, was clearly more picturesque than a palaver hut full of wrangling Old Men of Makin who were probably as silly as they were old. Besides, the friendship and protection of such an autocrat added much—everything—to the security, comfort and prestige of the visiting fireman. No wonder Stevenson cultivated him, and rejoiced in the increase of favour he won by prescribing bicarbonate of soda for the uneasiness suffered by the tyrant after several days of gin-drinking on a visiting schooner. Even so there was some nervousness, for just as the party were privately discussing the possible danger of a revolution if the king kept up this debauch, they were startled by the crack of a rifle shot. It was, however, only the king dealing with a dog which had thoughtlessly invaded the precincts of his crone-guarded palace. He must have been a good shot since apparently he only hit those he wanted to shoot. All this Stevenson dealt with admirably and vividly, and the tale and character of Tembinoka rate high in his literary achievement. All the same it is hardly surprising to find Stevenson making this report to his mother just before they reached Samoa in December:

> 'Fanny has stood the hardships of this rough cruise wonderfully; but I do not think I could enforce her to another of the same. I've been first rate, though I am now done for lack of green food. Joe is, I fear, really ill; and Lloyd has bad sores on his leg.'

When Stevenson arrived in Samoa he had no intention whatever of settling there. He did not particularly like the place, and stayed in Apia solely for the purpose of collecting information for his account of the late 'war' which was intended as the final section of *In The South Seas*. Eventually this section became a separate book, *A Footnote to History*, which is redeemed from the ennui of petty local affairs by the masterly chapter on the hurricane at Apia. When his work was completed—it was still intended as Letters for the *New York Sun*—he planned to be back in England about June 1890, travelling by way of Sydney, Ceylon, Suez and

Marseille. On the 2nd December 1890 he wrote to Colvin: 'I am minded not to stay very long in Samoa. . . .' Only seven weeks later he wrote Lady Taylor that he was 'the owner of an estate upon Upolu, some two or three miles above Apia' (Vailima, of course) and that he would come to England 'to break up my establishment'. In the end, he sent Lloyd to do this for him, and never saw England again.

Why this sudden change of plans, and the determination to bind himself to Samoa with a home and property? I think I have read most of the accounts, from Stevenson's own letters to the recollections of H. J. Moors, the prosperous American trader with whom Stevenson lodged at Apia and with whose help and financial aid Stevenson bought the land and eventually built his home. And none of them really explains this sudden but definitive resolve to settle, especially since at the start of the *Equator* voyage he had planned to write the book which became *The Wrecker* in order to buy a trading schooner of his own, and to travel continually around the islands selling and buying with Lloyd under the appropriate trade name of Jekyll, Hyde and Co.

Fanny, no doubt, had much to do with the decision. In contradiction to what he wrote his mother, Stevenson wrote Lady Taylor: 'My wife suffered a good deal in our last, somewhat arduous voyage. . . .' It is true that she did later go with him on the *Janet Nicholl*, but that was a steamer, not a small sailing schooner. And what she really enjoyed was arranging and bossing a household, and growing things, fruits and vegetables in preference to flowers. They had talked at one time of making a winter home in Madeira, but experience had shown that Louis was only well when cruising in warm seas or living close to the equator. That situation might have suggested the compromise of a home in the South Seas, as between perpetual cruising and a return to any colder climate. There were minor objections to Samoa, and there were the major ones that it was exposed to hurricanes, was in a disturbed political situation of the natives which might and did lead to head-hunting skirmishes and disorders dignified as 'war', with a tri-consular régime of Germany, U.S.A. and England; all of which led Stevenson into a morass of petty local politics he took most seriously and wasted much time and ink on. But the climate suited his health, and there was the most important consideration for a professional writer that the mail service was nearly as good in Samoa as in Hawaii and certainly better than in any other of the island groups. Here is the account by H. J. Moors, the man who was most closely connected with the whole business:

> 'At last one day Stevenson told me he would like to make his home in Samoa permanently. "I like this place better than any I have seen in the Pacific," he said. He had been to Honolulu, and liked it; Tahiti and the Marquesas had pleased him; but of all places he liked Samoa the best. "Honolulu's good—very good," he added, "but this seems more savage!"
>
> 'I laughed, but understood. "Then," said I, "as you can't live in Scotland, in France, or in the States, and as there's more of the savage in you than Honolulu can satisfy, why not pitch your camp near the capital of Samoa?"
>
> 'Beyond a little desultory conversation on the subject, he said they had not seriously discussed it. He promised, however, that the matter should be decided without much delay. As soon as the decision was reached, he hastened to inform me, and we shook hands on it. "Barkis is willin'," he said—and "Barkis" stood for "Fanny".
>
> 'He now asked me to look out for a nice piece of property that would suit him. Money matters seemed to trouble him, however—not so much the first cost of the land, but the cost of the improvements that would necessarily have to follow. Finally, after several fine properties had been submitted to him for inspection, he decided that the Vailima land was the most attractive. At his request I negotiated the purchase. There were four hundred acres, and I paid 4,000 dollars.'

This tells us what happened, but not why it happened. Probably, Stevenson did not quite know himself why he so suddenly made this important decision. His life shows more than one occasion when on a sudden impulse he committed himself to a serious determination and stuck to it. We may think of his resolve to marry Fanny at all costs, although she was a married woman with children at the time; and his reckless paying away of £2,000 for the *Casco*, purely on impulse. At all events, when he authorized Moors to buy that Samoa land in January 1890 he made a decision which bound him, in spite of some future sea excursions, to Samoa for the rest of his life.

12

To buy an estate in Samoa and then leave almost immediately for Sydney looks like a typical piece of Stevensonian fantasy and restlessness; but as a matter of fact there were perfectly sensible reasons for the move. There was not even a hut on the land they had bought, and the dense second-growth jungle and big trees had to be cleared and a temporary cottage built before they could start to make a real home. Moors took charge of these operations and cleared about eight of the fifteen acres which were all the Stevensons cultivated of their property. When he left for Sydney in February 1890, Stevenson still meant to carry out his plan of returning to England to dispose of 'Skerryvore', and then to go out permanently to Vailima with his mother—by which time Moors would have something ready for them. Moreover, something had to be done for Belle, who was more or less stuck in Sydney with her not-too-satisfactory Joe. It is hinted that in Honolulu Joe had developed over-convivial habits, for which reason he was taken away from temptation on the *Equator* cruise; but sending him from Honolulu to Sydney was out of the frying-pan into the fire.

And Sydney was not propitious to Stevenson's health. He told Moors that as he voyaged into colder latitudes his health failed, and he could scarcely get ashore when he reached Australia. This may be so, though February in Sydney is the height of summer; but the lung haemorrhage which abruptly cut short the pleasant social and literary life he started to lead there must have been due to the 'colds' inseparable from any large town. He was forced to cancel the voyage to England, and instead started on a cruise (11th April to 25th July, 1890) in the *Janet Nichol*, a combined steaming and sailing ship of about 600 tons. The voyage took the party (Stevenson, Fanny and Lloyd only) to about thirty islands, including a short time at Apia and a brief reunion with Tembinoka for whom Fanny had designed a picturesque royal standard. But they stayed nowhere for long—in some cases Fanny did not risk the dangers of landing through heavy surf—and most of the islands they saw were 'low' or atolls. As Stevenson remarked, hansom cabs are less like one another than low islands! They certainly did not visit Raratonga and Easter, as Moors thought, but they did see Niue, the Maniki Islands (including the pearl island, Penryn), Tokelau, Ellice and Marshal groups, as well as revisiting the Gilberts. The worst misfortune on the trip was a fire caused by the spontaneous combustion of fireworks bought by a rather foolish trader, known as 'Tin' Jack, to amuse his customers. Lloyd lost photographs and most of his clothes, and only Fanny's quick wit and action saved from being thrown overboard a burning trunk containing her husband's MS. The cruise may be followed almost day by day from the pages of Fanny's diary, who later with typical verbal exuberance refers to these uncomfortable days in a ship which rolled abominably as 'perhaps the happiest period of my life' which she remembered with 'thrilling interest'! Stevenson in a contemporary letter records that his health had not improved as much as he had hoped, but that the others 'seem less run down than they were on the *Equator*, and Mrs. Stevenson very much less so'. By August (1890) they were back in Sydney, whence Lloyd left for England to clear up, while in October Fanny and Stevenson returned to Samoa. The first of the Vailima Letters to Colvin is dated 2nd November, 1890. They had then begun to live in the original four-roomed cottage, a little above which the real house or double-house was afterwards built.

Partly as a result of the newspaper publicity and partly of the irrepressible gossip of small places, Vailima and its inhabitants became the subject of innumerable legends, including such fantasies as that Belle was Louis's daughter by a native woman, that Louis was 'the uncrowned king of Samoa', and that the Vailima house was a palace of stupendous luxury. It must be admitted that for what it was the place cost a lot of money, on top of which the expense of bringing from England and Scotland all kinds of necessary and unnecessary household articles must have been considerable, while money must have been poured out for equipment and labour on the cacao plantation side which was never able to show a profit. If any further evidence is needed that Louis and Fanny (that 'good manager') were really a couple of infantile spendthrifts, here it is. But surely that is far more creditable and loveable than if they had been cheese-paring scrapers and savers? Still, there is a no-man's-land between meanness and extravagance, and the Stevensons seem to have kept far to the spending side of it.

On this point we again have the evidence of Moors, who eventually became rather hostile to Fanny, but had no valid reason for giving wrong figures; and he must have known the correct ones since he was in charge of the building and supply of materials. After a great deal of discussion over plans Stevenson brought one back from Sydney which Moors calculated would have cost at least 20,000 dollars. This was abandoned for a more modest plan. Moors gives the following figures: Land, 4,000 dollars; cottage, 1,000 dollars; first section of Vailima house, 7,400 dollars, and second section, 7,500. Which makes 20,000; and when at last Fanny sold it somewhere about 1900 the utmost she could get was 10,000. Moors estimates the 'upkeep' of Vailima at about 6,500 dollars a year, adding that 'Mrs. Stevenson and Mrs. Strong were not the most economical women in the world'. One expense which might well have been spared in building the house was 1,000 dollars for a brick chimney and fire-places—only thirteen degrees south of the equator! The explanation that Stevenson felt that home is not home without a hearth seems inadequate for such an expense; while the alternative theory that a fire was needed to warm his sheets seems ridiculous, especially since such a proceeding, even if necessary in that climate, would normally take place in the kitchen and not in the living-room. On the other hand, the ice-machine, which they certainly did need in that climate, was so carelessly selected that it never worked.

There seems no way of verifying Moors's statement that the household expenses at Vailima ran as high as £1,300 a year. It seems colossal for the epoch, until we discover that Stevenson in his own way followed the example of Scott in spending, and made himself something like the head of an extempore clan rather than a distinguished Scottish author living quietly in a Pacific island for the sake of his health. Certainly he was worried about earning enough money to the end of his life, although he must have been making between £3,000 and £4,000 a year, while he knew that under the revised terms of his father's will Fanny and even Lloyd and Belle would be provided for after his mother's death. Stevenson excused the lavish outlay on Vailima as being a provision for his family, but it never was. As he poured out money to increase the house accommodation and to develop the cacao land he acquired more and more dependants and guests. In addition to Fanny and Lloyd, he had for considerable periods to support Joe Strong and Belle and their boy, Austin. Mrs. Stevenson of course was in a position to make a financial contribution, and after a lifetime's experience of 'Lou' no doubt expected to do so. Guests such as Graham Balfour made long visits; there was frequent entertaining of visiting warships such as H.M.S. *Curaçao*; and constant feasting of native chiefs and their followers. Three or four saddle horses were kept as well as two large cart horses from New Zealand. The cows and pigs and poultry were of course essential to the supply system, but almost certainly were run at a loss. Rats and native Rob Roys carried off chickens, while Joe in his zeal as poultry overseer insisted on feeding lime to new-hatched chicks which Fanny thought accounted for the high casualties.

In addition to the 'boys' hired to clear away 'bush' and otherwise work on the land Stevenson kept a varying number of native retainers, after he and Fanny gave up trying to keep white servants—apart from old Mrs. Stevenson's maid. In a footnote to one of Stevenson's letters of 1893, Lloyd Osbourne notes:

> 'Talolo was the Vailima cook; Sina, his wife; Tauilo, his mother; Mitaele and Sosimo his brothers; Lafaele . . . was married to Faauma.'

And he mentions that Iopo and Tali, who 'had long been in our service' still considered themselves part of Stevenson's family. In 1891 Stevenson lists several of the same names to Colvin, totalling seven indoor and two outdoor servants; and reports eight horses and five cattle. On ceremonial occasions the staff were garbed in loin-cloths of Royal Stewart tartan, though one would have thought the Macgregor tartan more suitable for one who hoped and indeed believed he was distantly related to Rob Roy. After Louis's death the American consul reported to Washington that 'Mr. Stevenson was the first citizen of Samoa'. Doubtless Fanny would not have put up with any status below that of first lady, and we may perhaps attribute some of the entertainment and display to her social ambitions, just as she probably influenced Stevenson's decision to set up an amateur plantation and to meddle in local politics. In the same way old Mrs. Stevenson was responsible for his regular church-going, which he went through in order to please her, but the household prayers which so much scandalized Henley seem to have been his own doing—Henley didn't realize how impossible it was to omit such formalities, though very likely the Shorter Catechist and the submerged yet surviving preacher in Stevenson not only enjoyed but was edified by them. Still, it is not fair to attribute everything to Fanny however much she bossed the establishment, as her husband admitted she did. If Moors's recollection is accurate the proposal to settle in Samoa started with Stevenson, and there can be no doubt that he hugely enjoyed his position as head of the 'Tusitala clan' and his influence in local politics. Fanatical as Fanny was in her championship of the defeated king, Mataafa (apparently because he was the 'under-dog') she doubtless encouraged but could not compel Louis to write his Samoan political letters to *The Times* and *Pall Mall Gazette*. Moreover, he so much enjoyed working on the land that he had to confine himself to the house from time to time in order to avoid going bankrupt through neglecting his writing. One might have thought that such strenuous physical work as he describes himself as doing under that sun would have been very bad for his lungs; but no! the work suited him, and of course there is always immense benefit for the sedentary worker in getting back to the realities of earth.

Yet Stevenson's own life was simple and laborious, and we must not be duped into giving false emphasis to lavish entertainments which are recorded simply because they were rare and therefore 'news'. In the Vailima Letters Stevenson has given two 'specimen days' from his ordinary life there, and they should be carefully read to dispel illusions of undue luxury and feudal splendour. The first is dated 19th March, 1891:

> 'I sleep now in one of the lower rooms of the new house, where my wife has recently joined me. We have two beds, an empty case for a table, a chair, a tin basin, a bucket and a jug; next door is the dining-room, the carpenters' camp on the floor, which is covered with their mosquito nets. Before the sun rises, at 5.45 or 5.50, Paul brings me tea, bread, and a couple of eggs; and by about six I am at work. I work in bed—my bed is of mats, no mattress, sheets,* or filth—mats, a pillow, and a blanket—and put in some three

* So what happens to the story that the fireplaces were built to warm his sheets?

hours. It was 9.5 this morning when I set off to the stream-side to my weeding; where I toiled, manuring the ground with the best enricher, human sweat, till the conch-shell was blown from our veranda at 10.30. At eleven we dine; about half past twelve I tried (by exception) to work again, could make nothing o't, and by one was on my way to the weeding, where I wrought till three. Half past five is our next meal, and I read Flaubert's Letters till the hour came round; dined, and then, Fanny having a cold, and I being tired, came over to my den in the unfinished house, where I now write. . . .'

Six months later we get another specimen day of a period when he had temporarily abandoned work as a tropical farmer, and was evidently giving more time to his literary work:

'Awoke somewhere about the first peep of day, came gradually to, and had a turn on the veranda before 5.55, when "the child" (an enormous Wallis Islander) brings me an orange; at 6, breakfast; 6.10, to work; which lasts till, at 10.30, Austin comes for his history lecture; this is rather dispiriting, but education must be gone about in faith—and charity, both of which pretty nigh failed me today about (of all things) Carthage; 11, luncheon; after luncheon in my mother's room, I read Chapter XXIII of *The Wrecker*, then Belle, Lloyd and I go up and make music furiously till about 2 (I suppose) when I turn in to work again till 4; fool from 4 to half past, tired out and waiting for the bath hour; 4.30, bath; 4.40, eat two heavenly mangoes on the veranda, and see the boys arrive with the pack-horses; 5, dinner; smoke, chat on veranda, then hand of cards, and at last at 8 come up to my room with a pint of beer and a hard biscuit, which I am now consuming, and as soon as they are consumed, I shall turn in.'

These first-hand accounts of Stevenson's working day invite at least a glance at the books produced during this last epoch of his life, a list of which was given in the last chapter. With many writers a decline of powers towards the end of their career has to be recorded. This was not the case with Stevenson. True, not all the later books are at his highest level, but that was true all along, for with him the work of art and the pot-boiler were always contending. His sudden death ended his writing career when he was half-way through *Weir of Hermiston*, which many admirers believe was his greatest achievement in novel-writing. If he had lived another ten or twenty years there is no reason to think that his standards of achievement would have been lowered, though obviously he worked himself to death and could not if he had lived have kept up such a rapid production. Not from any lack of fertility, however. It is usual to praise Stevenson as a stylist, and barring some early affectations and mannerisms, the praise is deserved, especially since stylists in English fiction are not numerous and some of those counted as stylists are not enjoyable. Style perhaps may be acquired by long study and practice, but invention is native—a writer is born with it and if he lacks it cannot acquire it. In his early days Stevenson sometimes seemed to be writing for writing's sake, without anything particular to say; but as he developed, his gift of invention became more and more conspicuous. He was never at a loss for a theme, projected and even started many more books than he ever had time to complete, and seemed almost inexhaustible in devising episodes and adventures for his characters. Certainly there is at times something factitious about both characters and adventures, and Addington Symonds quite plainly hints at something approaching a formula of picturesque bloodshed, even in a work on so high a level as *The Master of Ballantrae*. Symonds, however, was an epicure in violence and bloodshed, taking as his standard Cellini and the terrific crimes of Renaissance Italy which form often the basis of the Elizabethan tragedies of blood. Stevenson wrote—whether he wanted or not—for a bourgeois audience of narrow views and perceptions, some of which he shared, while he fretted against others. To blame him for not attaining the tragedy and violent passions of Webster and Tourneur is as unfair as reproving Dickens for not reaching the heights of Shakespeare. So much are all men unconsciously involved in the common life of their epoch that only the greatest writers are greater than their own times. How much of young Stevenson's energy was frittered away in useless strife with the prejudices of Edinburgh, and how much the expanding creative genius of the maturing Stevenson was thwarted or diverted by the preconceived ideas and limitations of the Anglo-American 'public'! The speculation is futile—he had to do the best he could in the circumstances given him by his 'romance of destiny'.

Although not published until April 1892, *Across The Plains* consisted chiefly of the essays written for *Scribner's*, mainly if not wholly at Saranac Lake. This was the last collection of his essays published in Stevenson's lifetime (the *Juvenilia* were posthumous) and show no decline in strength although some of the charm of youth has been shed along with its innocent pretensions and self-deceptions. Looking over these most carefully constructed essays a reader cannot help smiling at the thought that the young eulogist of idling became one of the most conscientiously industrious literary workers of his time. If Stevenson mostly goes back to the memories of youth for his themes the reason perhaps was that he unconsciously felt that his American readers were mainly interested in him rather than in his philosophical speculations, and as it was a taste he shared he could write with gusto. In any case he had not lost his gift of telling phrases:

> 'The area railings, the beloved shop-window, the smell of semi-suburban tanpits, the song of the church-bells upon a Sunday, the thin, high voices of compatriot children in a playing-field—what a sudden, what an overpowering pathos breathes to him from each familiar circumstance!'

The anonymous 'him' refers to Stevenson himself, and the evocation is of his own Edinburgh childhood. In the next quotation about his education as an engineer the experiences are wholly personal, for they are quite outside the lives of ordinary engineering students whose fathers don't happen to be lighthouse-builders:

> 'It takes a man into the open air; it keeps him hanging about harbour-sides, which is the richest form of idling; it carries him to wild islands; it gives him a taste of the genial dangers of the sea; it supplies him with dexterities to exercise; it makes demands upon his ingenuity; it will go far to cure him of any taste (if he ever had one) for the miserable life of cities. And when it has done so, it carries him back and shuts him in an office!'

Here once again was Stevenson the charmer, perhaps with more graces and fewer airs than in previous collections of essays, but certainly essentially the same Stevenson even to that elusive Shorter Catechist who lurks under much of his view of life in spite of the other aspect of irresponsible bohemianism. *Pulvis et Umbra* he meant as 'a Darwinian sermon' which concludes with a peroration which would scarcely have been ill received by the Kirk:

> '. . . God forbid it should be man that wearies in welldoing, that despairs of unrewarded effort, or utters the language of complaint.

Let it be enough for faith, that the whole creation groans in mortal frailty, strives with unconquerable constancy: Surely not all in vain.'

This in turn is followed by *A Christmas Sermon*, which ends with a graceful tribute to Henley. Considering that this piece was written in Saranac some magnanimity and sweetness were required of Stevenson for him to write of Henley's poem in memory of his sister that it is 'beautiful and manly' and that 'it says better than I can, what I love to think'. For some men in Stevenson's situation *vis-à-vis* Henley such words might come barbed with irony, but Stevenson really meant what he said; and as late as 1893 we find him writing to congratulate Henley on his latest book of poems.

Unfortunately, although Stevenson for once had been lucky enough to receive handsome payment for these essays in serial form, he knew well enough that such a book could not sell sufficiently to meet his greatly increased rate of spending. As he said himself 'such books pay only indirectly', though they pleased reviewers for what that was worth, and brought in 'a few shillings a year for a while'. His main effort was necessarily turned to the more saleable fiction which was also, perhaps, the more effective expression of his versatile literary genius. At the head of these novels of his maturity stands the weird and desolate tragedy of *The Master of Ballantrae*, which succeeds, where success was most difficult, by welding together in one story such very disparate and heterogenous elements—Scottish Jacobitism, a fraternal blood feud, misunderstanding between husband and wife, a servitor as faithful but not so grotesque as Caleb Baldeston, an Indian fakir with incredible miracles and devotion to the Master, a storm at sea with an attempted murder by an honest man, adventures in eighteenth-century America. . . . It is a tragedy in which the hero is a villain.

Stevenson has left a brief, tantalizingly brief, account of what he calls 'the genesis' of this book. This is worth the attention of every Stevensonian since it reveals what was probably his method of planning stories when they were not suggested in sleep by the 'little people'. One cold night at Saranac Stevenson finished re-reading Marryat's *The Phantom Ship* (a book I have not read, though I infer it is a variant of the *Flying Dutchman*) and deliberately set out 'with the spirit of emulation' to make a story of his own. He was looking in his memory for some similar thread of universal folk-lore when he remembered a tale of his father's about 'a buried and resuscitated fakir'—so that, strange to relate, he started off with Secundra Dass! One may be forgiven for thinking him the weakest link in the story, since far from embodying some superstition of our own he raps in vain against the thick plate glass of our occidental disbelief.

The next step was a recollection of a story conceived nine years earlier 'in Highland rain, in the blend of the smell of heather and bog-plants, and with a mind full of the Athole correspondence and the memories of the dumlicide Justice'. Hence the family of Durrisdeer and their 'mutual tragic situation'. And then for various reasons he invented the chevalier Burke, basing him on a young Irishman Stevenson had known long before, 'a youth of an extraordinary moral simplicity—almost vacancy; plastic to any influence, the creature of his admirations. . . .' Here was a fantastic assortment of literary ingredients which almost any writer could have converted by industry into an unpalatable mess—Stevenson was needed to apply the correct recipe. Not all have enjoyed the result without reservations. Symonds, who criticized Stevenson with all the unsparing candour of an old friend, thought the novel did not deserve the praise it received for its 'psychological analysis' and that no adequate explanation is given of the Master's power over the family he hurt so cruelly. But was he right? Symonds was a dutiful only son without Stevenson's experience of the repeated forgiveness which may await the prodigal; and then the Master was the eldest son, he had forfeited estate and the promised wife who married his rival brother because he had been 'out' for the 'lawful King' in the '45. He had claims which he could exploit until he exasperated his brother to a fratricidal duel, and finally hounded to madness and death. Stevenson knew the prejudices and beliefs of the eighteenth-century Highland gentry, and was probably right. As to the 'psychological analysis'—its success or failure in a reader's opinion must depend on whether he thinks Stevenson's characters historically true. As usual with him the woman is the weak thread in the fabric. And there are those who, like George Moore and Swinnerton, thought the fabric shoddy. As E. F. Benson thought the man shoddy. There are always these differences of opinion.

The Master of Ballantrae belonged to Scotland's past and Stevenson's past. It was still in the Scott-Dumas-Marryat tradition brisked up, and given style. *The Beach of Falesà* is by far the best piece of work to come out of his new experiences in the Pacific. There is violence in it, but nothing factitious. Stevenson himself thought highly of it, and wrote (28th September, 1891) to Colvin:

> 'There is a vast deal of fact in the story, and some pretty good comedy. It is the first realist South Sea story; I mean with real South Sea character and details of life. Everybody else who has tried, that I have seen, got carried away by the romance, and ended in a kind of sugar-candy sham epic, and the whole effect was lost—there was no etching, no human grin, consequently no conviction. Now I have got the smell and look of the thing a good deal. You will know more about the South Seas after you have read my little tale than if you had read a library.'

Now, critics have come along and have turned against some of Stevenson's more obviously fabricated 'romance' his own phrase, 'kind of sugar-candy sham epic', but nobody has dared to do this to *The Beach of Falesà*. What the contemporary editor and publisher did was to try to bowdlerize the story in the interests of an idiotic prudery. Commenting on that to Colvin (31st January, 1892) Stevenson says ruefully:

> 'This is a poison-bad world for the romancer, this Anglo-Saxon world; I usually get out of it by not having any women in it at all; but when I remember I had *The Treasure of Franchard* refused as unfit for a family magazine, I feel despair weigh upon my wrists.'

Here we touch a serious fault in Stevenson's books which has frequently been pointed out—the absence of women in some of his books and the conventional treatment of those who are introduced. Even in *The Master of Ballantrae* Alison Durie and her feelings are not properly worked out. In a letter to Bob Stevenson, written only three months before Louis's death, he says:

> 'If I had to begin again—I know not—*si jeunesse savait, si vieillesse pouvait* . . . I know not at all—I believe I should try to honour sex more religiously. The worst of our education is that Christianity does not recognize and hallow sex. It looks askance at it, over its shoulder, oppressed as it is by reminiscences of hermits and Asiatic

self-torture. It is a terrible hiatus in our modern religions that they cannot see and make venerable that which they ought to see first and hallow most. Well, it is so; I cannot be wiser than my generation.'

What Stevenson could not or would not attempt was dared by the courage and genius of D. H. Lawrence, who was martyred by Anglo-Saxon hypocrisy and philistinism, but won. And Stevenson changed his mind late in life. Thomas Hardy has recorded that he read a newspaper interview in which Stevenson stated that he 'disapproved of the morals of *Tess of the d'Urbervilles*', which (Hardy thought) might account for the fact that Stevenson never thereafter communicated with him.

The Beach at Falesà was included in *The Island Nights' Entertainment* (Cassell, April 1893) along with *The Bottle-Imp* and *The Isle of Voices*. *The Bottle-Imp* is a variation on the theme of Balzac's *Peau de Chagrin*, and the story had the unique fate of being first printed in a Samoan translation made by a missionary, who gave Stevenson his native name of 'Tusitala'. An unforeseen result was that Samoans who read or heard the story did not distinguish religious stories from avowed fiction or for that matter from history. The king of Apemama refused to believe in the reality of Captain Cook since he found no mention of him in the Bible of the Gilbert Islands, while the Stevensons unconsciously staged a religious revival by showing magic lantern slides of Bible events which the Gilbertians held to be proof positive of their reality—the magic lantern cannot lie. In a similar spirit the Samoans accepted the Bottle-Imp, to whose magic aid they attributed Tusitala's supposedly limitless wealth; and chiefs visiting Vailima were known to ask shyly for a glimpse of this interesting imprisoned devil.

The other novels of this epoch all tend towards compromise with popular taste, if they do not deliberately aspire to boil the pot. The best of them (apart from the unfinished *Weir of Hermiston*) is probably *Catriona*, the sequel to *Kidnapped*, which has some excellent episodes and revives the characters of David Balfour and Alan Breck, though hardly with the success of the first volume. *St. Ives*, which was not quite finished, suffers from the fact that it is rather in the manner of Stanley Weyman, while parts of it were dictated to Belle in such evil conditions of health that he had to use the deaf and dumb alphabet, as speech was forbidden him. The *Wrecker* was planned quite frankly with Lloyd, on board the *Janet Nichol*, as a best seller with the idea of buying a schooner and, as we have seen, they succeeded so well that the American serial rights brought 15,000 dollars. After expressing to Colvin his gratification that the English books sales had been highly successful, Stevenson, like Puck, reflected, 'What fools these mortals be!' As for *The Ebb-Tide*, which like *The Wrecker* was written in collaboration with Lloyd, it is indisputably an excellent thriller, but Stevenson was 'discontented' with it, 'there seems such a veil of words over it'. And again to Gosse he spoke of it (10th June, 1893) as:

'. . . a dreadful, grimy business in the third person, where the strain between a vilely realistic dialogue and a narrative style pitched about (in phrase) "four notes higher" than it should have been, has sown my head with grey hairs; or I believe so—if my head escaped, my heart has them.'

This disparagement of his book should not be taken too literally, for it may have been no more than a symptom of weariness and ill health. Assuredly in those years he was over-working in order to maintain the scale of expense of Vailima. *Weir of Hermiston*, the book on which Stevenson was working when he died, looked as if it might have become one of the best if not the best of his novels; but it remains a broken torso. For the figure of the Justice-Clerk Stevenson reverted to Lord Braxfield whose portrait by Raeburn had so much impressed him as a young man, and once more he took up the familiar theme of strife between father and son, though the characters of the two women are far more effective than is usual with Stevenson. Unfortunately half a novel however excellent is not a novel. Belle, the amanuensis, has left a summary of what she believed Stevenson intended to do with the story, but though interesting that is far from being a real substitute for Stevenson's complete narrative.

There is another book besides this romance which Stevenson never saw in print—his Letters. Unfortunately, more than sixty years after his death the world of Stevensonians still awaits a reasonably complete and unexpurgated edition. In order to comply with Victorian notions of 'reticence' and 'good taste', to meet Fanny's exigencies and his own stiff ideas of propriety, Colvin expurgated some of the letters he published, omitted others, while there were still others he never saw. Among the last group is an amusing letter to Henley in which Stevenson jokes at the expense of Colvin, sarcastically sketching the kind of 'Life' Colvin would write of him and how he would turn the rather scandalous days of Stevenson's youth into something correct and proper. Which of course is exactly what Colvin and Graham Balfour with the aid of Fanny actually did. One result of suppressing letters to Mrs. Sitwell, for example, was inevitably the arousing of unjustified suspicions of their intimate relations. Another was to create the impression that Stevenson was rather more of a prig than in fact he was. And everything was eliminated which tended to throw any shadow on Fanny's sunny picture of herself as the devoted artist-wife nursing her beloved husband and acting as unerring critic—which led one of the hangers-on who inevitably cluster round every publicized character to write a book about Fanny as Stevenson's '*sine qua non*'.

Every man writes himself down in his letters even if it is only as a business man dictating to his secretary. And Stevenson put much of himself into his letters. The fact that the Colvin collection is incomplete and to some extent censored does not prevent it from being a fair reproduction of the writer's mind—it is perhaps no more than the difference between an untouched photograph and the same portrait after being touched up by a sentimental photographer. In accordance with Victorian standards the portrait had to be made 'appealing', just as Royal Academy portraits had to flatter their sitters. The unexpurgated Stevenson is much more fun, but the man as revealed in the Colvin Letters is not so seriously falsified as he is in Graham Balfour's *Life*. There is nothing calculated or false in these letters; they are spontaneous, often amusing and witty, often vivid in description, and sincere in feeling. To be sure, he writes an enormous amount about himself and his concerns; but that is almost unavoidable in personal letters. Most of us if suddenly confronted with a collection of our letters would be disagreeably shocked to find what egotists we are, and probably none of us as good-tempered and light-hearted as Stevenson was. There may be a little posing here and there especially in the early letters to Mrs. Sitwell, but it is harmless. On the whole, the 'charm' of Stevenson which is marked enough in his early essays and travel-books is even more potent in the letters, and there are fewer affectations of style and mannerisms to be pardoned. The youthful Stevenson gained by writing without his theories of literary perfection, and the mature Stevenson had either discarded or made them second nature. Moreover, he had the art of writing letters which are nearly as interesting to persons who came into the world after he was dead as they obviously were to those for whom they were written. It is merely a biographer's growl, but one could wish that Stevenson had dated his letters more accurately, especially as Colvin's conjectural dating is not always convincing. The need is for a new complete edition of all Stevenson's letters, from the originals—a formidable task only to be discharged by Mr. J. C. Furnas who unquestionably knows more about Stevenson than any person living.

At the risk of knocking down an open door one must insist on Stevenson's devotion to his art. This praiser of idleness was a lifelong worker. Here is what he wrote to George Meredith (5th September, 1893) and in a few sentences that part of his life is epitomized:

> 'For years after I came here, the critics (those genial gentlemen) used to deplore the relaxation of my fibre and the idleness to which I had succumbed. I hear less of this now; the next thing is they will tell me I am writing myself out! and that my unconscientious conduct is bringing their grey hairs with sorrow to the dust. I do not know—I mean I do know one thing. For fourteen years I have not had one day's real health; I have wakened sick and gone to bed weary; and I have done my work unflinchingly. I have written in bed, and written out of it, written in haemorrhages, written in sickness, written torn by coughing, written when my head swam for weakness; and for so long, it seems to me I have won my wager and recovered my glove. . . .'

A few lines further on he apologizes to Meredith for being so 'devilish egotistical', but at all events there is Stevenson's view of his life as a battle, a view which was taken up and exaggerated by the early Stevenson hagiographers. This was reduced to its real value—many would think, reduced below it—by Henley in his celebrated review of Balfour's *Life*. The difficulty is to reconcile Stevenson's account of himself here, not so much with his half-jesting praise of idlers (which was meant ironically, to deride the philistine idea of art as idleness) as with his more serious belief that the artist is a kind of *fille de joie*, selling his pleasure. He retracted that in a letter to Le Gallienne, but allowed the essay to stand.

All this to the contrary, we must not suppose that Stevenson's life in Samoa was all work and the weariness of sickness. He had a horse, 'Jack', of which he was fond; and frequently rode for exercise and pleasure, though he was not strong enough to make long excursions on Upolu like Lloyd and Graham Balfour. He not only entertained but went out to dinners and lunches, and under Belle's tuition learned to dance. When his mother arrived he became a regular church-goer; and he had daily—later weekly—prayers in his house and composed those Vailima prayers which aroused the wrath of Henley who remembered the scoffer and libertine of Edinburgh days. He made ship voyages—to the island of Tusitala with the American consul, two excursions to Sydney—one of them to meet his mother on her way out from Scotland—and a journey to Honolulu with Balfour. Away from Samoa he invariably fell sick with some lung complaint, and at Honolulu had pneumonia so badly that Fanny had to come by the next boat to nurse him and take him home. So much was this adventurer and would-be warrior dependent on women. Fanny, gardening and planting cacao fiercely, brooding over Stevenson's too successful home-thrust that she had the soul of a peasant and not of an artist, bossing the 'boys', more and more abandoned him to Belle who served him in a multitude of ways, from acting as amanuensis to cutting his finger-nails.

Probably the greater part of his leisure was devoted to the natives and the affairs of Samoa. Obviously the Stevensons could not cut themselves off from the life of the place and remain austerely aloof, but, whatever the cause, they and especially Stevenson became more involved than was approved by their friends in England and America. Anybody reading the Vailima letters must notice how much attention is given to the servants, their behaviour, sayings and doings, and private and matrimonial affairs. You might paraphrase Villiers de l'Isle-Adam's famous remark and turn it to: 'As for living, we'll do that for our servants'. Much of this was genuine kindness and perhaps a necessity of the situation, part was due to the fact that he and Fanny took on themselves the functions of local chieftains, and part to the white man's irresistible urge to patronize the native from the height of his incomparable superiority. The praying was inevitable, and Henley himself in their position would have held prayer-meetings simply because the missionaries had made such a fetish of it that it couldn't be omitted without being anti-social. As it was, poor Stevenson was bitterly censured for joining a paper-chase on a Sunday afternoon. Unfortunately, he and the rest of them inevitably became involved in the venomous local gossip of a small Pacific island, and, what was worse, in the parochial politics of the place. There was a tri-consular foreign government, and a rivalry which ended in head-hunting skirmishes between the two 'kings' Malietoa and Mataafa, with the Stevensons strongly supporting the Mataafa faction. Fanny, in her accustomed manner, expressed her feelings energetically on these local politics:

> '... when I look at the white men at the head of the government and cannot make up my mind which is the greater coward, my woman's heart burns with shame and fury and I am ready for any madness.'

And again:

> 'Suddenly I rose up and said vehemently that all the white men in Samoa were cowards, and left the party. I am afraid I behaved very badly. At luncheon healths were being drunk and I drank the health of "H. J. Moors, my worst enemy and the only white man clinging to Samoa who is not a coward".'

Moors had become Fanny's 'worst enemy' because he backed Louis in any little attempts at rebellion against the Vailima regiment of women, and because he had stood by his friend Joe Strong when Belle decided to divorce him. Fanny doesn't say what she wanted the white men to do, for they could hardly take up arms and go head-hunting with Mataafa. Stevenson's reaction was characteristic. On the 28th June, 1893, he rode out with Graham Balfour to look at the then incipient 'war'. Crossing a ford into Mataafa's country he came on seven natives armed with Winchesters, and further on passed about a dozen armed men 'and the cheerful alacrity and brightness of their looks set my head turning with envy and sympathy'. And after other little episodes he concludes:

> 'No, war is a huge *entrainement*; there is no other temptation to be compared to it, not one. We were all wet, we had been about five hours in the saddle, mostly riding hard; and we came home like schoolboys, with such a lightness of spirits, and I am sure such a brightness of eye, as you could have lit a candle by!'

As Fanny's enemy, Moors, remarked—if there was something

of Don Quixote in Stevenson, there was also something of Tartarin de Tarascon.

How seriously Stevenson took the playing at Chieftain may be seen from several passages in the later Vailima letters. Writing in November 1893 he describes how 'our Protestant boys' went to some festival 'in the Vailima uniform', presumably of Royal Stewart tartan loin-cloths and 'coats' made by Belle, and were 'hailed as they marched in as the Tama-ona—the rich man's children. This is really a score; it means that Vailima is publicly taken as a family'. A little later he describes his 1893 birthday feast with pride and satisfaction:

> 'The feast was laid in the hall, and was a singular mass of food; 15 pigs, 100 lb. beef, 100 lb. pork, and the fruit and filigree in proportion. We had sixty horse-posts driven in the gate paddock; how many guests I cannot guess, perhaps 150. They came between three and four and left about seven. Seumanu gave me one of his names; and when my name was called at the ava drinking, behold it was *Au mai taua ma manu-vao*! You would scarce recognize me, if you heard me thus referred to!'

And indeed he had come a long way and seen changes since the day when a shabbily dressed bohemian with the poems of Charles d'Orléans in his rucksack had been imprisoned by the *gendarmerie* of Chatillon under the belief that he was a German vagabond street-singer without identification papers. It is not surprising that a couple of days later, after drinking ava with the imprisoned chiefs of Mataafa's party, he remarked to Fanny as they rode home: 'Could we ever stand Europe again? did she appreciate that if we were in London, we should be *actually jostled* in the street? and there was nobody in the whole of Britain who knew how to take ava like a gentleman?'

These captive chieftains are connected with one of Stevenson's many acts of generosity and in this case with a unique form of acknowledgment. We must not take leave of Stevenson without again paying tribute to a kindness and generosity in him which more than atone for all and any of the—mostly rather harmless—faults in him which have to be admitted if the record is not to be falsified. In Edinburgh, in London, in Paris and Grez he was always ready to share what little money he had with fellow-bohemians in distress, while he could not resist even the professional beggars who were generally frauds. In Paris he heard of an

American artist in financial trouble, and Stevenson's only worry was how to convey fifty francs he badly needed himself without hurting his friend's feelings—of course, he bought a sketch. In San Francisco he went out of his way to bring succour to a sick journalist of whom he had heard, going to his bedside with money and the kindly saying, 'we writers are always hard up'. A Scottish book-keeper who had lost his job through the continual Australian strikes instantly got help from him at Apia. A musician out of work with a pregnant wife was cared for, and a job found for him. When famine came to one of the Pacific islands he had visited, he sent a gift of fifty pounds. There are many other instances recorded—and not by him.

The story of the captive chieftains and the 'Road of Loving Thoughts' would be perfect but for the fact that half the motives were political on their side, and even Robert Louis must have been influenced by Fanny's violent prejudices in favour of Mataafa. At all events, after his defeat over twenty chiefs were held in Apia jail, uncomfortably housed but well looked after in the matter of food by their families. When Stevenson made his remark to Fanny about being 'actually jostled' in Europe, they had been carrying large gifts of tobacco and kava to the prisoners, who of course were delighted to have the support of the 'first citizen of Samoa'. In December (1893) they went again to a feast in the prison! In the ceremonial drinking of kava, Fanny was called first, before her husband, which indicates that the ceremony was intended to mark their sense of gratitude to political supporters; and after dinner the white guests were loaded with all kinds of gifts, which would be seen by the 'usurping king' as they went back to Vailima. After the chiefs were released they cleared a Road of Loving Hearts or Road of Gratitude for the use of Vailima. Stevenson was particularly pleased by this acknowledgement. As he wrote:

> 'Now, whether or not their impulse will last them through the road does not matter to me one hair. It is the fact that they have attempted it, that they have volunteered and are now really trying to execute a thing that was never before heard of in Samoa. Think of it! It is road-making—the most fruitful cause (after taxes) of all rebellions in Samoa, a thing to which they could not be wiled with money nor driven by punishment. It does give me a sense of having done something in Samoa after all.'

The address he made the chiefs at the feast is printed as an appendix to the *Letters*. This was in October 1894, and on the 13th November there was the usual native feast for his forty-fourth birthday. He was working hard on *Weir of Hermiston*, and in good spirits since he felt he was working at his best, and luckily Fanny agreed with him. There was a Thanksgiving dinner for American friends on the 29th November. On the 3rd of December he came down from his work and found Fanny still in the state of uneasy foreboding which had been with her for two or three days—the sense that something grievous was about to happen to someone they cared for—though they agreed it could not be either of them. Trying to cheer her, he brought up a bottle of burgundy for dinner and was helping to make a salad when he suddenly collapsed with a cerebral haemorrhage, and within two hours was dead.

The sudden and unexpected shock of his death may be imagined, not only at Vailima—where it was the end of all happy days—but in England and America where most of his friends learned the news from the headline or newspaper poster: 'Death of R. L. Stevenson'. Much of the responsibility fell on Lloyd, who buried his friend and stepfather in the selected site on top of Mount Vaea, where later a tomb was built whose inscriptions include the *Requiem* he had written for himself years before.

Twenty-one years later, in 1915, when Samoa had passed into the protection of New Zealand, the ashes of Fanny were brought from California and placed beside her husband's. It is the inevitable end, yet with a special twist which makes the lonely grave of those two the only possible epilogue to the romance of their destiny.

SELECTED BOOK LIST

(For Stevenson's works the Swanton and Tusitala editions were used. I have limited this list strictly to books which are really helpful.)

BAILDON, H. BELLYSE. *Robert Louis Stevenson. A Life Study in Critciism.* London, 1901.

BALFOUR, GRAHAM. *The Life of Robert Louis Stevenson.* London, 1901.

CHARTERIS, Hon. EVAN. *The Life and Letters of Sir Edmund Gosse.* London, 1931.

CHESTERTON, GILBERT KEITH. *Robert Louis Stevenson.* London, 1927.

COLVIN, SIDNEY. *Memories and Notes of Persons and Places,* 1852–1912. London, 1921.

COLVIN, SIDNEY, Edited by. *Robert Louis Stevenson: His Work and Personality.*

CONNELL, JOHN. *W. E. Henley.* London, 1949.

ELWIN, MALCOLM. *The Strange Case of Robert Louis Stevenson.* London, 1950.

FERGUSON, DE LANCEY and MARSHALL WAINGROW, Edited by. *R. L. Stevenson's Letters to Charles Baxter.* London, 1956.

FIELD, ISOBEL OSBOURNE STRONG. *And Lloyd Osbourne: Memories of Vailima.* New York, 1902.

GOSSE, EDMUND. *Critical Kit-Kats.* London, 1896.

HAMMERTON, J. A., Edited by. *Stevensoniana.* Edinburgh, 1910.

HELLMAN, GEORGE S. *The True Stevenson, a Study in Clarification.* Boston, 1925.

JAMES, HENRY and STEVENSON, ROBERT LOUIS. *A Record of Friendship and Criticism,* edited by Janet Adam Smith. London, 1948.

LOW, WILL H. *A Chronicle of Friendships,* 1873–1900. London, 1908.

MASSON, ROSALIND, Edited by. *I Can Remember Robert Louis Stevenson.* Edinburgh and London, 1922.

MASSON, ROSALIND. *The Life of Robert Louis Stevenson.* Edinburgh and London, 1923.

MOORS, HARRY JAY. *With Stevenson in Samoa.* London, 1910.

OSBOURNE, LLOYD. *An Intimate Portrait of R.L.S.* New York, 1924.

RALEIGH, WALTER. *Robert Louis Stevenson.* London, 1895.

SANCHEZ, NELLIE VAN DE GRIFT. *The Life of Mrs. Robert Louis Stevenson.* London, 1920.

STEUART, J. A. *Robert Louis Stevenson: Man and Writer.* 2 vols. London, 1924.

STEVENSON, FANNY VAN DE GRIFT OSBOURNE. *The Cruise of the* Janet Nichol *Among the South Sea Islands: A Diary by Mrs. Robert Louis Stevenson.* London, 1915.

STEVENSON, FANNY VAN DEGRIFT OSBOURNE (edited by Charles Neider). *Our Samoan Adventure.* London, 1956.

SWINNERTON, FRANK. *R. L. Stevenson: A Critical Study.* London, 1914.

SYMONDS, JOHN ADDINGTON. *A Biography compiled from his Papers and Correspondence,* by Horatio F. Brown. London, 1903.

SYMONDS, JOHN ADDINGTON. *Letters and Papers,* edited by Horatio F Brown, 1923.

Especially valuable:

FURNAS, J. C. *Voyage to Windward: The Life of Robert Louis Stevenson,* New York (N.Y.) 1951.

INDEX